The Politics of Care in
Habermas and Derrida

The Politics of Care in Habermas and Derrida

Between Measurability and Immeasurability

Richard Ganis

LEXINGTON BOOKS
A division of
ROWMAN & LITTLEFIELD PUBLISHERS, INC.
Lanham • Boulder • New York • Toronto • Plymouth, UK

Published by Lexington Books
A division of Rowman & Littlefield Publishers, Inc.
A wholly owned subsidiary of The Rowman & Littlefield Publishing Group, Inc.
4501 Forbes Boulevard, Suite 200, Lanham, Maryland 20706
www.lexingtonbooks.com

Estover Road, Plymouth PL6 7PY, United Kingdom

British Library Cataloguing in Publication Information Available

Library of Congress Cataloging-in-Publication Data

Ganis, Richard.
  The politics of care in Habermas and Derrida : between measurability and immeasurability / Richard Ganis.
     p. cm.
  Includes bibliographical references (p.   ) and index.
  ISBN 978-0-7391-5009-2 (cloth : alk. paper) — ISBN 978-0-7391-5011-5 (electronic)
  1. Caring. 2. Habermas, Jürgen. 3. Derrida, Jacques. I. Title.
  B3258.H324G36 2011
  170.92'2—dc22   2010038560

Contents

Acknowledgments   vii

Introduction   1

1   Care and Justice: Competing Conceptions of the Moral?   25

2   Care as Unqualified Gift: Derrida's (Im)possible Visitation   43

3   Caring for Nature in Habermas and Derrida: Reconciling the Speaking and Nonspeaking Worlds at the Cost of "Re-enchantment"?   63

4   "Habermasian Care" versus "Derridean Care": Asymmetry or Accord?   95

5   Taking the Measure of Care   121

Bibliography   147

Index   157

About the Author   163

Acknowledgments

The Politics of Care in Habermas and Derrida is the fruit of my longstanding interest in Jürgen Habermas's effort to critically defend the "unfinished" political and emancipatory project of Enlightenment modernity against the ever-rising tide of detractors who have convened to dance upon its grave. Whatever its proposed criticisms and interventions, this book remains significantly informed by Professor Habermas's seminal reconstruction of the Frankfurt School's critical-theoretic project and in solidarity with its overarching philosophical and political aims. Yet I must likewise underscore my intellectual indebtedness to the imposing body of work that Jacques Derrida has bequeathed to us. Indeed, the towering figure of Derrida poses perhaps the most formidable challenge to Habermas's program, and it is precisely on this conviction that I have brought these two philosophers together in this volume. My hope is that the ensuing encounter will be both illuminative of each author's perspective and generative of new ideas.

I am extremely grateful for the support and good counsel that I have received from a number of associates and friends throughout the genesis and development of this book. These colleagues include Peter Bratsis, Peter Buse, Carlos Frade, and Jane Kilby, my advisors at the University of Salford, where this book—an outgrowth of my doctoral dissertation—began its conceptual life. I am likewise indebted to the instructive insights and criticisms of Eduardo Mendieta, who served as external examiner on my viva committee. Special thanks are also due to the anonymous reader of my manuscript commissioned by Lexington Books. In response to the thoughtful and enormously helpful comments of this reviewer, I have endeavored to clarify and explicate a number of issues that were left hanging in an earlier draft of the book. In addition, I must thank Jana Wilson, my editor at Lexington Books, for her interest in the project, and for her invaluable guidance and assistance throughout the publication process. For their help with the final production of the book, I am grateful to Victoria Koulakjian, assistant editor at Rowman & Littlefield, and Jo-Ann Parks, who proofread the manuscript. Inestimable debts are also owed to a long list of at once uncountable and counted upon friends and fellow doctoral researchers at the University of Salford and the University of Manchester, who graciously offered me support and intellectual sustenance as I carried forth my work on Habermas and Derrida in the cold, rain-sodden environs of Northwest England. Finally, I am grateful to Safina M. L. Joseph of the Lahore University of Management Sciences for her immeasurable kindness, encouragement, patience, and care during the final phases of this project.

Of course, all of the deficits and weaknesses that remain in this work are my responsibility alone.

Introduction

I will seek someone who understands that justice isn't about some abstract legal theory or [a] footnote in a case book. It is also about how our laws affect the daily realities of people's lives—whether they can make a living and care for their families; whether they feel safe in their homes and welcome in their own nation.

I view that quality of empathy, of understanding and identifying with people's hopes and struggles as an essential ingredient for arriving as [*sic*] just decisions and outcomes.[1]

> —President Barack Obama, in a press release announcing some of the attributes that are in his view essential for a replacement for retiring Justice David Souter on the U.S. Supreme Court

While the courts of many countries run roughshod over people's rights, American courts are tightly bound to the words of the Constitution and must defend the rights of every single American—regardless of a judge's personal or political feelings in a case.

But President Obama and Judge Sotomayor have expressed a very different view of judging. This view says that justice should not be blind, that it should not be based only on the law and the Constitution, but that it should take a judge's own personal and political feelings into account. . . .

Empathy-based rulings, no matter how well-intentioned, do not help society, but imperil the legal system that has been so essential to our liberties and so fundamental to our way of life.[2]

> —Republican Senator Jeff Sessions, in an editorial expressing his opposition to Obama's nomination of Judge Sonia Sotomayor to the U.S. Supreme Court

1

While cloaked in customary displays of grandstanding and political theater, the 2009 senatorial confirmation hearings for U.S. Supreme Court Justice Sonia Sotomayor brought a salient political question of our times into the media spotlight: In the process of adjudicating matters of universal justice, is there a legitimate and indeed necessary place for the standpoint of "care" for the other, as President Obama intimates in his statement on Justice Souter's imminent retirement from the Court? Or should the asymmetrical perspective of care remain wholly and unequivocally dissociated from the principle of impartial treatment for all? The efforts of confirmation committee members like Senator Sessions to defend the imperative of strict impartiality against Obama's plea for the inclusion of an "empathy standard" on the judicial bench drew immediate censure from many pundits and commentators. Sessions, after all, was himself denied a seat on a U.S. District Court in Alabama in 1986, on the grounds that his biases against organizations such as the National Association for the Advancement of Colored People and the American Civil Liberties Union rendered him bereft of the very juristic detachment that he demanded of, and found lacking in, Judge Sotomayor's legal temperament.[3] The seeming duplicity of his objections to Sotomayor's Supreme Court appointment aside, other members of the senatorial committee were quick to join Sessions in vociferously upholding the doctrine of "judicial restraint." To this end, they invoked with some frequency Chief Justice John Roberts's famous claim that the role of a judge can be likened to that an umpire in a game of baseball. Both judges and umpires, Roberts maintained, are tasked with calling "balls and strikes," fairly and objectively, without consideration of their own personal viewpoints. Notably, during the hearings Judge Sotomayor was at great pains to defend her fealty to the impartiality principle, repeatedly assuring her critics that were she appointed to the high court, she would adopt the attitude of a neutral umpire and allow only the "facts" of the case, rather than her own personal convictions, to guide her judicial rulings.[4]

With nominee and committee members alike engaged in an apparent competition over who could construct the solemnest platitude to the impartiality norm, President Obama's initial argument for carving open a place for the standpoint of empathy on the high court attracted few fervent champions. Democratic senators such as Charles Schumer were notable exceptions. In contrast to much of the prevailing rhetoric, Schumer did not hesitate to affirm the propriety of granting the empathetic perspective entrée into the legal sphere. Indeed, far from being antithetical to the principle of judicial neutrality and equal treatment, as Sessions and other detractors of Obama's position alleged, Schumer suggested that it is both appropriate and essential for a jurist to evince empathetic concern for the litigants who stand before her in a court of law. The empathy standard, he declared, "is the opposite of indifference, the opposite of having icewater in your veins."[5]

Over the last several decades, many thinkers within the academy have likewise voiced displeasure with the contention that an objective arbitrator—a "feeling-neutral" umpire, as Justice Roberts would have it—is sufficient, or indeed even necessary, when addressing questions of universal justice. This view is linked in many respects to a new conception of "the other"[6] that has emerged within a wide range of academic disciplines: literary criticism, feminist historiography, postcolonial studies, cultural sociology, to name but a few. According to this revised idea, to speak of the other is to allude to something that cannot be represented, measured, or made repeatable. It has been alleged, in other words, that the other is other precisely because it is "wholly other." At the level of moral and legal theory, this perspective has led many authors to accord more weight to the obligation to care than the philosophical tradition of moral universalism has been willing to allow.

A central concern for the present investigation is whether the theoretical "turn" toward care entails certain "costs" at the level of ethics and politics. These potential shortcomings come into view not only with respect to questions such as whether or not the inclusion of an empathy standard on the U.S. Supreme Court promises to compromise the impartiality of judicial rulings. Indeed, formidable challenges arise whenever the care perspective is brought to bear on matters that have been customarily arbitrated from the vantage point of universal justice and equal treatment alone. On what terms, for example, are ethicists of care positioned to adjudge the actions of contemporary terrorist organizations and organized crime syndicates? Can the acts of political and social violence perpetrated by such groups be understood as expressions of "care" for beloved others? If so, are agents are free to commit such actions absent any injunction to provide universally defensible reasons? In what sense are care ethicists poised to distinguish violence-oriented expressions of care morality from forms of affective sociation—spousal and parental love, for example—in which the nonuniversalizability of the self's relationship to the other is seldom regarded as objectionable? Lastly, in view of the increasing degradation of the natural environment for which modern human societies are responsible, should the prevailing anthropocentric conception of the nonhuman world be abandoned in favor of a new ethics of care for both insensate nature and nonspeaking animals?

On the conviction that their respective texts are exemplarily well positioned to engage such questions, this book foregrounds the thought of Jürgen Habermas and Jacques Derrida, two of the most formidable philosophers of the late twentieth and early twenty-first centuries. The discussion of Derrida places particular emphasis on the deconstructive effort to position the attitude of limitless concern for the "irreducible alterity" of the other in an unsettled yet productive relationship with the moral standpoint of equal treatment. Derrida's approach is contrasted with Habermas's discourse-ethical model, which insists that the injunction to care unconditionally must always be constrained by obligations of mutual understanding and impartial, reciprocal respect.

In its consideration of the problem of care in Habermas and Derrida, the study highlights an often overlooked point of contention between the two thinkers—namely, their contrasting accounts of the principle of measure. Unlike Derrida, Habermas sets forth a categorical distinction between instrumental measure (oriented toward the world of objects) and noninstrumental measure (appropriate to the realm of the social). From this vantage point, not every effort to "count" is as injurious to "difference" as Derrida alleges. Indeed, in distinguishing "communicative reason" from "instrumental reason," Habermas is able to envisage a type of measurable equality that is facilitative of human flourishing rather than a hindrance to it. To Habermas, a principal deficit of Derrida's deconstructive care ethics is its failure to provide moral agents with a common intersubjective standpoint from which to adjudicate conflicting validity claims and value orientations. In addition, in refusing to categorically demarcate instrumental problem-solving languages from noninstrumental ones, the difference-ethical standpoint of deconstruction appears to shear itself of the theoretical resources needed to guard against a "re-teleologized" conception of nature and the knowledge of nature.

While sympathetic to the overarching philosophical itinerary of the discourse-ethical model, I take seriously Derrida's contention that a rather sterile, cognitive-centric account of ethicopolitical life is precisely the consequence of Habermas's uncompromising commitment to principles of *Aufklärung*, a standpoint that leads him to subordinate the attitude of unconditional concern for the other's absolute otherness to reciprocative procedures of moral argumentation. To Derrida this deficit is endemic to the broader framework of Kantian moral universalism upon which Habermas draws. Indeed, to Derrida the perspective of communicative rationality under which Habermas labors is to be found guilty—to invoke Senator Schumer's metaphor—of having ice water in its veins. Giving this objection its due, this book appeals to the dialogue that the two writers have initiated in an effort to lay the groundwork for a reconstructed critical theory that is more accommodative of the gesture of unlimited care for a single unrepresentable individual than Habermas's discourse-ethical project has being willing to countenance. Yet in so doing, it is at pains to assure that such an intervention does not undermine the categorical primacy accorded to universalistic moral rights and duties in the philosophical tradition of Kant. Although I find the recognition theory advanced by Axel Honneth to be encumbered by a number of conceptual difficulties, I position Honneth's framework as a promising launching point for such a proposed reconstruction (whose basic terms I shall attempt to delineate in chapter 5). The study's emphasis on theoretical reconstruction distinguishes it from recent writings that are more sanguine about a possible reconciliation, if not outright "marriage," between Habermas and Derrida. Indeed, despite what thinkers such as Simon Critchley and Martin Matuštík regard as a move toward rapprochement in their later writings, I maintain that significant conceptual incongruities persist between the two interlocutors, distinctions that ultimately consign their respective engagements with the problem of care morality to rather disparate spaces at the level of ethics and politics.

To broach this argument and introduce the terms in which each author has approached the problem of care for the other, the following section considers Derrida's idea of incalculably unconditional hospitality alongside Habermas's communicative-theoretic defense of the Kantian ideal of measurable toleration. This discussion will be followed by an outline of the thematics to be discussed in subsequent chapters.

DERRIDEAN HOSPITALITY: A VISITATION
WITHOUT MEASURE OR CONDITIONS

The problem of the irreducible "otherness of the other" has preoccupied thinkers in the Western academy since at the least the early 1960s. At this time, anthropology and other disciplines within the social sciences and humanities began to express frustration with the limitations of paradigmatic conceptual systems as systems.[7] In opposition to these "totalizing" frameworks, newer "postparadigmatic" approaches emerged, calling attention to issues such as contextuality, indeterminacy, intractable contradiction, paradox, irony, and the meaning of social life to those who enact it.[8] Problems of grand-theoretic description thus gave way to questions of intimate representation, difference, and diversity. An older social-scientific imaginary linked to the idea of a unified, disciplined, and inner-directed subject was displaced by partial, perspectival, and culturally embedded modes of inquiry carried out in alliance with sociocultural sites, positionalities, and claims construed as radically unpredictable and contestable.

For many of those drawn to this new conception of the other, the writings of Jacques Derrida have been propaedeutic and indeed requisite. While myriad *topoi* animate Derrida's framework, the present investigation will place particular emphasis on its endeavor to deracinate the "constituent subject" from the epistemological firmament of *logos* and its attendant principle of "identity." To this end, Derrida proceeds from the assumption that the structure of

language and being cannot be located in what the tradition of Western metaphysics sees as the commensurable relationship between signifier and signified. "Simply," he observes, "[the signifier] has no 'natural attachment' to the
signified within reality."[9] Radically disjoined from the *telos* of identity, signifier and signified emerge as a constantly sliding, shifting, and circulating pro-
cession of signs, with no structural anchor to impart meaning or stability to a
conceptual system. Here Derrida's target is nothing less than the foundational-
ism of ultimate groundings, the link between language and representation. En
rapport with the "death" proclamation that thinkers such as Nietzsche and
Heidegger level against "Man, Metaphysics, and History,"[10] his deconstructive maneuver dismantles the epistemological scaffolding of modern "subject-
centered reason"—namely, the correspondence theory of truth. The latter
perspective seeks to position words and concepts in an identarian relationship
to objects in the noumenal world. Yet from Derrida's standpoint, we are enjoined, as Edith Wyschogrod observes, to contest the proposal that truth can
be viewed "as a matching of event or pattern with what is said about it, a relation of homology between propositions and referent."[11]

On this move, Derrida dispatches us to an ineliminably indeterminate and
liminal discursive space; unmoored from the epistemological imperative of
identification, we are free to speak of signification as a "play of differences,"
a situation in which "no element can function as a sign without referring to
the other elements," and where each element is "constituted of the trace
within it of the other elements of the chain."[12] Here, as Thomas McCarthy
notes, all signifiers inevitably bear the residue of "the tissue of relations and
difference"; we can therefore "never achieve a simple univocality of meaning
. . . for language, as 'writing,' inevitably harbors the possibility of an endless
'dissemination,' an indefinite multiplicity of recontextualizations and
reinterpretations."[13] In valorizing the principle of *nonidentity* over and against
the dedifferentiating mastery of *logos*, Derrida is in fact positioned to disarticulate the entire occidental discourse of stereotomic inside/outside, space/
time, subject/object, true/false binaries. He can disrupt the idea of the subject
as a unitary narrative perspective; the conception of moral-ethical norms as
universalistic and universalistically negotiable; and the viability of all "ontotheological" conceptualizations of the relation between ethics and politics.

Notably, with respect to the latter objective, Derrida has insisted that deconstruction has been an intrinsically ethical and political practice from its
inception, famously disavowing all intimations that his writing underwent an
ethicopolitical "turn" in the 1980s and 1990s.[14] Such protestations aside,
commentators were quick to detect in Derrida's later texts a shift away from
an earlier preoccupation with the language-theoretic subversion of reason,
metaphysics, and the totalizing ideals of the Western metaphysical tradition:

the emphasis now was on specifying the normative-political orientations toward the "heterogeneous," according to which that radical criticism was to be carried out.[15] Among other motivations, Derrida's move was likely precipitated by a desire to gird deconstruction against charges of moral-ethical prevarication and/or indifference, which many critics (including some with unmistakable allegiances to "postmodernism") lamented as the cost of a philosophical critique that ultimately exhausted itself in the incessant disarticulation of *logos*.

Whether or not one perceives his later interest in the ethicopolitical as a "turn," Derrida was clearly at pains to pursue it without giving up on his initial impulse to situate the deconstructive maneuver in unrelenting disjuncture with Enlightenment frameworks of moral universalism. This resolve is clearly in evidence in works such as *Politics of Friendship* and *Rogues*, which continue to rigorously interrupt all efforts to anchor the construction of otherness in a single set of constitutive criteria. Reading against the conceptual grain of received understandings of liberalism and Marxism alike, Derrida disfigures the textual field as a matrix of interstitial sites, discursive spaces that allow the other's internal frames of reference to live, multiply and unpredictably, outside subject-centered reason's *telos* of inviolable universal facticity. His deconstructive "thinking of the trace" emerges, in this context, as a new "non-way of walking"—an ethicopolitical opening to an other whose irreducible otherness is "stabilized" by the logo-, andro-, and ethnocentrism[16] of the modern *ratio* at the cost of epistemic "disqualification" and "annihilation."[17]

This philosophical itinerary is carried forth in Derrida's idea of "unconditional" hospitality. Developed in his later writings, this category seeks to disfigure the ideal of limited or conditional hospitality, which receives its seminal treatment in Immanuel Kant's short treatise *Perpetual Peace*. Here Kant tasks modern nation-states with the responsibility of securing the conditions of an eternal peace, rather than a merely provisional one—the kind that might be secured through an armistice or a ceasefire, for example. To carry out the mandate of perpetual peace, nation-states are obliged to extend the summons of universal hospitality to the foreigner who comes. Yet such hospitality is not without its stipulations: the newcomer must be a citizen of another nation-state and behave "peaceably" in the host country. She, moreover, is not accorded the right to remain but only the right to visit. In Kant the circuit of hospitality is therefore one of a qualified "invitation" or "gift": the guest is bidden to arrive and reciprocates by offering something in gratitude. At the level of the nation-state, adherence to a regime of hospitable reciprocity means that the host remains the master: "he," writes Derrida, "controls the threshold, he controls the borders, and when he welcomes the guest he wants to keep the mastery."[18]

Taking important cues from Emmanuel Levinas's ethics of the "altogether-other," Derrida introduces the idea of unreserved hospitality in a bid to break this well-ordered, circular movement of reciprocity and exchange, extending to both host and *arrivant* the pleasures of the "absolute surprise." Pure hospitality, insists Derrida, "implies that you don't ask the other, the guest, to give anything back, or even to identify himself or herself. . . . For pure hospitality or a pure gift to occur . . . there must be an absolute surprise."[19] On this view, Derrida transfigures Kant's invitation into an idea more closely resembling the traditional and religious concept of "visitation," in which the newcomer is at liberty to arrive unbidden, unexpectedly, and at any time, without horizon or expectations. For Kant such pure hospitality cannot be countenanced, as it threatens to remove a vital mechanism of "immunity" or systematic defense against the other, opening the door to an anarchic war of each against all. With unconditional hospitality, there is always the possibility, notes Derrida, "of the other coming and destroying the place, initiating a revolution, stealing everything, or killing everyone."[20] Notwithstanding such risks, deconstructive ethics remains vitally invested in dethroning the host as master of its home, its space, its nation-state, and reconfiguring our reciprocal relations with the other as a discourse of "pure gift."

Among the metaphysical conceits that Derrida's maneuver aims to disrupt is the strong undercurrent of Christian evangelism at the spine of Kant's tolerant invitation. Indeed, to Derrida, Kant's ideal is little more than a fundamentally religious endeavor cloaked beneath the veil of a putatively secular morality. As Giovanna Borradori notes, Derrida views tolerance as "the quintessential example of this Kantian double bind: it presents itself as being religiously neutral and yet it contains a strong Christian component."[21] Kant and his followers commit the critical misstep of failing to recognize the religious etiology of their own stipulative frames: they cling paradoxically to a secularized idea of tolerance without recognizing its imbrication within the moral idiom of the Christian, from whence it is cast forth as an inflexible or "scrutinized hospitality, always under surveillance, parsimonious and protective of its sovereignty."[22] It is only upon redeployment to the spatiotemporally liminal register of the deconstructive trace that tolerance, cosmopolitan right, and the right of invitation are released from their boundedness to the heritage of Christian, Judaic, and Islamic ontotheology.

Derrida expresses similar misgivings about "forgiveness," an act that he likewise posits in the double register of the conditional and the unconditional. On his account, limited forgiveness circulates within the spheres of politics and law as a purposive-rational therapy of punishment and reconciliation. With unconditional forgiveness, however, the utilitarian calculus is removed, such that the possibility of forgiving the unforgivable becomes imaginable.

As an intervention that can be conceived only in terms of its own epistemic incongruity, pure forgiveness positions itself alongside pure hospitality and pure gift as admitting of a certain "madness." Indeed, Derrida's "unconditionals" present themselves as "transpolitical political principles," rules for position-taking that cannot be enframed within the nation-state's legal-juridical conventions of pragmatic negotiation and equal exchange. Insofar as Kant and his followers imprison these concepts within the confines of the nation-state's legal-juridical *ratio*, they destine them to circulate in their theories as schemas for something like a politicoprogrammatic dream.

Derrida's notion of hospitality without conditions, in contrast, is one that can never be accorded political or juridical status: because states cannot include it within their laws, such hospitality is fundamentally incompatible with the very idea of a sovereign nation-state. To be just and responsible, in other words, the overture of hospitality must be dislodged from the epistemological imperatives of calculation, measurability, and infallible truth that found and delimit all modern constructions of law, ethics, and politics. Pure hospitality responds to the call of the wholly other—the other of another culture, another place, another time—from within liminal spaces of perspective taking that are absolutely heterogeneous to knowledge and unlocatable within the regulative ideals that circumscribe the sociation of rational, self-legislating Kantian men. The unconditionally hospitable visitation can thus be construed as an essentially nonappropriative, noninstrumental, and nonviolent friendship—a "relation as nonrelation" that is for Derrida "radically messianic" precisely insofar as it raises a performative ethicopolitical call for a democratic future to come (*avenir*).

In distinction to the teleoeschatologies of Judaeo-Christendom, Islam, or—for that matter—Soviet Marxism, Derrida's aim is not to ossify the promise of democracy-to-come as an ontotheological program, but rather to subject it to the profoundly heterogeneous ordeal of undecidability. Indeed, with his idea of a "messianic without religion, without messianism," Derrida seeks to displace the promise of a democratic future from the de-eventalized *telos* of ideal finality, such that it is no longer circumscribed by a specific, originary content. Nor is it on this view presupposed or issued by a self-legislating subject—the kind of subject that Derrida evokes with his famous account of *ipseity*. Ipseity, he observes, suggests "some 'I can,' or at the very least the power that *gives itself* its own law, its force of law, its self-representation, the sovereign and reappropriating gathering of self in the simultaneity of an assemblage or assembly, being together or 'living together,' as we say."[23] It is precisely the metaphysical sameness of selfhood as ipseity that Derrida's radically asynchronous messianic time is poised to disturb; fundamentally heterogeneous to every other time, the messianic is directed "toward the utterly indeterminable aspect of the future beyond horizons, expectations, planning, or awaiting."[24] As we shall see in chapter 4, this effort to disarticulate the *ratio* of Western metaphysical spatiotemporality resonates notably with both Ernst Bloch's idea of noncontemporaneity as well as with Walter Benjamin's concept of *Jetztzeit*, the "now time" threatened with collapse by the shards of messianic time that shoot through it.[25]

Yet whatever its affinities with the proposals of Bloch and Benjamin, Derrida's notion of a persistent slippage of the present out of simultaneity with itself aims at something rather different: a situation in which both the *ethical* gesture of unrestricted care for an intrinsically unknowable, unanticipatable, and immeasurable other is thought alongside a *political* idea of democracy-to-come. Significantly, for Derrida the latter conception bears no resemblance to an existing liberal democracy, the regulative ideal of a Kantian kingdom of ends, or a utopia understood as a future modality of presence. Instead, in Derrida, democracy-to-come is linked "to the messianic experience of the *here and now* (*l'ici-maintenment*), without which justice would be meaningless."[26]

As already intimated, this book will argue that Derrida's gesture of unconditional care for the absolutely other aims not at a wholesale overthrow of the principle of quantifiable measure, but rather at placing the calculable and the incalculable into an unsettled yet fruitful relationship with one another. In fact, according to Derrida, it is precisely its acknowledgment of this uneasy alliance between the measurable and the immeasurable that makes the deconstructive ethics of difference *reasonable*. "What is called reason," he writes, "from one language to another is thus found on both sides. According to a transaction that is each time novel, each time without precedent, reason goes through and goes between, on the one side, the reasoned exigency of calculation or conditionality, and on the other, the intransigent, nonnegotiable exigency of unconditional incalculability . . . *both* calculation *and* the incalculable *are necessary*. This is the responsibility of reason."[27] Accordingly, from Derrida's standpoint, the overture of unreserved hospitality admits of justice and responsibility only insofar as it entails a decision that is "*both regulated and without regulation*," a decision that endeavors to "confirm the law and also to destroy it or suspend it enough to have to reinvent it in each case . . . in the affirmation of the new and free confirmation of its principle."[28] Here Derrida breaks importantly with the pessimistic appraisal of the calculably rational advanced in first-generation critical theory, which offers little hope for any such accord between the calculable and the incalculable. Yet this divergence aside, he evinces a striking kinship with authors like Max Horkheimer and Theodor Adorno, in that he likewise sees the standpoint of calculative measure as entailing an inviolable injury to the incalculably singular. Moreover, to redress this wound, his framework—whatever its claims on behalf of the principle of reason—accords architectonic primacy to that which is antinomical to the epistemology of correspondence and identity. "One must know," says Derrida in "Force of Law," that the standpoint of measurable justice must always address "itself to singularity, to the singularity of the other, despite, or even because it pretends to universality."[29]

We will consider some of the aporias that attend to Derrida's effort to tensely ally the perspective of calculable justice with the standpoint of the unsubsumable example in chapter 2. However at present, a brief overview of Jürgen Habermas's effort to uphold tolerative measurability as the categorically preeminent standpoint of moral reason is in order.

HABERMAS'S DEFENSE OF TOLERANCE

Although it too tenders a rich and complex arc of thematics—many of which have been elaborated, discarded, or otherwise modified over the course of a half century–long career—a core set of proposals have distinguished Habermas's framework from the outset. In a word, he has consistently aligned himself with the critical force of a "demystified" communicative rationality.[30] Through a methodical appropriation of a wide range of theoretical traditions and idioms, Habermas endeavors to defend a view of human social life that is predicated on our capacity to engage in clear and successful dialogue with one another. He therewith preserves in the notion of communicative action a Socratic and utopian belief in the propriety of debate, discussion, and the rational adjudication of contested validity claims. In recent years, one of Habermas's key aims has been to locate the possibility of speech without coercion in the normative and legal-juridical topography of modern constitutional democracies, which, he claims, announce procedures conducive to the formation of rationally conceived agreements among communicative actors. The domains of norm and legality are therefore essential to any framework of democratic action and organization in the present; without them, philosophy cannot address questions of morality, ethics, social transformation, and—crucially for the present study—sociocultural heterogeneity and otherness.

These preliminary remarks offer a sense of why Habermas is drawn to a modified version of the Kantian ideal of tolerance over the unqualified visitation proposed by his colleague Derrida. Habermas concedes that with the ascendancy of the Catholic Church, the principle of toleration has been enacted for centuries in a paternalistic spirit, one that "retains an element of an act of mercy or of 'doing a favor.'"[31] However, he refuses to endorse Derrida's portrayal of the notion as patronizing, Christocentric, and ultimately delimited by the ineliminable residue of violence at the root of its own calculative *telos*. In Habermas's communicative-theoretic reconstruction, Kant's category is positioned in the normative and legal-juridical framework of modern constitutional democracies, whose deliberative procedures enjoin full and equal participants in public spaces of shared citizenship to reach uncoerced and rationally conceived agreements about competing value orientations and ideals of life, even if mutual cognitive dissonances remain unresolved for the time being.[32] Anticipating objections from deconstruction and other quarters, Habermas maintains that the "peculiar character of reflexivity" of the modern constitution has emerged as a bulwark against any sovereign or culture of the majority that endeavors to endow itself with the authority to one-sidedly establish a normalized "threshold of tolerance" to which so-called deviant minorities are obliged to adhere. In a move that recalls Locke's claim that the sovereign loses its legitimacy and can be justly overthrown upon the abrogation of its responsibilities, Habermas argues that

> [i]n its tolerance of civil disobedience, the constitution self-reflexively stretches to cover even the conditions for overstepping its own boundaries. A democratic constitution can thus tolerate resistance from dissidents who, after exhausting all legal avenues, nonetheless oppose legitimately reached decisions. It only imposes the condition that this rule-breaking resistance be plausibly justified in the spirit and wording of the constitution and conducted by symbolic means that lend the fight the character of a nonviolent appeal to the majority to once again reflect on their decisions.[33]

For Habermas, it is precisely the modern constitution's self-reflexive tendency to feed off the resistances of minorities that positions tolerance and its right of invitation as part of the groundwork for cosmopolitan conventions among modern nation-states. Moreover, the "weak" normative assumptions of modern sociocultural forms of tolerance uphold "a non-defeatist concept of reason against contextualism and a nondecisionist concept of the validity of law against legal positivism."[34]

Against Derrida, then, Habermas's aim is not to disabuse Enlightenment modernity of its logocentric impulses, but rather to show how the derailment of its initial deployment of the critical force of reason has opened the door for political violence and domination—a problem theorized under the rubric of "reification" by his predecessors at the Frankfurt School. In elaborating his communicative-theoretic reconstruction of this concept, Habermas hopes, in fact, to circumvent many of the "prerational" aporias attendant to the earlier critical theory's attempt to theorize a way out of Weber's "iron cage" of bureaucratic reason via "teleologized" prescriptions for modern science and technology. For Habermas, a key advantage of positing a distinction between strategic and communicative action and an associated differentiation between "system" and "lifeworld"[35] is that we are no longer obliged to subscribe to the one-dimensionality thesis—championed famously by Herbert Marcuse—that sought to portray modern instrumental reason as an *intrinsically* totalitarian enterprise. In conceiving of the rationalization of modern complex societies as an essentially "double-sided" process, his framework allows for the theorization of an at least partially dereified contemporary public sphere, in which communicative actors retain the capacity to internalize and appeal to intersubjective norms in order to simultaneously identify with and differentiate themselves from other subjects in a social, i.e., communicative, context. Ideals of equal rights and reciprocal respect thematized by the modern bourgeois democratic revolutions are thus preserved as a normative ground for a self-reflexive, or immanent, critique of contemporary social conditions. Communications theory, it has been said, "marches to the tune of the *Marseillaise*."[36]

Thus, whatever his arguments with Derrida, Habermas has likewise located the "promise" of something like a violence-free future within the structure of all language. Yet as Bill Martin observes, there is a basic disagreement over what the "something" that language "intends" *is*.[37] For Habermas, the potential for a democratic future is by no means always already deferred (in the deconstructive sense), but prefigured in the norms of communicative reason to which real-world dialogic subjects must appeal in order to reach collective decisions about contested validity claims. Habermas maintains that precisely insofar as it is oriented toward resolving disagreements guided by the "force of the better argument," each *existing* act of uncoerced, reciprocative discussion and debate is inscribed at its normative core with both a negative claim against distorting, pathological forces of instrumental-technical manipulation and a concomitant promissory demand for material social arrangements consonant with the normative principles in the name of which interlocutors speak. "[W]ith each act of unconstrained understanding, with each moment of living together in solidarity, of successful individuation," says Habermas, "[c]ommunicative reason operates in history as an avenging force."[38]

Seen in this light, it is clear that Habermas follows Marx in retaining Hegel's at once negating, preserving, and transcending operation of *Aufhebung*, even if he breaks with both Hegel and Marx at the level of theoretical categorization. Indeed, while he deploys the method of immanent exposition and defetishizing critique adopted by both of these thinkers, Habermas wants to move social criticism beyond the metalinguistic frame of human intentionality in which both remained moored. To this end, Marx's analysis is taken to task for according analytical primacy to an overarching set of "determinant contradictions" within the capitalist political economy. To Habermas, this bias leads Marx, and indeed much of the ensuing Marxist tradition, to envisage capitalist modernity as a rather homogeneous "realm of necessity," the terms of whose transcendence are prefigured in a simulacrum of "extrasocial" guarantees. This is especially true of the later Marx, who, like the later Hegel, abandoned an earlier interest in "using the idea of uncoerced will formation in a communication community existing under constraints of cooperation as a model for the reconciliation of a divided bourgeois society"; instead, the Marx of *Capital* sought to trace the "unfettering of productive forces . . . back to a principle of modernity that is grounded in the practice of a producing subject rather than the reflection of a knowing subject."[39] The classical Marxian model therefore remains circumscribed by a latent analytical monism that militates against the full expression of its own self-reflexive critique of the a priori categories of thought and action inscribed in the *ratio* of modern bourgeois society. So encumbered, it invites the prospect of making

> use of a consciousness burdened with the feeling of a crisis merely to integrate empirical history as a whole into the cycles of a superhistory; it derails the open historical process of possible self-determination and redirects it back into the received contours of a naturelike occurrence: The book of history gets translated back into a book of geological lore concerning the ages of the world.[40]

From the vantage point of its latently positivistic philosophy of history,[41] the liberated society is all too quickly conceived "as a historically privileged concrete form of ethical life (*Sittlichkeit*)" rather than "as the set of necessary conditions for emancipated forms of life about which participants *themselves* would have to reach an understanding."[42]

The crucial question for Habermas is thus, "How can an intrinsic ideal form be constructed from the spirit of modernity, that neither just imitates the historical forms of modernity nor is imposed on them from the outside?"[43] To this address this problem, Habermas reconstructs Marx's monistic forces of production/relations of production model, repositioning it in the dualistic framework of system/lifeworld. The potential for a human future free from the violence of instrumental-technical control is on this view not grounded—with Marcuse and others—in an eschatological rupture with a modernity putatively aimed at bringing all spheres of life under the fetters of purposive-rational administration; rather, it is located in moral-practical norms of communicative sociation that have *already* differentiated themselves from scientific-technical and aesthetic-expressive problem-solving languages in modern complex societies. Habermas's communicative-theoretic reconstruction can thus be read as an effort to retain the Marxian framework's conception of philosophy and social praxis as immanent critique while at the same time rendering it better equipped to carry forth its own emancipatory aims.

It is against this philosophical backdrop that Habermas begins his engagement with Derrida's thought. Although his reception of his colleague's work would soften somewhat in later years (largely in response to Derrida's heightened level of engagement with the tradition of Kant), Habermas has never quite distanced himself from the view of deconstruction that he adopted in two 1985 essays in *The Philosophical Discourse of Modernity.*[44] Here, as will be discussed at length in chapter 4, Habermas contends that deconstruction remains trapped in a "performative double bind"; articulated within a single "poetic" or "impaired" linguistic idiom, it fails to see that it cannot carry out its own ethicopolitical objectives without express recourse to the very normative traditions and rationalist criteria of defensibility it aims to unravel. Indeed, from the standpoint of Habermas's discourse-ethical defense of Kantianism's tolerative ideal, Derrida's unconditional visitation with the other deprives moral agents of a common intersubjective framework for reaching (at least provisional) unforced agreements about competing propositions of truth, rightness, and sincerity. While a deconstructive ethics of unreserved care for the other may position itself as critical of orientations such as xenophobia, racism, and anti-Semitism, it remains Janus-faced in insisting that it can guard against such practices without "parasitically [feeding] upon what it deconstructs," as Seyla Benhabib notes in a sympathetic reading of Habermas's argument.[45] This parasitism takes the form of a performative double bind inasmuch as Derrida (working within the shadow of a thinker like Nietzsche) has blurred the "genre distinction" between literature and philosophy, thereby allowing the critical orientation of the latter to be consumed by a "bad" aestheticism. Habermas argues that "[i]f thought can no longer operate in the realms of truth and validity claims, then analysis and critique lose their meaning": we are thus left with the enthronement of "*taste*, the 'Yes' and 'No' of the palate . . . as the sole organ of knowledge beyond Truth and Falsity, beyond Good and Evil."[46] For precisely this reason, whatever its self-professed efforts to disarticulate the philosophical foundations of the Western metaphysical tradition, a deconstructive care ethics remains ensnared in the very "philosophy of subjectivity," "Absolute System," and "the last word" that it purports to undermine.

For his part, Derrida views such readings of his text as entirely misguided, insisting that deconstruction (at least as he has portrayed it) can pursue its own ethicopolitical aims only upon express recognition of the philosophical traditions of modernity that Habermas seeks to critically defend. As Richard Bernstein observes, "Derrida is acutely aware that we cannot question or shake traditional ethical and political claims without at the same time also drawing upon these claims. The very dichotomy of 'inside-outside' is also deconstructed. We are never simply 'inside' or 'outside' metaphysics."[47] Habermas is indeed highly uncharitable to Derrida to the extent that he has charged him with "advocating a total rupture with metaphysics, as if some apocalyptic event might occur that would once and for all release us from the metaphysical exigency."[48] As we have noted, Derrida's aim is not to eviscerate the *topos* of Enlightenment rationality *tout court* but to forge a *reckoning* between its calibrative ideals and the perspective of the incalculably singular, from which standpoint the deconstructive ethics of radical difference takes its moral bearings. Consequently, for the purposes of the present study, the question will not be *whether* Derrida has endeavored to ally the vantage points of the measurably identical and the immeasurably asymmetrical. Rather, we shall consider whether his *prioritization* of the latter orientation leads to certain ethicopolitical culs-de-sac, and whether Habermas's framework is in fact better equipped to attend to these problems.

LOCATING A "POLITICS OF CARE" IN THE HABERMAS/DERRIDA EXCHANGE

Put differently, a central question for this book is whether Habermas is justified in upholding the critical force of communicative rationality as a bulwark against the putative dangers of an approach like Derrida's—namely, contextualism, perspectivism, decisionism, "bad" historicism and aestheticism, and "re-teleologized" nature speculation. With Habermas, I will argue that whatever its protestations to the contrary, Derridean care ethics is ill equipped to corral such outcomes from the standpoint of its own categorical resources—a defect that underscores the propriety of the discourse-ethic's prioritization of impartialist procedures of universal will-formation. I will nevertheless criticize Habermas, not so much for ignoring or devaluing the orientation of care—he is acutely aware of the relevance of care as a source of "nourishment" for moral discourse—but rather for disregarding what Axel Honneth has characterized as the "genetic and conceptual priority" of the care perspective. I shall maintain that were Habermas's moral theory to acknowledge the gesture of care as antecedent to detached modes of thought and action within the sphere of social integration, it would be better positioned to defend itself against charges of cognitive centrism.

To commence the discussion, chapter 1 opens with an examination of Habermas's initial efforts to situate the standpoint of one-sided concern for the other within the contours of his broader discourse-ethical program. Here, in response to the arguments of feminist thinkers such as Carol Gilligan, Habermas contends that the unilateral orientation of care must be placed at express conceptual remove from questions of universal justice. The chapter then considers Seyla Benhabib's "sympathetic" critique of Habermas's proposed division between moral norms and ethical values. In line with Gilligan, Benhabib faults Habermas for discounting questions of affective sympathy, needs, and the good life as largely private matters with little or no bearing on the impartial, justice-oriented discourses of moral agents. In a move that is in some sense accommodative of the deconstructive posture of unconditional openness to the other's irreducible alterity, she maintains that the asymmetrical perspective of care must be accorded a place in moral discourse, such that the goal of solidarity no longer looms as an empty abstraction. Unlike Derrida, however, Benhabib remains circumspect of the risks of disseminating a morality of care throughout the entire discursive field: there is always the danger, she notes, of according to the "concrete other" the authority to present its own parochial and potentially immoral claims as those that are best for all. The fruitfulness of any communicative-theoretic effort to link the moral identity of the contextual other to that of the "generalized other" thus hinges upon positioning the particularistic concerns of a given care ethos in an ultimately subordinate relationship to questions of universal justice. The chapter concludes by engaging the arguments of Stella Gaon, James Gordon Finlayson, Sharon Krause, Steven Hendley, and William Rehg. These authors likewise find defects in Habermas's theorization of care but are nevertheless dissatisfied with aspects of Benhabib's proposed solution to this problem.

Having surveyed a range of largely sympathetic objections to Habermas's approach, I turn in the second chapter to a consideration of Derrida's endeavor to displace the question of care morality outside the regulative confines of the discourse-ethical model. Three salient deconstructive tropes are highlighted in this context: gift giving, friendship, and hospitality. To flesh out the discussion of these notions and gain further purchase on the status of symmetrical versus asymmetrical moral obligations in deconstructive thought, I consider Derrida's engagement with the work of Emmanuel Levinas. Here I place particular emphasis on Derrida's claim that despite its efforts to the contrary, Levinas's concept of the "altogether-other" fails to extricate itself from a certain "transcendental phenomenology." In light of this critique, I argue that Iris Marion Young is correct to characterize the moral standpoint of deconstruction as "asymmetrically reciprocal," but dispute Young's contention that Derrida has fashioned a productive association between the perspectives of communicative reciprocity and the dissymmetricality of the care attitude. Instead, I maintain that Derrida disfigures the standpoint of measurable equality on terms that eviscerate needed intersubjective constraints, not only on the orientation of care, but also on the disparate yet similarly unilateral standpoint of "terrorism." To support this claim, the chapter considers the arguments of Michel Rosenfeld, as well as Axel Honneth's recognition-theoretic critique of Derrida's deconstructive moral standpoint.

Building on the discussions of care morality advanced in the first two chapters, chapter 3 considers the conceptual tensions between Habermas's and Derrida's respective engagements with the question of care for "the other of nature"—disparities that are no less palpable than those that demarcate their approaches to the problem of care for the human other. I note that a Kantian distinction between human and nonhuman nature is at the core of Habermas's discourse-ethical defense of Enlightenment modernity as an "unfinished" political and emancipatory project. From this vantage point, Habermas upholds the legitimacy and permanence of Galilean science's anthropocentric view of the natural world and discounts the possibility—entertained by first-generation critical theorists such as Marcuse—of "re-teleologizing" both nature and the knowledge of nature.

Habermas's "disenchanted" view of science and technology raises the question of whether it is possible (or indeed desirable) to construct an "ecological ethics" from the standpoint of an anthropocentric theory that avoids all references to nature as an end-in-itself. In an attempt to address this problem, I call attention to Steven Vogel's important "constructivist" critique of Habermas's methodological dualism, along with Derrida's kindred argument against the idea of an originary nature, a nature construed as wholly independent of the social. *Pace* such objections, I defend the viability of Habermas's dualistic epistemological standpoint and argue for an ecological ethics that formalistically links the "good-for-nature" to the communicatively conceived "good-for-humanity." Such an ethics prevents what Habermas understands as humanity's "knowledge-constitutive interest" in the instrumentalization of the environment from being carried forth as a project of limitless domination and mastery. Habermas is nevertheless rightly taken to task for precluding the attitude of affective sympathy from being extended toward the nonhuman world. In this context, I find Axel Honneth's idea of a "derivative" recognitional orientation toward the objective realm a useful intervention, in that it opens up the possibility of an ethics of felt concern for the domain of objects, but without obliging us to abandon the communicative-theoretic distinction between an eternally objectified, ahistorical natural world on the one hand, and a nonreified sphere of human sociation on the other. In sharp contrast, the monistic vantage points upheld by writers like Derrida and Vogel lack the categorical resources needed to stave off the prospect of a re-teleologized account of nature and the knowledge of nature.

Foregrounding the problem of care morality, chapter 4 draws attention to the arguments of commentators such as Martin Matuštík and Simon Critchley, who discern grounds for a fertile accord between Habermasian discourse ethics and Derridean deconstruction. While I find these interventions interesting and fruitful, I remain far less sanguine about the prospects for a rapprochement between the two thinkers. Indeed, authors like Lasse Thomassen and Martin Morris are in my view correct to portray the categorical gulf separating Habermas and Derrida as formidable if not insurmountable, even if I am reluctant to follow them in weighing in on Derrida's side of the philosophical divide. To shore up this claim of conceptual incongruity, the chapter calls attention to the two thinkers' contrasting receptions of Martin Heidegger's account of care, as well as their dispute over the legacy of Ernst Bloch and Walter Benjamin. While there are important conceptual differences between the perspectives of Heidegger, Bloch, and Benjamin, each represents an effort to in some sense bring the standpoint of the spatiotemporally disjointed trace to the fore of social critique. To the extent that he inherits this legacy and prioritizes, under the sign of the event, the perspective of irreducible incalculability and nonprogrammability over that of the measurably equal, Derrida, I maintain, opens the door to dangers considered in earlier chapters—that is, the prospect of a "reenchanted" conception of the natural world, as well as the lack of a common intersubjective framework to which moral agents can appeal as they endeavor to adjudicate among competing validity claims and arrive at unforced, universally binding agreements about them.

In my view, Habermas offers a more fruitful vantage point from which to frame the relationship between the symmetrical standpoint of equal treatment and the asymmetrical attitude of care, albeit one that requires theoretical reconstruction so that it can more adequately deflect the accusation of cognitive centrism leveled by Derrida and other critics. In an attempt to rectify the care-theoretic deficits of Habermas's framework, chapter 5 highlights the recognition theory of Axel Honneth, an approach that is in my estimation the most promising launching point for any such revision of Habermas's program. With Honneth, my proposal is to allow more of the "recognitional" attitude into the domain of social integration than can be tolerated on rigorously Habermasian premises. At the same time, against Honneth's perspective of "recognitional monism," I maintain that critical social theory is better positioned to vouchsafe its own *critical* character by retaining, rather than abandoning, the Habermasian account of knowledge-constitutive interests and its associated distinction between social integration and system integration. From this vantage point, the epistemological compass of the reifying disposition is expressly and rightly confined to the extranormative object domains of nature and the "media-steered" political and economic subsystems of modern complex societies. It is kept, on these terms, categorically distinct from both the immeasurability of the care perspective and the noninstrumental type of rationality that undergirds reciprocative norms of moral argumentation. Honneth's portrayal of recognitional care as conceptually and genetically antecedent to *all* incarnations of measure is criticized for leaving the status of the objectivating disposition ambiguous at the level of epistemology and human interests.

---∞∞---

Through its attempts to enlarge existing ideas, redress theoretical gaps, and tender new philosophical overtures, this book's overall aim is to contribute to a more robust and fruitful understanding of the problem of care morality at the level of both ethics and politics.

NOTES

1. Barack Obama, "The President's Remarks on Justice Souter," *The White House Blog*, 1 May 2009, www.whitehouse.gov/blog/09/05/01/The-Presidents-Remarks-on-Justice-Souter/ (12 July 2010).

2. Jeff Sessions, "Confirmation Hearing: 'Our Chance to Get It Right,'" *Richmond Times-Dispatch*, 12 July 2009, www2.timesdispatch.com/news/2009/jul/12/ed-sessions12_20090710-195407-ar-37551 (12 July 2010).

3. Sarah Wildman, "Closed Sessions: The Senator Who's Worse than Lott," *The New Republic*, 30 Dec. 2002, www.tnr.com/politics/story.html?id=8dd230f6-355f-4362-89cc-2c756b9d8102 12 (12 July 2010).

4. Eager to suggest otherwise, several Republican members of the confirmation committee made much political hay out of a 2001 comment in which Sotomayor suggested that a "wise Latina" judge could arrive at better legal decisions than a white male counterpart. Expectedly, Sotomayor downplayed the remark as "a rhetorical flourish that fell flat. . . . [I]t left an impression that I believed that life experiences commanded a result in a case, but that's clearly not what I do as a judge." In Susan Ferrechio, "Sotomayor: 'Wise Latina' Line Was a Rhetorical Flourish That Didn't Reflect Her Real Views," *The Washington Examiner*, 14 July 2009, www.washingtonexaminer.com/opinion/blogs/beltway-confidential/Sotomayor-wise-Latina-line-was-rhetorical-flourish-that-didnt-reflect-her-real-views-50732192.html (12 July 2010).

5. In Andrew Quinn and James Vicini, "Sotomayor Cool under Republican Grilling," *Reuters*, 14 July 2009, www.reuters.com/article/idUSTRE56B0TA20090714 (12 July 2010).

6. Taking note of its often lackadaisical usage in the contemporary literature, the psychoanalyst Jacques Lacan famously cautioned his students against using the term *the other* "as a mouthwash." Jacques Lacan, *The Seminar of Jacques Lacan: Book II: The Ego in Freud's Theory and in the Technique of Psychoanalysis, 1954–55*, ed. Jacques-Alain Miller, trans. Sylvana Tomaselli (Cambridge, UK: Cambridge University Press, 1988), 7. Throughout this study, an effort has been made to abide by Lacan's admonition.

7. See Sherry B. Ortner, "Theory in Anthropology since the Sixties," in *Culture/Power/History: A Reader in Contemporary Social Theory*, ed. Nicholas B.

Dirks, Jeff Eley, and Sherry B. Ortner (Princeton: Princeton University Press, 1994), 372–411.

8. See George E. Marcus and Michael J. Fischer, *Anthropology as Critique: An Experimental Moment in the Human Sciences* (Chicago: The University of Chicago Press, 1986).

9. Jacques Derrida, *Of Grammatology*, trans. Gayatri Spivak (Baltimore: Johns Hopkins University Press, 1997), 46.

10. See Jane Flax, "Transitional Thinking: Psychoanalytic, Feminist, and Postmodern Theories," in *Thinking Fragments: Psychoanalysis, Feminism, and Postmodernism in the Contemporary West* (Berkeley: The University of California Press, 1990), 14–43.

11. Edith Wyschogrod, *An Ethics of Remembering: History, Heterology, and the Nameless Others* (Chicago: The University of Chicago Press, 1998), xi.

12. Jacques Derrida, *Positions*, trans. Alan Bass (Chicago: The University of Chicago Press, 1981), 26, in Thomas McCarthy, "The Politics of the Ineffable: Derrida's Deconstructionism," in *Hermeneutics and Critical Theory in Ethics and Politics*, ed. Michael Kelly (Cambridge, Mass.: The MIT Press, 1991), 148.

13. McCarthy, "The Politics of the Ineffable," 148.

14. Here and elsewhere in the Introduction I draw upon my "Derrida and Habermas: Asymmetry and Accord." Review of *The Derrida-Habermas Reader*, ed. Lasse Thomassen. *Radical Philosophy Review* 10, no. 2 (2007): 197–203.

15. Such a view of Derrida's shift toward the ethicopolitical is advanced in Axel Honneth, "The Other of Justice: Habermas and the Ethical Challenge of Postmodernism," in *Disrespect: The Normative Foundations of Critical Theory* (Cambridge, UK: Polity Press, 2007), 99–128.

16. For Derrida, the historical confluence of the demise of ethnocentrism and Enlightenment transcendentalism is by no means coincidental: "One can say with total security that there is nothing fortuitous about the fact that the critique of ethnocentrism—the very condition for ethnology—should be systematically and historically contemporaneous with the destruction of the history of metaphysics." Jacques Derrida, *Writing and Difference*, trans. Alan Bass (Chicago: The University of Chicago Press, 1978), 282. This is indeed the philosophical legacy that thinkers like Nietzsche and Heidegger have bequeathed to the contemporary ethnologist. Yet as we shall emphasize throughout this study, Derrida maintains that every effort to disfigure the inside/outside binaries of the Western metaphysical tradition from the deconstructive standpoint of the trace, arche-writing and *différance* is always already coimbricated with the transcendental perspective of the Same. Indeed, "whether he wants to or not—and this does not depend on a decision on his part—the ethnologist accepts into his discourses the premises of ethnocentrism at the very moment when he denounces them." Derrida, *Writing and Difference*, 282.

17. The echo of Derridean deconstruction and the broader poststructuralist turn in continental philosophy reverberates widely in contemporary feminist, multiculturalist, postcolonial, and subaltern historiographic writing. Homi Bhabha, *The Location of Culture* (New York: Routledge, 1994) and Gayatri Spivak, *In Other Worlds: Essays in Cultural Politics* (New York: Routledge, 1988) are but two of the many important texts to consider in this context.

18. Jacques Derrida, "Hospitality, Justice and Responsibility: A Dialogue with Jacques Derrida," in *Questioning Ethics: Contemporary Debates in Philosophy*, ed. Richard Kearny and Mark Dooley (New York: Routledge, 1999), 69.

19. Derrida, "Hospitality, Justice and Responsibility," 70.

20. Derrida, "Hospitality, Justice and Responsibility," 71.

21. Giovanna Borradori, ed., *Philosophy in a Time of Terror: Dialogues with Jürgen Habermas and Jacques Derrida* (Chicago: The University of Chicago Press, 2003), 161.

22. Jacques Derrida and Giovanna Borradori, "Autoimmunity: Real and Symbolic Suicides—A Dialogue with Jacques Derrida," in *Philosophy in a Time of Terror: Dialogues with Jürgen Habermas and Jacques Derrida*, ed. Giovanna Borradori (Chicago: The University of Chicago Press, 2003), 128.

23. Jacques Derrida, *Rogues: Two Essays on Reason*, trans. Pascale-Anne Brault and Michael Nass (Stanford: Stanford University Press, 2005), 11.

24. Matthias Fritsch, "Derrida's Reading of Marx," in *The Promise of Memory: History and Politics in Marx, Benjamin, and Derrida* (New York: The State University of New York Press, 2005), 71. Fritsch's account is especially concerned with interrogating the decentered understanding of memory and loss that emerges from Derrida's "hauntological," or spectral, reading of Marx.

25. See "Theses on the Philosophy of History," in *Illuminations*, ed. Hannah Arendt (New York: Schocken, 1969), 253–64. Benjamin's *Jetztzeit* and Bloch's notion of nonsimultaneity will be discussed in relation to Derrida's complementary idea of *khôra* in chapter 4. In this context, it is also interesting to note the affinities between Derrida's endeavor to dislocate the spatiotemporal fixity of the social text and Michel Foucault's notion of "eventalization." With this concept, Foucault contests the logocentrism and linearity of positivist causality by construing the singular event as a "'polygon' or, rather, a 'polyhedron' of intelligibility, the number of whose faces is not given in advance and can never be taken as finite. One has to proceed," says Foucault, "by progressive, necessarily incomplete saturation." Michel Foucault, *Power: The Essential Works of Foucault, 1954–1984, Volume 3*, ed. James D. Faubion (New York: The New Press, 1994), 227.

26. Simon Critchley, "Frankfurt Impromptu—Remarks on Derrida and Habermas," in *The Derrida-Habermas Reader*, ed. Lasse Thomassen (Chicago: The University of Chicago Press, 2006), 108.

27. Derrida, *Rogues*, 150.

28. Jacques Derrida, "Deconstructing Terrorism," in *Philosophy in a Time of Terror: Dialogues with Jürgen Habermas and Jacques Derrida*, ed. Giovanna Borradori (Chicago: The University of Chicago Press, 2003), 169; my emphasis.

29. Jacques Derrida, "Force of Law," in *Acts of Religion*, ed. Gil Anidjar (New York: Routledge, 2002), 248.

30. In contrast to some readers, I will argue throughout this study that whatever its terminological and conceptual shifts, there is more continuity than discontinuity in Habermas's decades-long project. Particular emphasis will be placed on Habermas's dualistic account of human reason, which has in my view underlain the basic philosophical itinerary and trajectory of his thinking over the years.

31. Jürgen Habermas and Giovanna Borradori, "Fundamentalism and Terror—A Dialogue with Jürgen Habermas," in *Philosophy in a Time of Terror*, 40.

32. Jürgen Habermas, "Religious Tolerance—The Pacemaker of Cultural Rights," in *The Derrida-Habermas Reader*, ed. Lasse Thomassen (Chicago: The University of Chicago Press, 2006), 200.

33. Habermas and Borradori, "Fundamentalism and Terror," 41–42.

34. Jürgen Habermas, "On the Relation between the Secular Liberal State and Religion," in *The Frankfurt School on Religion: Key Writings by the Major Thinkers*, ed. Eduardo Mendieta (New York: Routledge, 2005), 340.

35. Elaborated out of the Husserlian tradition of phenomenology, the lifeworld, in Habermas's rendering, "forms a horizon and at the same time offers a store of things taken for granted in the given culture from which communicative participants draw consensual interpretative patterns in their efforts at interpretation." Jürgen Habermas, "An Alternative Way Out of the Philosophy of the Subject: Communicative versus Subject-Centered Reason," in *The Philosophical Discourse of Modernity: Twelve Lectures*, trans. Frederick G. Lawrence (Cambridge, Mass.: The MIT Press, 1990), 298. In contrast, action in the economic and political subsystems is coordinated via strategic organizing directives (undergirded by the "delinguistified" steering media of money and administrative power, respectively), without reference to reciprocal argumentation procedures aimed at mutual understanding.

36. Joel Whitebook, "The Problem of Nature in Habermas," *Telos* 40 (Summer 1979): 65.

37. Bill Martin, "What Is at the Heart of Language?" in *Matrix and Line: Derrida and the Possibilities of Postmodern Social Theory* (New York: The State University of New York Press, 1992), 85. Martin's account offers a useful overview of the problem of language in the two thinkers' writings, raising a number of forceful arguments against Habermas.

38. Jürgen, Habermas, "A Reply to My Critics," in *Habermas: Critical Debates*, ed. John B. Thompson and David Held (Cambridge, Mass.: The MIT Press, 1982), 221, 227.

39. Habermas, "Three Perspectives: Left Hegelians, Right Hegelians, and Nietzsche," in *The Philosophical Discourse of Modernity*, 63.

40. Jürgen Habermas, "Ernst Bloch: A Marxist Schelling," in *Philosophical-Political Profiles*, trans. Frederick G. Lawrence (Cambridge, Mass.: The MIT Press, 1983), 64–65.

41. For an important elaboration of this idea, see Albrecht Wellmer, "The Latent Positivism of Marx's Philosophy of History," in *Critical Theory of Society*, trans. John Cumming (New York: Continuum, 1971), 67–119.

42. Jürgen Habermas, *Between Facts and Norms: Contributions to a Discourse Theory of Law and Democracy*, trans. William Rehg (Cambridge, Mass.: The MIT Press, 1996), 478.

43. In Richard Rorty, "Habermas and Lyotard on Postmodernity," in *Habermas and Modernity*, ed. Richard J. Bernstein (Cambridge, Mass.: The MIT Press, 1985), 167.

44. Jürgen Habermas, "Beyond a Temporalized Philosophy of Origins: Jacques Derrida's Critique of Phonocentrism" and "Excursus on Leveling the Genre Distinc-

tion between Philosophy and Literature," in Habermas, *The Philosophical Discourse of Modernity*, 161–84, 185–210.

45. Seyla Benhabib, "Democracy and Difference: Reflections on the Metapolitics of Lyotard and Derrida," in *The Derrida-Habermas Reader*, ed. Lasse Thomassen (Chicago: The University of Chicago Press, 2006), 144.

46. Jürgen Habermas, "The Entwinement of Myth and Enlightenment: Re-Reading *Dialectic of Enlightenment*," *New German Critique* 26 (Spring-Summer 1982): 25, 27, in Richard J. Bernstein, "An Allegory of Modernity/Postmodernity: Habermas and Derrida," in *The Derrida-Habermas Reader*, ed. Lasse Thomassen (Chicago: The University of Chicago Press, 2006), 78.

47. Bernstein, "An Allegory of Modernity/Postmodernity," 81.

48. Bernstein, "An Allegory of Modernity/Postmodernity," 81.

Chapter One

Care and Justice:
Competing Conceptions of the Moral?

This chapter begins by surveying the theoretical contours of Jürgen Habermas's proposed distinction between an ethics of care and a morality of justice. It then considers the arguments of several authors who are sympathetic to the overarching philosophical aims of Habermas's discourse-ethical program, but who nevertheless object to its insistence upon a strict partitioning of the two perspectives. These critics include Seyla Benhabib, whose feminist critique of communicative ethics has been enormously influential, helping to set the terms of much of the contemporary debate about how the relation between moralities of care and justice should be conceptualized in critical social theory. To conclude the chapter, I examine the arguments of Stella Gaon, James Gordon Finlayson, Sharon Krause, Steven Hendley, and William Rehg. While these writers are likewise critical of the strict partition between moral norms and ethical values drawn by Habermas, they are also dissatisfied with aspects of Benhabib's proposed corrective to this problem.

HABERMAS'S ACCOUNT OF THE CARE/JUSTICE SCHISM

One of Habermas's first attempts to situate care and justice as distinct moral orientations appears in an essay entitled "Justice and Solidarity."[1] Here his communications theory acknowledges its indebtedness to Lawrence Kohlberg's account of moral ego development, whose final, postconventional "stage 6" is dependent for its attainment upon the satisfaction of certain formal, cognitively concordant criteria—namely, ideal role taking, reversibility of perspectives, and universalizability. The stage 6 moral ego, Habermas notes, assumes that the project of perspective taking is not one-sided but reciprocal. Alter is expected to take Ego's perspective in the same way, so that the contested mode of action can be perceived and thematized in mutual agreement, taking into consideration the interests affected on both sides. . . . This [therefore] requires a universal interchangeability of perspectives of all concerned; Ego must be able to imagine how each person would put herself in the place of every other person.[2]

While Habermas recognizes the importance of universalizability, reversibility, and perspectivity as intersubjective criteria for a postconventional moral orientation, he is critical of Kohlberg's attempt to derive from these norms as a "common higher principle" encompassing both "equal treatment" and "benevolence." Indeed, Kohlberg is faulted for envisaging the two moral outlooks as in some sense reconcilable, notwithstanding Kohlberg's concession that the standpoint of "concern for the welfare of the other, compassion, love of one's fellow man, and willingness to help in the broadest sense" stands in a "tense relationship" with the principle of respect for the dignity of all as equal and autonomous individuals.[3] According to Habermas, Kohlberg fails to appreciate just how tense the relationship between care and universal justice is. The latter theorist incorporates the principle of benevolence into the principle of equal respect for all persons only to commit what Habermas sees as a tacit shift in meaning—namely, privileging the capacity for empathy and strengthened social ties at the expense of the purely cognitive and impartial ideal role–taking procedures of moral judgment.

To avoid Kohlberg's presumed category mistake and the "emotivistic bias" to which it gives rise, Habermas seeks to uphold the principles of benevolence and justice as discrete, indeed *competing*, moral standpoints. His first step is to resituate the procedural conditions of postconventional morality identified by Kohlberg in the expressly dialogical framework of discourse ethics, which enjoins subjects to *publicly* justify and adjudicate contested validity claims and value convictions. So positioned, the procedural criteria of stage 6 morality are no longer anticipated, as in Kohlberg, by a private, inner-directed moral ego, but become the abstract normative ballast for the real-world discourses of communicative consociates. This move allows Habermas to transfigure Kohlberg's notion of benevolence into what he calls "solidarity":

[T]he perspective complementing that of equal treatment is not that of benevolence but solidarity. . . . Justice concerns the equal freedoms of unique and self-determining individuals, while solidarity concerns the welfare of consociates who are intimately linked in an intersubjectively shared form of life—and thus also the maintenance of the integrity of this form of life itself. Moral norms can-

not protect one without the other: they cannot protect the equal rights and freedoms of the individual without protecting the welfare of one's fellow man and
of the community to which the individuals belong.[4]

Note that on this deontological, discourse-ethical conception of moral
rights and duties, the effort to carve open a place for the "reverse side of
justice" via the category of solidarity can be pursued only so far: at a certain
point, Habermas must accede to the limitations of his rationalist account of
discursive universal will-formation and expressly distinguish the idea of
solidarity from questions of care, needs, and the good life—i.e., precisely
those questions that Kohlberg hopes to encompass under the rubric of benevolence. With Hegel, then, Habermas sets out to shear solidarity of "the
particularism of the concrete other" (as set forth in Aristotle's ethics of the
polis and Thomistic ethics of goods, for example) in recognition of the
"strictly postmetaphysical premise that evaluative questions concerning the
good life must remain separate from normative questions concerning a just
communal life—because, unlike the latter questions, the former are not capable of being formulated theoretically, that is, they are not accessible to rational discussion that claims to be universally binding."[5] As Axel Honneth
notes, Habermas's idea of solidarity resonates with the idea of care insofar as
it acknowledges that the concern expressed for the existential welfare of others admits of an affective dimension. The principle of solidarity nonetheless
"differs from care in that it applies equally to all human beings without any
privileging or asymmetry. For Habermas, solidarity is the other of justice
because it entails that all subjects reciprocally attend to the welfare of the
other, with whom they also share the communicative form of human life as
equal human beings."[6]

In keeping one-sided acts of care at an unambiguous conceptual remove
from the symmetrical norms of equal treatment, Habermas is well positioned
to defend the fundamental moral standpoint of discourse ethics, as encapsulated in the now well-known "principle (U)." According to its initial formulation in 1983's *Moral Consciousness and Communicative Action*, (U) holds
that a controversial norm can admit of validity only if *all* who stand to be affected by it "can accept the consequences and the side effects [that its] general
observance . . . can be anticipated to have for the satisfaction of the interests
of each individual."[7] With (U), then, matters bearing on the welfare of concrete others remain in direct competition with universalistic principles of equal
treatment. Habermas is at pains, indeed, to remand the viewpoints and concerns of particular communities of value to the heading of the "ethical," which
is thereby clearly differentiated from the strictly "moral" standpoint of generalized justice articulated in principle (U). The ethical, on this account, always

presumes a "shared ethos" that places "at issue how we understand ourselves as members of our community, how we should orient our lives, or what is best for us in the long run and all things considered."[8] Accordingly, the universalization test (U) commends participants in moral discourses to adopt a dialogic stance distinct from both the objectivating attitude of instrumental rationality as well as the particularistic perspective attendant to questions of needs, affective attachments, and the good life. Indeed, only upon cleansing itself of such asymmetrical orientations is the moral reason of the discourse ethic poised to "authorize the universal norms that justice entails."[9]

SEYLA BENHABIB'S CRITIQUE

Since its publication in 1992, Seyla Benhabib's essay, "The Generalized and the Concrete Other,"[10] has been widely read and acknowledged (by some) as a "classic" and indeed "groundbreaking"[11] work. Here Benhabib appeals to some of the key findings of Carol Gilligan's *In a Different Voice* (itself a highly influential study) to contest both Habermas's and Kohlberg's depiction of care and justice as "incompatible," even "antagonistic" moral standpoints. In Benhabib's view, Gilligan is rightly far more sanguine about the ability—shown by the women subjects of her study[12]—to display affective sensitivity to situational complexities rather than abstract from particulars and provide abstract, universally defensible reasons for given validity claims and value convictions. Indeed, for Gilligan the propensity to eschew abstract moral reasoning and evince compassion and empathy in concrete situations must be understood as a mark of *moral maturity*. Significantly, however, Gilligan sees both the impartialist "justice" perspective and the contextualist and interpersonal "care" perspective as counterposed and incapable of reconciliation. As William Rehg observes, she maintains that "for a given moral situation, one simply has to take one perspective or the other, but one cannot simultaneously entertain both, or bring both together in a single moral perspective."[13]

Dissatisfied with this nonintegrationist view, Benhabib's idea is to reposition the two perspectives as lying "along a continuum," such that obligations and relations of care present themselves as "genuinely moral ones, belonging to the *center* and not the margins of morality."[14] Accordingly, Benhabib does not so much reject Habermas's distinction between care and justice as challenge his resolve to exclude acts of affective attachment from the domain of the "moral," strictly speaking. The main difficulty, she suggests, lies with Habermas's conceptualization of principle (U), which privileges the moral argumentation norms of rational, generic, "disembedded" interlocutors at the expense of the particular needs, viewpoints, and goods of "concrete others"—

that is, persons recognized as unique individuals "with a concrete history, identity and affective-emotional constitution."[15] Indeed, this bias toward the "generalized other" positions (U) to effectively expunge matters of care from the purview of legitimate moral deliberation: it sentences the concrete other to recede epistemologically "behind the façade of a definitional identity of all as rational beings," where a universalist morality of justice secures the dignity and worth of the moral subject "at the cost of forgetting and repressing our vulnerability and dependency as bodily selves."[16] As Benhabib sees it, Habermas must therefore be deemed guilty of a certain "substitutionalist universalism"—that is, a privileging of the moral sphere of the generalized other over and against that of the concrete other.[17]

To guard against this substitutionalist fallacy (an error that neo-Kantians such as Kohlberg and John Rawls are likewise accused of committing), Benhabib argues for an "interactive universalism" that takes full account of Gilligan's resolve to accord everyday, interactional problems pertaining to care, needs, and the good life a place in moral-practical discourses.[18] The effort here is to enrich and extend Habermas's view of solidarity and the moral, such that they are no longer strictly circumscribed by the cognitive-centric argumentation rules undergirding the discourses of disembodied selves. Benhabib is nevertheless well aware of a basic risk that attends to any effort to nudge asymmetrical gestures of care within the orbit of generalized criteria of equal treatment—namely, the danger of according to the concrete other the authority to present its own parochial and potentially immoral claims as those that are best for all. Benhabib cites the clan-centric morality of organized crime syndicates such as the Mafia as a case in point. She notes that any effort to universalize the Mafia's asymmetrical value orientations would undermine the fundamental discourse-ethical objective of vouchsafing the dignity and autonomy of all as free and equal citizens.[19] To guard against such a relativist outcome—which is of course also precisely the aim of Habermas's critique of Kohlberg's proposed reconciliation between the standpoints of benevolence and justice—Benhabib maintains that the fruitfulness of any communicative-theoretic effort to link the moral identity of the concrete other to that of the generalized other must rest on a clear categorical distinction between each domain, such that the particularistic concerns of a given care ethos are in the end always subordinated to questions of universal justice. "Such a universalism supplies the constraints within which the morality of care must operate."[20]

For Benhabib, the task is thus to reconcile such "constraining" moral universalism with the asymmetrical gesture of felt concern for the other as a concrete, vulnerable, and dependent bodily self. To this end, she avers that there are in fact good grounds for abandoning Habermas's principle (U) in favor of the less "abstract," less "consensus-guaranteeing" principle of discourse ethics (D), which accords validity to only those norms "that meet (or could meet) with the approval of all concerned as participants in practical discourse."[21] For Benhabib (D) coupled with the principles of universal moral respect and egalitarian reciprocity (i.e., the argumentation rules undergirding practical discourses) amount, in and of themselves, to a sufficient universalizability test. There is no need whatsoever for (U), which does little more than excise ethical orientations such as love and friendship from "the phenomenology of moral experience" while remanding the universal core of morality to the exclusive custody of disembedded communicative consociates.

On this move, Benhabib invites objections from Derrideans and kindred critics, who argue—as we shall see in chapter 2—that in affirming the ascendancy of the universal moral standpoint, she is ultimately no less guilty than Habermas of sacrificing the other's irreducible alterity to the logocentric violence of the Same. To fend off such charges, Benhabib appeals to Hannah Arendt's notion of an "enlarged mentality." Positioned at the normative core of her proposed framework, Arendt's category helps Benhabib argue that precisely because it is attuned to a multiplicity of viewpoints and subject positions, "and precisely because it is ready to submit all its fundamental principles to debate, [interactive universalism] can provide the bases for the public philosophy of a pluralist, tolerant, democratic-liberal polity."[22] Her claim here is that the discourse ethic is structurally equipped with a certain pluralizing self-reflexivity (or, as Arendt would have it, an enlarged mentality): it commends interlocutors to reverse perspectives and face the irreducible distinctiveness of the other through something like a Hegelian "struggle for recognition," rather than to simply ignore or project this difference away as mere illusion.[23]

With this effort to bring the ethical values, needs, and affects of particular subjectivities to the fore of moral disputation, Benhabib extends one of the principal intercessions of her first major work, *Critique, Norm, and Utopia*, which mobilizes a certain Hegelian reading of discourse ethics in order to articulate two complementary visions of politics—one normative (the "politics of fulfillment"), and the other utopian (the "politics of transfiguration"). The former, claims Benhabib, "envisages that the society of the future attains more adequately what the present society has left unaccomplished," while the latter "emphasizes the emergence of qualitatively new needs, social relations, and modes of association, which burst open the utopian potential within the old."[24]

Some Initial Rejoinders to Benhabib

Many of Benhabib's objections to Habermas's discourse-ethical conception of morality have been affirmed, reinforced, and extended in significant terms by other thinkers. These writers include Stella Gaon, who, in line with Benhabib, criticizes Habermas for prioritizing the cognitive perspective of equal treatment and mutual understanding. She too finds Habermas's model guilty of devaluing the asymmetrical concerns, needs, and affects of concrete bodily selves to the point of transcendentalizing and teleologizing "the figure of a fully autonomous, unambiguously rational, Kantian 'Man.'"[25] Gaon departs from Benhabib, however, in maintaining that a sharp schism between moral norms and ethical values is a necessary, indeed "structurally indispensable," condition of Habermas's program: it cannot simply be reconstructed away by moving the attitude of affective sympathy and questions of the good life to the fore of moral discourse—as Benhabib proposes—without undermining the basic philosophical scaffolding of discourse ethics (which Benhabib, no less than Habermas, is committed to upholding). In Gaon's view, Habermas's "theory is caught between the equally undesirable choices of either having to derive the legitimacy of *the* moral point of view from an unthematized reference to transcendence, or falling prey to the charge of relativism Habermas has consistently sought to refute. Consequently, discourse ethics can be shown to privilege a subject that is removed, *in essence and by definition*, from the contingencies of everyday life."[26]

Habermas's framework is on this conviction portrayed as congenitally unable to accord individual self-understandings and identities "full play" in moral discourses, as this would undermine the strict criteria of impartiality that such dialogues impose. *Contra* Benhabib, Gaon maintains that it is simply not the case that "concrete selves can engage in the full reversal of interpretative structure that Habermas demands. . . . For concretely-situated others, in contrast to general and abstract ones, are decidedly partial, precisely to the extent that they cannot be said to be removed from the normative spectrum of their everyday lives."[27] Try as she might to thematize the empathetic dimension of communicative ethics—that is, to coax the concerns, affects, and needs of concrete subjectivities within the compass of the symmetrical norms of moral argumentation—Benhabib, in Gaon's view, cannot overcome the discourse ethic's constitutive incapacity to reconcile human plurality and concrete "definitional identities" with its own procedural norms of ideal role taking, universalizability, and symmetrical reversibility of perspectives. Since definitional identity presupposes *incomplete reversibility*, Gaon adjudges Habermas's model to be ensnared in the same theoretical quagmire in which other universalistic moral philosophies find themselves: like them, it has little choice but to privilege "a 'generalized' concept of the self," in full awareness of its own inherent inability to account "for concrete differences among actual moral discussants."[28] Put differently, "unless (U) is virtually inescapable, there is no basis for Habermas's claim that the empty procedure of discourse ethics is structurally related to the substantive, ethical interests of all communicative agents."[29]

Gaon's analysis is sharply at odds with the arguments of James Gordon Finlayson, who insists—correctly in my view—that Habermas is by no means guilty of transcendentalizing the moral subject, precisely insofar his framework consigns the adjudication of moral norms to the *terra firma* of real-world discourses. Indeed, Finlayson denies that Habermas has theorized anything resembling a "generalized" or "abstract" other at all, let alone positioned it to obliterate the viewpoints of actual bodily selves. He insists, rather, that all participants in principle (U)–governed discourses are in fact real, concrete persons; in no sense are they situated as

> abstract, "disembodied and disembedded" individuals as Benhabib claims. In which case, it is not true that moral discourse (at least as Habermas understands it) makes the concrete other vanish, or blinds agents to the *viewpoint* of the concrete other. Participants in discourse have to adopt the (myriad) points of view of every other concrete person in order to ascertain whether their values and interests are generalizable or not. And contra Benhabib even the hypothetical others whose viewpoints we take up, and whose interests we must determine in the course of advocatory discourses, are in fact concrete, particular others.[30]

As Habermas has not actually differentiated the contextual other from the generic other in the sense that both Gaon and Benhabib suggest, the claim that (U) entails the subsumption of the former by the latter in moral discourses cannot be sustained.[31]

To Finlayson, a logical fallacy undergirds Benhabib's argument. On the one hand, principle (U) is criticized for shunting obligations and relations of care to the margins of morality, rather than commending them to their rightful place at the center of that domain. Yet on the other hand, Benhabib denies the universalizability of care, love, friendship, and conceptions of the good, and insists that generalized principles of justice must always "trump" and "constrain" partialistic and personal expressions of concern for the other. According to Finlayson, Benhabib is therefore ill positioned to carry forth her criticism of Habermas, as "she too allows that morality has a central core of universal and impartial principles, and arguably even allows that this central core can be captured by a single principle."[32] Seen in this light, there is in fact an irreconcilable tension, he suggests, between Benhabib's desire to prioritize care in moral discourses and her overarching commitment to the theory of moral universalism set forth in discourse ethics, which imposes clear limitations on any effort to smudge the distinctions between care and justice. Ultimately, Benhabib, no less than Habermas, must accede to those limitations and subordinate one-sided expressions of concern for the existential welfare of others to the moral standpoint of universal justice and equal treatment. As Finlayson comments, Habermas would have little difficulty with Benhabib's contention that the moral arena is not exhausted by relations of justice: he would simply maintain, as she is likewise obliged to do, that principles of equal treatment must occupy a central position within morality.[33]

Finlayson finds less to quibble with, however, when it comes to a second line of argument taken up by Benhabib—that is, her contention that Habermas has tendered a too-sharp distinction between the good/ethics and justice/morality. Agreeing with Benhabib, he maintains that "Habermas needs to say something more about the relation between ethical values and moral norms, since he claims both that valid norms protect universalizable interests, and that interests are needs that are interpreted in light of values. However, his strict distinction between morality and ethics prevents him from doing just this."[34]

An interesting attempt to draw Habermas out on the question of the relation between the moral and the ethical is set forth by Sharon Krause. According to Krause, in forging a sharp categorical divide between these two arenas, Habermas's theory saddles itself with a troubling "motivational deficit." Krause puts the difficulty this way: discourses duly uncoupled "from questions of the good and the affective attachments that go with them" appear to offer little impetus for communicative consociates to engage in moral deliberation in the first place.[35] At the level of moral psychology, the injunction to subject each and every claim and conviction to the universalization test of discourse ethics would seem, in other words, to be a wholly insufficient incentive to participate in moral dialogue. Indeed, one could imagine a scenario in which adherence to (U) yields little more than "endless iterations of rational discourse aimed at reaching understanding," and a consequent "loss of confidence in reason and the end of rational discourse as a normative ideal."[36]

The idea that a project of discourse-ethical decision making could ultimately exhaust itself in a "joyless reformism" has not been lost on Habermas. In his 1972 essay on Walter Benjamin, for example, he asks,

> Is it possible that one day an emancipated human race could encounter itself within an expanded space of discursive formation of the will and yet be robbed of the light in which it is capable of interpreting its life as something good? The revenge of a culture exploited over millennia for the legitimation of domination would thus take this form: Right at the moment of overcoming age-old repressions, it would harbor no violence but it would have no content either. . . . The structures of practical discourse—finally well established—would necessarily become desolate.[37]

In *Between Facts and Norms*, Habermas returns to this theme, noting that the banalization of everyday political discourse carries with it the danger of eroding the semantic potentials of the "uncanny," from which moral communication must draw its nourishment. To guard against this potential "entropy of meaning," it simply won't do, he argues, to invoke the "transcending" power of dialogical reasonableness alone. Rather, if the trivial and the everyday are to "remain open to the shock of what is absolutely strange, cryptic, or uncanny," we must have recourse to *other kinds* of transcendence, those that "refuse to be assimilated to pregiven categories."[38] Examples of such transcendent potentialities include "the unfulfilled promise disclosed by the critical appropriation of identity-forming religious traditions . . . and the negativity of modern art."[39] In this context, Habermas even allows for a certain permeability between the private and public spheres. Although marked by different conditions of communication, he maintains that "the public sphere draws its impulses from the private handling of social problems that resonate in life histories."[40]

Such proposals are indicative of the effort that Habermas has made in recent years to nudge what he earlier referred to, with Benjamin, as an "influx of semantic energies"[41] within the normative orbit of discourse ethics. This move has been undertaken on the conviction that questions of norm justification cannot be successfully resolved "without empathetic sensitivity by each person to everyone else": a "mature capacity for moral judgment" requires the "integration of cognitive operations and emotional dispositions and attitudes."[42] Habermas underscores this point in developing his notion of "constitutional patriotism." According to this idea, my own existential commitment to discourse-ethical norms enjoins my corollary, affective allegiance to the democratic-constitutional principles, institutions, and practices that enable me to engage with others in a consociative project aimed at reaching mutual understanding about our contested value convictions. Precisely because constitutional patriotism makes "the subjective feelings and attitudes of participants toward the norms under deliberation relevant to the validity of these norms," it is able to mediate "between the cognitive standpoint that justifies norms and the affectivity that normally animates action."[43] From its vantage point, we can readily see that "every legal community and every democratic process for actualizing basic rights is inevitability permeated by ethics."[44]

To Krause, Habermas has on these terms accorded ethical goods and value orientations entrée into the justification procedures of the universalization test, making them *in some sense* cohabitable with its reason and interests.[45] Viewed in these terms, Habermas's account of the justice perspective places itself at some remove from the model of pure proceduralism that it is often presumed to represent. In fact, according to some commentators, Habermas has muddied the boundaries between care and justice to the point where they are no longer, strictly speaking, in schism. This is in fact the interpretation of

Steven Hendley. Hendley maintains that in portraying the attitude of affective concern for the vulnerable bodily self as a prerequisite for the cognitive adjudication of contested moral validity claims, Habermas has established the propriety and significance of care for discourse ethics.[46] Hendley's diagnosis is affirmed by William Rehg in his well-known study of Habermas's discourse ethics, *Insight and Solidarity*. According to Rehg, grounds for a rapprochement between the ethics of care and the impartialist perspective of justice embodied in principle (U) are readily apparent when we consider the problem of "application." Rehg notes that from a discourse-ethical vantage point, every attempt to apply a moral norm in a concrete situation "is potentially open to the whole gamut of considerations raised in the ethics of care"; in fact, "the discourse-ethical practice of application requires something like a concrete moral solidarity . . . [that] turns the participant's gaze on the quite particular aspects of one another's welfare."[47]

To illustrate this point, Rehg considers a hypothetical example of moral norm application, which has been cited in the ensuing literature on discourse ethics with some frequency. In this scenario, a philosophy professor, whom Rehg calls John, has taken employment at a university on a year-to-year contract basis in hopes of eventually obtaining a tenure-track position.[48] A number of years pass, at which point the university suddenly announces that it will conduct nationwide merit-based searches for all tenure-track appointments, throttling John's expectations about where his contract work at the university was ultimately leading him. Rehg considers various circumstances under which the actors involved in this case might decide whether or not the moral norm at play (the expectation of fair and equal treatment from the university's hiring bureaucracy) has been justly applied. Perhaps John's personal situation is such that requiring him to compete with other job seekers on a merit basis would leave him vulnerable to a wholly unsupportable existential injury (e.g., the loss of his familial relationships and his longstanding geographic ties to the local community), whereas other potential applicants would face no such threat. Under such circumstances, the university would be obliged to qualify its merit norm, applying it only in instances where it would not mean subjecting those already employed on a contract basis to the sorts of existential damages faced by John. Countless other permutations of mitigating circumstances and corresponding qualifications to the university's merit norm are of course possible. The central point for Rehg, however, is that the moral standpoint of discourse ethics enjoins us to see that "even the straightforward application of general rules must presuppose . . . a sensitive apprehension of situational particulars, especially those pertaining to the 'weal and woe' of other persons."[49] Rehg argues that inasmuch as both standpoints have underscored the importance of interpersonal responsiveness to the "nonrepeatable particularity" of the concrete situation, discourse ethics is well positioned and indeed well counseled to forge an alliance with the ethics of care.

As with Benhabib, however, Rehg's attempt to fashion such a rapprochement is pulled short, in the end, by his allegiance to the basic conceptual morphology of the discourse-ethical model, which imposes intractable limitations upon one's ability to reconcile the asymmetrical gesture of care with the symmetrical norms of moral argumentation. While Rehg, no less than Habermas, may be keen to associate the procedures of universal will formation with an ethics of care—to retain, in other words, "a remnant of good at the core of the right,"[50] the demand that moral discussants abstract from concrete situations and subject their particular validity claims to the universalizability test remains ascendant in Habermas's account of norm application. Even if discourse ethics does not quite relegate the standpoint of care to "second-class status,"[51] its prioritization of principle (U) means that controversial moral norms, and any qualifications or exceptions that might be made to them, must meet with the universally binding consensus of the persons affected if they are to be adjudged rational. Habermas's perspective therefore faces inflexible barriers when attempting to conceptualize an orientation of care for the truly particularistic, or nonrepeatable, example. As Hendley observes, what gets lost in Habermas is precisely "the moral significance of this substantive relation to the other that is constitutive of care and that establishes the point of my engagement to discursive procedures with the vulnerable other."[52]

It would appear, then, that whatever his efforts to theorize the care perspective as a necessary source of "nourishment" for moral discourse, Habermas ultimately prioritizes the "cognitive rather than affective dimensions of the self."[53] In my view, such a valorization of the cognitive aspects of moral argumentation is indeed essential in order to avoid the potentially unsavory moral implications of allowing particular *ethoi* of care to claim the field of universal moral disputation as their own (recall Benhabib's warnings about a Mafia-style care perspective "gone wild"). Yet the terms in which Habermas—as well as sympathetic care-ethical critics such as Benhabib—have prioritized the impartialist standpoint are beset by a basic deficit: they neglect to conceptualize relations of care and affective attachment as "conceptually and genetically antecedent" to the efforts of self and other to understand one another from the standpoint of detached moral cognition. In this regard, I break with Habermas and follow Axel Honneth, who maintains that because it labors under a "simplistic conception that every form of detached observation is opposed to antecedent recognition," the discourse-ethical model does not "take sufficient account of the fact that the neutralization of recognition and [affective] engagement normally serves the purpose of intelligent problem solving."[54] In other words, from Habermas's standpoint, one fails to appreciate that the structure of moral argumentation originates in a prereflexive orientation of "existential engagement" or "caring." Such a Honnethian conceptualization of care eludes even a critic like Rehg, who, as we have seen, argues quite forcefully for the coextensivity of the asymmetrical care perspective and the impartial, universalistic moral standpoint of discourse ethics.

Interestingly, writers like Georg Lukács and Martin Heidegger are not guilty of such an oversight, inasmuch as they—in Honneth's estimation at least—have situated the attitude of recognitional concern in precisely such a precursive relationship to the standpoint of detached cognition. Whatever the (undeniably considerable) disparities between their respective frameworks, both authors acknowledge that "the elementary structures of the human form of life characterized by 'care' [in Heidegger's terms] and existential interestedness [in Lukács's] are always already there."[55] Yet what Honneth understands as the conceptual and genetic primacy of caring recognition is obscured in Habermas's model; from its vantage point, it is difficult to see that this earlier perspective adds "an element of affective disposition, even of positive predisposition, which is not appropriately expressed by the notion that subjects always seek to understand each other's reasons for acting."[56]

In response to such charges, Habermas would no doubt insist that there are in fact good grounds for prioritizing the impartialist standpoint of norm justification on the terms that he proposed. He would argue that in failing to do so, a thinker like Honneth will be hard pressed to preserve the "razor-sharp cuts" between evaluative claims and normative ones, between the good/ethics and the just/moral, which are needed to keep the specter of relativist prevarication at bay.[57] As Krause observes, "the more the right is embedded within the good—the more justice makes reference to ethical life—the disagreements about the good found in all modern societies will . . . [render] liberal-democratic justice controversial in precisely the way Habermas seeks to avoid."[58] Indeed, however much Habermas may tinker with the idea of allying subjective needs, affects, and goods with the detached, cognitivist procedures of moral discourse, the requirements of his deontological, universalistic moral theory constrain him from fully bridging the conceptual gulf between the two standpoints. Krause concedes that Habermas is correct to worry that the more that moral reasoning is allowed to cohabitate with ethical life, the more likely it is that the "feeling-neutral" standpoint of justice will be infected by a destabilizing influx of competing conceptions of the good—a danger that attends, for example, to Rawls's idea of "primary goods" (see note 45 of this chapter). She argues that one is nevertheless well instructed to undertake such a move and abide by its limitations in the interest of forestalling the motivational deficit that attends to the ascendant standpoint of moral cognitivism in Habermas's theory.

While I sympathize with the impetus behind Krause's proposal, I am more wary than she perhaps is of the prospect of undermining or subverting the conceptual priority of the impartialist standpoint of moral discourse. Indeed, I maintain that Habermas is correct to give categorical precedence to this orientation so that the relativist dangers just underscored can be staved off. I do, however, insist that Habermas as well as his care-ethical critics would be better positioned to defend themselves against charges of cognitive centrism were they to acknowledge, with Honneth, the conceptual and genetic primacy of the care perspective—at least at the level of social integration. This thesis—which is in fact one of the central intercessions of this book—will be developed at length in chapter 5, where I present a detailed examination and critique of Honneth's proposed epistemology of care.

However, before mounting this argument, I shall consider, in the next chapter, the deconstructive framework of Jacques Derrida, which attempts nothing less than a thoroughgoing disarticulation of the kinds of discourse-ethical negotiations of care morality that we have considered thus far. Indeed, Derrida's aim is to transfigure the gesture of care so that it can attend to the radical—indeed irreducible—differences between the self and its other at the level of both ethics and politics. It is to this effort that we shall now turn.

NOTES

1. Jürgen Habermas, "Justice and Solidarity: On the Discussion Concerning 'Stage 6,'" in *Hermeneutics and Critical Theory in Ethics and Politics*, ed. Michael Kelly (Cambridge, Mass.: The MIT Press, 1991), 32–52.

2. Habermas, "Justice and Solidarity," 39.

3. Habermas, "Justice and Solidarity," 45.

4. Habermas, "Justice and Solidarity," 47.

5. Habermas, "Justice and Solidarity," 42.

6. Axel Honneth, "The Other of Justice: Habermas and the Ethical Challenge of Postmodernism," in *Disrespect: The Normative Foundations of Critical Theory* (Cambridge, UK: Polity Press, 2007), 123.

7. Jürgen Habermas, *Moral Consciousness and Communicative Action*, trans. Christian Lenhardt and Shierry Weber Nicholsen (Cambridge, Mass.: The MIT Press, 1990), 65.

8. Jürgen Habermas, *The Inclusion of the Other: Studies in Political Theory*, ed. Ciaran P. Cronin and Pablo De Greiff (Cambridge, UK: Polity Press, 1998), 26.

9. Habermas, *The Inclusion of the Other*, 26.

10. Seyla Benhabib, "The Generalized and the Concrete Other: The Kohlberg-Gilligan Controversy and Feminist Theory," in *Situating the Self: Gender, Community and Postmodernism in Contemporary Ethics* (New York: Routledge, 1992), 148–77.

11. Andrea Maihofer's characterization. See her essay, "Care," in *A Companion to Feminist Philosophy*, ed. Alison M. Jaggar and Iris Marion Young (Oxford: Blackwell, 1998), 386.

12. Benhabib discusses the controversy generated by *In a Different Voice* in some detail, including the debate over whether Gilligan has conceived of care as a moral faculty exclusive to women, effectively recapitulating patriarchal accounts of "nurturant" feminine subjectivity under the cover of putatively feminist social-scientific research. Such an essentialist view of women as "caregivers" is defended by, among others, Robin West, who has no compunction whatsoever about declaring that women "are actually or potentially materially connected to other human life. Men aren't." Robin West, *Caring for Justice* (New York: New York University Press, 1997), 14. Benhabib insists that such a position is in large measure wrongly ascribed to Gilligan, and in any case demurs from postulating any hard and fast associations between care and gender. I am likewise disinclined to make this problem a focal point of my study. The question of whether or not there is a gendered dimension to moral reasoning is discussed at some length in Joan C. Tronto, *Moral Boundaries: A Political Argument for an Ethic of Care* (New York: Routledge, 1993). I am grateful to Lorraine Pannett for calling my attention to Tronto's work.

13. William Rehg, *Insight and Solidarity: The Discourse Ethics of Jürgen Habermas* (Berkeley: University of California Press, 1994), 186.

14. Benhabib, "The Generalized and the Concrete Other," 158, 186; my emphasis.

15. Benhabib, "The Generalized and the Concrete Other," 159.

16. Benhabib, "The Generalized and the Concrete Other," 165, 189.

17. Benhabib, "The Generalized and the Concrete Other," 164.

18. Benhabib, "Feminism and the Question of the Postmodern," in *Situating the Self*, 227.

19. Benhabib, "The Debate over Moral Theory Revisited," in *Situating the Self*, 187.

20. Benhabib, "The Debate over Moral Theory Revisited," in *Situating the Self*, 187.

21. Benhabib, "In the Shadow of Aristotle and Hegel: Communicative Ethics and Current Controversies in Practical Philosophy," in *Situating the Self*, 37.

22. Benhabib, "In the Shadow of Aristotle and Hegel," in *Situating the Self*, 44.

23. The "enlarged mentality" of such a post-Enlightenment politics can be receptive, moreover, to an array of specifically gendered concerns, including various feminist struggles against the instrumentalization of the lifeworld—issues, affirms Benhabib, that are often glossed over in Habermas's disgendered account of discourse ethics. Similar objections are raised by Jean Cohen, who upbraids Habermas for treating gender as a category "incidental" to modern processes of system/lifeworld differentiation: "The most significant flaw in Habermas's work is his failure to consider the gendered character roles of worker and citizen that emerged with the differentiation of the market economy and the modern state from the lifeworld"—a defect that in turn leads him to overlook a certain fluidity between the public and private spheres. Jean L. Cohen, "Critical Social Theory and Feminist Critiques: The Debate with Jürgen Habermas," in *Feminists Read Habermas: Gendering the Subject of Discourse*, ed. Johanna Meehan (New York: Routledge, 1995), 71. Nancy Fraser agrees, noting that a thoroughly disgendered model of system/lifeworld and discourse ethics is inca-

pable of perceiving "that feminine and masculine gender identity run like pink and blue threads through the areas of paid work, state administration, and citizenship as well as through the domain of familial and sexual relations. That is to say that gender identity is lived out in all areas of life." Nancy Fraser, "False Antitheses: A Response to Seyla Benhabib and Judith Butler," in Seyla Benhabib et al., *Feminist Contentions: A Philosophical Exchange* (New York: Routledge, 1995), 36.

24. Seyla Benhabib, *Critique, Norm, and Utopia: A Study of the Foundations of Critical Theory* (New York: Columbia University Press, 1987), 13.

25. Stella Gaon, "Pluralizing Universal Man: The Legacy of Transcendentalism and Teleology in Habermas's Discourse Ethics," *The Review of Politics* 60, no. 4 (1995): 717.

26. Gaon, "Pluralizing Universal Man," 693; my emphasis.

27. Gaon, "Pluralizing Universal Man," 700–701.

28. Gaon, "Pluralizing Universal Man," 698.

29. Gaon, "Pluralizing Universal Man," 713.

30. Finlayson, "Women and the Standpoint of Concrete Others," 20.

31. Rainer Forst likewise argues that it is precisely "concrete" bodily selves that principle (U) enjoins to participate in moral discourses, leaving us with good grounds to reject Benhabib's claims about the ascendancy of the "generic other" in Habermas's model. Forst, "Situations of the Self: Reflections on Seyla Benhabib's Version of Critical Theory," *Philosophy and Social Criticism* 23, no. 5 (1997): 79–96.

32. James Gordon Finlayson, "Women and the Standpoint of Concrete Others: From the Criticism of Discourse Ethics to Feminist Social Criticism," 21. Unpublished manuscript, cited with permission from the author.

33. Finlayson, "Women and the Standpoint of Concrete Others," 21.

34. Finlayson, "Women and the Standpoint of Concrete Others," 21.

35. Sharon Krause, "Desiring Justice: Motivation and Justification in Rawls and Habermas," *Contemporary Political Theory* 4, no. 4 (2005): 374.

36. Krause, "Desiring Justice," 379.

37. Jürgen Habermas, "Walter Benjamin: Conscious-Raising or Rescuing Critique," in *Philosophical-Political Profiles*, trans. Frederick G. Lawrence (Cambridge, Mass.: The MIT Press, 1983), 158.

38. Jürgen Habermas, *Between Facts and Norms: Contributions to a Discourse Theory of Law and Democracy*, trans. William Rehg (Cambridge, Mass.: The MIT Press, 1996), 490.

39. Habermas, *Between Facts and Norms*, 490.

40. Habermas, *Between Facts and Norms*, 366.

41. Habermas, "Walter Benjamin," 158. See chapter 4 of this book for a further discussion of this idea and its reception by both Habermas and Derrida.

42. Habermas, *Moral Consciousness and Communicative Action*, 202, 182.

43. Krause, "Desiring Justice," 374.

44. Jürgen Habermas, "Struggles for Recognition in the Democratic Constitutional State," in *Multiculturalism: Examining the Politics of Recognition*, ed. Amy Gutmann (Princeton: Princeton University Press, 1994), 126.

45. See Krause, "Desiring Justice," 377. Here Habermas appears to have moved discourse ethics into a loose alliance with John Rawls's attempt to theorize the moral standpoint as coextensive with subjective feelings, attitudes, and conceptions of the good life. This point of convergence is tenuous, however, insofar as important differences remain between Habermas's position and the Rawlsian concepts of "primary goods" and the "original position." Whereas Rawls posits the latter as a hypothetical thought experiment aimed at *establishing* principles of justice, Habermas seeks to *derive* justice norms from the structural attributes of "real-life argumentation." Gaon, "Pluralizing Universal Man," 700. From this discourse-ethical vantage point, Habermas takes Rawls to task for infusing practical reason with affectivity and binding it to a pregiven horizon of accepted values and meanings. As Krause observes, for Habermas such features serve only to render Rawls's "theory vulnerable to the charge that it cannot account for genuinely universal obligations. Moreover, because it incorporates rather than transcends particular conceptions of the good and the affective attachments to which they give rise, the fact that there is disagreement about these goods in modern society makes [Rawls's] theory unstable." Krause, "Desiring Justice," 371.

46. Steven Hendley, *From Communicative Action to the Face of the Other: Levinas and Habermas on Language, Obligation, and Community* (Lanham, Md.: Lexington Books, 2000), 36–37.

47. Rehg, *Insight and Solidarity*, 208.

48. I revisit Rehg's hypothetical in chapter 5, where I attempt to illustrate the deficits that befall Axel Honneth's recognition theory as it allows the dualistic framework of knowledge and human interests to recede from its conceptual compass.

49. Rehg, *Insight and Solidarity*, 10–11.

50. Habermas, *The Inclusion of the Other*, 29.

51. Rehg, *Insight and Solidarity*, 188.

52. Hendley, *From Communicative Action to the Face of the Other*, 41.

53. Mark E. Warren, "The Self in Discursive Democracy," in *The Cambridge Companion to Habermas*, ed. Stephen K. White (Cambridge, UK: Cambridge University Press, 1999), 181.

54. Axel Honneth, *Reification: A New Look at an Old Idea* (Oxford: Oxford University Press, 2008), 56.

55. Honneth, *Reification*, 32.

56. Honneth, *Reification*, 35.

57. Habermas, *Moral Consciousness and Communicative Action*, 104.

58. Krause, "Desiring Justice," 380.

Chapter Two

Care as Unqualified Gift:
Derrida's (Im)possible Visitation

In setting forth his riposte to the kinds of perspectives on care morality that we encountered in the preceding chapter, Jacques Derrida underlines the intractable theoretical impasse to which we have already been alerted: however determined Habermas and his more or less like-minded critics may be to prod the concrete needs, goods, affective attachments, and pluralistic definitional identities of real-world bodily selves within the compass of the "just/moral," their efforts are ultimately constrained by the procedural criteria of ideal role taking, universalizability, and symmetrical reversibility of perspectives prioritized in the framework of discourse ethics. Yet unlike writers like Benhabib, who imagine that this difficulty can be surmounted without injuring the overarching conceptual terrain of discourse ethics, Derrida affirms the objections of commentators like Stella Gaon. Like them, he maintains that Habermas's approach is structurally incapable of according discursive space to the ineradicable epistemic incongruities at the core of all self-other relations. Indeed, to paint with broad philosophical brushes, the presumed incommensurability of ego and alter is the launching point for Derrida's reception of Habermas's theory, along with the broader tradition of Enlightenment modernity that Habermas seeks to critically defend.

The present chapter considers Derrida's effort to disarticulate the distinction between our symmetrical and asymmetrical moral obligations, and thereby displace the question of care morality outside the ratiocinative confines of Habermas's communications theory. To this end, I foreground the key Derridean tropes of gift giving, friendship, and hospitality. To flesh out this discussion and gain further purchase on the status of symmetrical versus asymmetrical moral obligations in deconstructive thought, I overview Derrida's critique of Emmanuel Levinas, with emphasis on the former's claim that despite its intentions to the contrary, Levinas's notion of the "altogether-other" fails to extricate itself from a residual "transcendental phenomenology." In view of this reading of Levinas, I argue that Iris Marion Young is correct to characterize the moral standpoint of deconstruction as "asymmetrically reciprocal," but dispute Young's contention that Derrida has forged a fruitful alliance between the orientations of communicative reciprocity and asymmetrical care. Instead, I maintain that he has failed to adequately theorize a common intersubjective standpoint from which moral agents can valorize conflicting value orientations and conceptions of the good—not just those that arise out of discourses of care or affective sympathy, but also those that issue from the disparate yet similarly one-sided discourses of "terrorism." To lend to support to this claim, the chapter considers the arguments of Michel Rosenfeld, as well as Axel Honneth's recognition-theoretic critique of Derrida's asymmetrically reciprocal moral standpoint—an appraisal about which we shall have more to say in chapter 5.

GIFT GIVING, FRIENDSHIP, AND HOSPITALITY: THE INCALCULABLE UNCONDITIONALITY OF DERRIDEAN "CARE"

While the term "care" is not invoked with exceptional frequency in Derrida, it is in my view an ethical impulse that shoots through the conceptual fabric of his expansive text. Let us begin by considering his account of gift giving without measure or conditions, a gesture in which the perspective of care is squarely situated. In Derrida's view, for a gift to be "unconditional," it must be shorn of any and all symmetrical obligations: "there must be no reciprocity, return, exchange, countergift or debt."[1] An unqualified gift, that is to say, entails precisely the refusal of all regimes of reciprocal equivalence, measurability, and calculability—such as those set forth in modern legal contracts and in the rules governing the exchange of money and commodities in the capitalist market ("M—C—M," in Marx's famous formulation). Such well-formed, synchronically balanced circuits are ruptured with the unreserved gift, which imposes no duty on the recipient to return something back to the benefactor, nor indeed *owe* him or her anything. Moreover, the gift without qualifications releases both parties from the exchange relation's requirement of *temporal simultaneity*: the "demand of time," in other words, the demand for the gift to be "restituted immediately and right away" is renounced unequivocally.[2] Freed from the command of instantaneous reciprocation, expressions of unqualified gift giving open onto a radically *a*symmetrical horizon of time, in which the intervals between the receipt and future bestowment of a gift can be neither calculated nor known in advance.

We are thus positioned, with this gesture, rather far afield from Habermas's framework of communicative action, which attributes the forging of social bonds not to the locutionary content of given utterances but to *illocutionary* acts of offering and accepting meanings. Iris Young encapsulates Habermas's position neatly: "Every speech act that aims at understanding entails an *offer* by the speaker to make good on its meaning, and the understanding of the speech act entails an *acceptance* of that offer by a listener."[3] The deconstructive maneuver of unqualified gift giving radically dislocates precisely this even-keeled regime of communicative reciprocity, releasing ego and alter into asynchronous intervals and spaces that promise to safeguard the irreducibly different experiences, perspectives, and identities of each from the logic of calculation, equivalence, and sameness. This effort to radically disjoin the present out of contemporaneity with itself is carried forth in Derrida's discussion of *khôra*,[4] a category delineated in Plato's *Timaeus*. Used without a definite article (which would suggest fixity and thingness), *khôra* presents itself as a formless, structureless abyss or chasm that marks for ego "a place apart, the spacing which keeps a dissymmetrical relation to all that which, 'in herself,' beside or in addition to herself, seems to make couple with her."[5]

That self and other are in need of "protection" from the "homogenizing" *telos* of discursive symmetricality follows from Derrida's axiological principle that every identity is purely contingent, unanticipatable, and immeasurable—a postulate that reverberates widely in contemporary poststructuralist accounts of "difference." Among the numerous champions of this thesis is Chantal Mouffe, who likewise rejects all efforts to reabsorb the differing vocabularies of self and other into "oneness and harmony." With Derrida, Mouffe insists that "[i]t is because every object has inscribed in its very being something other than itself and that as a result, everything is constructed as différance, that its being cannot be perceived as pure 'presence' or 'objectivity.'"[6] Proceeding from this premise, Derrida's unconditional gift aims to perform the ethicopolitical work of safeguarding incommensurable singularities from the (presumed) threat of epistemic erasure by the idealized totalities of thought and action inscribed in the epistemological firmament of the Western ontotheological tradition.

Unreserved gift giving emerges on these terms as unmistakably homologous to the deconstructive idea of friendship. Unlike its metaphysical counterpart, such friendship, says Derrida, is not

the dream of a beatifically pacific relation, but of a certain . . . experience perhaps unthinkable today and unthought within the historical determination of friendship in the West. This is a friendship, what I sometimes call an *aimance*, that excludes violence; a non-appropriative relation to the other that occurs without violence and on the basis of which violence detaches itself and is determined.[7]

For Derrida, all of the universalistic moral theories that we encountered in chapter 1 are woefully ill equipped to accommodate the "nonappropriative" intervention of *aimance* (often translated as "lovence"): in their haste to subordinate this gesture to adjudicative principles of justice and norms of consensus, they take "something essentially unstable and chaotic" and turn it into a mere *stabilization*, which is by no means "natural, essential or substantial."[8] In this context, it is crucial to note that Derrida has positioned both the gift and friendship not simply as *ethical* expressions of felt concern for the other but as *political* intercessions against the ineradicable residue of violence at the core of all universalistic efforts to smooth away the intrinsic nonidentifiablity of self and other. At the level of both ethics and politics, that is to say, "[u]ndecidability continues to inhabit the decision. . . . The relation to the other does not close itself off, and it is because of this that there is history and one tries to act politically."[9]

In wresting the dissymmetrical orientation of concern for a single unrepresentable individual away from the strictly private realms of kinship, spousal relationships, and so forth, and designating it as an expressly *public* intervention, Derrida has indeed veered far beyond what can be permissibly envisioned as "care" from within the philosophical tradition inaugurated by Kant. From the latter perspective, our public obligations toward the other extend no further than the idea of *toleration*—a category that we overviewed in our introduction to the thematics of this study. To recapitulate briefly, the Kantian ideal of tolerance takes the form of an exactingly symmetrical "invitation": under the aegis of the nation-state, the guest is entreated to enter the host country's borders, but only on the condition that she agrees to abide by its clearly demarcated reciprocative norms. As Kant sees it, these rules oblige the newcomer to be a citizen of another nation-state; behave "peaceably" in the host country; partake of the right to visit but not the right to remain; and ultimately offer the state something in return for the welcome she has been extended. For Derrida, an irreducible residue of violence resides at the core of all such regimes of hospitable reciprocity, precisely because in controlling the threshold, borders, and terms of the invitation, the host retains mastery over the *arrivant*.[10]

Derrida deploys the gesture of unreserved hospitality to break toleration's well-ordered and ineradicably hegemonic circuit of symmetrical exchange: the newcomer is at liberty to arrive unbidden, unexpectedly, and at any time, without horizon or expectations, such that both she and the host are accorded the

pleasures of the "absolute surprise." Kant's normatively bounded ideal of toleration is thus transfigured into an im/possible promissory offer of limitless
openness to a wholly nonidentifiable, nonforeseeable, and unknowable other.
Fundamentally incompatible with the very idea of the sovereign nation-state
and its *ratio* of legal-juridical tolerance, Derrida's visitation presents itself as
a decidedly nonregulative, nonappropriative, noninstrumental, and nonviolent
"relation as nonrelation," which carries with it both an ethical impulse of concern for a completely unrepresentable other as well as an expressly political
demand for an always already deferred democratic future-to-come.

At this point, a question of conceptual clarification arises: Does Derrida's
account of *aimance* amount to a *subversion* of the Kantian distinction between the unilateral orientation of care and the universalistic perspective of
equal treatment? Or has he proposed something more akin to a *reconciliation*
of the moral standpoints of asymmetrical care and the orientation of egalitarian reciprocation? In an effort to address these questions, I turn now to a
closer examination of the terms in which the standpoints of measurability and
immeasurability are theorized in Derrida's framework.

IMMEASURE FOR MEASURE: DERRIDA'S UNEASY ALLIANCE

It should be clear from the foregoing discussion that to Derrida, the perspectives of measurable equality and immeasurable care are no longer to be envisioned, with Kantianism, as compartmentalized, mutually exclusive moral
standpoints. As Derrida writes in *Rogues*,

> Calculable measure also gives access to the incalculable and the incommensu-
> rable, an access that remains itself necessarily undecided between the calculable
> and the incalculable—and this is the aporia of the political and of democracy.
> But, by the same token, by effacing the difference of singularity through calcu-
> lation, by no longer counting on it, measure risks putting an end to singularity
> itself, to its quality or its nonquantifiable intensity. And yet the concept of mea-
> surable equality is not opposed to the immeasurable. That is why [Jean-Luc]
> Nancy is right to speak of "the equality of singularities in the incommensurabil-
> ity of freedom."[11]

In this passage, Derrida underscores his conviction that the standpoints of
measurable equality and immeasurable singularity are necessarily situated in
a tense but nonetheless productive relationship with one another. Here we are
reminded of a kindred claim that we underlined in the introduction—namely,
that if it is to be just and responsible, a decision must be "both regulated and
without regulation"; it must "confirm the law and also to destroy it or suspend

it enough to have to reinvent it in each case . . . in the affirmation of the new and free confirmation of its principle."[12] Such formulations depict the principle of egalitarian measure as a necessary counterpoint to the perspective of radical singularity, even if the latter must always remain on guard against a certain reifying violence within the soul of the former. In coimbricating the two orientations in these terms, Derrida aims to defend his deconstructive maneuver against charges that it is aimed at a wholesale overthrow of the principle of equal measurement. Rather than dismiss *tout court* the ideal of quantifiable equality heralded by the modern bourgeois democratic revolutions, Derrida proposes an unavoidably aporetic association between this principle and the deconstructive effort to persistently disarticulate *logos* on behalf of the unquantifiably singular. In fact, according to Derrida, calculable "equality is not simply some necessary evil or stopgap measure; it is also the chance to neutralize all sorts of differences of force, of properties (natural and otherwise) and hegemonies, so as to gain access precisely to the *whoever* and the *no matter who* of singularity in its very immeasurability."[13]

With this double gesture, Derrida seems keen to salvage something from the principle of measurability that eluded Frankfurt School thinkers like Marcuse and Adorno. As the following chapter will discuss in further detail, these writers understood measure as in some sense *the* category of modernity, a principle aimed at commandeering and subordinating all spheres of life to processes of instrumental-technical rationalization. For them liberation from late capitalism's "iron cage" of bureaucratic reason (as Max Weber memorably portrayed it) rests on an appeal to precisely that which is antinomical to subject-object epistemology and its *telos* of identity—namely, the nonidentical, the esoteric, the mythopoetic, the dream, the erotic, the playful, the aesthetic. By no means does Derrida reject the latter as the firmament for a deconstructive ethics of difference. Rather, his aim to forge a reckoning between the immeasurably singular and the quantifiably equal such that deconstruction might be better positioned to carry forth the ethicopolitical work of shielding the nonidentical from the cruelty of the identarian "inspection exercise" in which conventional frameworks of philosophy, metaphysics, and dialectics are caught up.[14] As he insists in *Politics of Friendship,*

> There is no democracy without respect for irreducible singularity or alterity, but there is also no democracy without "the community of friends" (*koína ta philōn*), without the calculation of majorities, without stabilizable, representable subjects, all equal. These two laws are irreducible to one another. Tragically irreconcilable and forever wounding. The wound itself opens with the necessity of having to *count* one's friends, to count the others, in the economy of one's own, there where every other is altogether other.[15]

Note that this effort to situate the measurable and the immeasurable in an unsettled but fertile relationship with one another bears little resemblance to Habermas's view that the revolutionizing processes of modernization have *differentiated out* three clearly demarcated problem-solving languages: the scientific, the moral-practical, and the aesthetic-expressive. With Weber, Habermas understands the disaggregation of these linguistic fields as a movement of *disenchantment*. "[W]ith the rise of civil society the economic and political subsystem was uncoupled from the cultural system and traditional world views were undermined by the basic ideology of fair exchange, thus freeing the arts from the context of ritual."[16] So too were the knowledge of nature and the knowledge of the social released from the ideological veil of premodern myths and cosmologies, and separated out into the respective epistemological frameworks of the *Naturwissenschaften* and the *Geisteswissenschaften*. Significantly, both the empirical-analytic orientation of the former and the hermeneutic-historical perspective of the latter are bound up with the principles of measure and universalizability: at the level of epistemology, both scientific and communicative rationality raise "universal validity claims which are necessarily open to ongoing criticism and revision."[17] The key difference is that the human sciences admit of an expressly *non*instrumental type of reason that befits their orientation toward the sphere of communicative action—in express contradistinction to the conceptual compass of the natural sciences, which is aimed at the investigation of the insensate, reified domain of nonspeaking nature. Thus, although the measurability principle is associated with both communicative and instrumental forms of reason, it is only the latter that is marked by an intrinsically objectivating attitude.

Contra Habermas, Derrida draws no such hard and fast distinction between reifying and nonreifying spheres of rationality. Indeed, as Bill Martin emphasizes, for Derrida a dividing line "between language's world-disclosive function and its pragmatic-instrumental function cannot be rigorously drawn."[18] Instead, Derrida aims to portray *all* regimes of measurability as entailing a necessary *wound* to the nonidentical: every effort to count, in other words, carries with it an ineliminable residue of violence. This is a conviction that he shares with a thinker like Adorno, even if he breaks with the latter in insisting on the need for an aporetic alliance between the countable and the uncountable. In chapter 3, I argue that in disfiguring the dualistic framework of reason set forth in the Kantian tradition, Derrida shears his approach of the categorical resources needed to guard against a "re-enchanted" account of nature and the knowledge of nature. However, at present I wish to focus on how Derrida's attempt to undermine the distinction between the instrumental and noninstrumental domains of measurability bears on his understanding of the relationship between symmetrical and asymmetrical intersubjectivity.

DERRIDA'S CRITIQUE OF LEVINAS: AN OVERTURE
OF "ASYMMETRICAL RECIPROCITY"?

The observations of several writers would seem to affirm our claim that Derrida's efforts to unchain moral philosophy from the normative constraints of the Kantian requirement of equal treatment must not be construed as a blanket renunciation of that obligation. For an author like Iris Young, for example, "equality" and "mutual recognition" do indeed adhere to Derridean tropes such as unqualified gift giving, friendship, and hospitality. However, for Young the principles of equivalent reciprocation that these interventions enjoin must be viewed as being "of *a different order*" from those that circulate within the liberal discourse of contracts and exchange.[19] Indeed, according to Young, the perspective of *a*symmetricality is precisely what distinguishes deconstructive reciprocation from its Kantian counterpart. Asymmetrical reciprocity, she contends, means that communication and moral respect arise not only out of "some sense of mutual identification and sharing," but also out of "a moment of *wonder*, of an openness to the newness and mystery of the other person."[20] From the "respectful stance of wonder" (an idea that Young derives and develops from Luce Irigaray), ego is commended to engage in reciprocal perspective taking with alter while also remaining self-reflexively open to alter's incommensurably different needs, interests, perceptions, and values— and even, indeed, to the "strangeness" of her own positions, assumptions, and perspectives in relation to those of her vis-à-vis.[21] Young's contention that Derrida's unconditionally hospitable overtures operate on simultaneously reciprocal and dissymmetrical planes suggests that he has placed the ethical impulse of felt concern for the other's immeasurable alterity into a fruitful alliance with the expressly political idea of an always already deferred universal justice-to-come. Indeed, according to Young, the dissymmetrically reciprocal vantage point of deconstruction allows gestures like "care-taking, deferential, [and] polite acknowledgement of the Otherness of others" to enter into the egalitarian framework of "communicative democracy" on terms that would be illicit from the dualistic moral vantage point of Kantianism.[22]

Axel Honneth concurs with Young's depiction of asymmetrical reciprocity as a distinguishing orientation of Derrida's framework, inasmuch as he likewise sees deconstruction as endeavoring to pull together the contrasting moral perspectives of reciprocal respect and boundless concern for a single, unrepresentable individual. To Honneth, Derrida has indeed pushed the conflict between affective sympathy for the other (the principle of "goodness") and the obligation to treat each person just like everyone else (the idea of "law") "one degree further" than, for example, Emmanuel Levinas, who sees both dispositions as lying along a continuum of "justice."[23] In fact, according to Levinas, the moral perspective of goodness is a vantage point from which we can see that law's requirement that all be treated on entirely equal terms inflicts inescapable injustices upon the incommensurable identities of individual moral selves. Levinas argues that in the phenomenological encounter of another "face" ego experiences the individuality of her vis-à-vis as so unrepresentable and incalculable that she is immediately burdened with the moral obligation to offer help and care everlastingly. It is only through forswearing the orientation of inner-directed self-interest that ego can mature into a "moral" self. Because Levinasian intersubjectivity finds the unintended deprivation of liberty to be a structural condition of "the infinite task of doing justice"—ego, that is to say, is always morally obliged to subordinate its own autonomy and interests to the needs of alter—we are led to "the surprising thesis that justice always transcends justice itself."[24]

It would thus appear that in Levinas an inherent tension exists between goodness's principle of one-sided concern for the other's infinite otherness and law's remit of universally equal and impartial treatment. A number of commentators have rejected this understanding, however, insisting that Levinas has not conceived of the relationship between these two orientations as one of tension but rather as one of concurrence. According to Steven Hendley, for example, Levinas's idea is that the reciprocal perspective of justice, encapsulated in the notion of the "third party," pervades and is coextensive with ego's obligations to care and respond deferentially to the singularly unrepresentable other. "The regulative priority of justice is not," insists Hendley, "something opposed to the imperative of care, for Levinas. Justice is best conceived as a complication of the perspective that originally opens up in my caring relationship with the concrete other. Justice in other words *is* care appropriately transformed by the requirements of multiple, competing obligations."[25]

Such a reading is roundly disputed by Derrida, who takes Levinas to task for neglecting—indeed refusing—to position the reciprocative, and necessarily violent, perspective of "the Same" as a counterpoint to the unconditionally sympathetic viewpoint of care for the other's absolute otherness. Although he is to be credited for attempting to undermine "a certain traditional humanism," Levinas, insists Derrida, remains guilty of a "profound humanism." Indeed, a residue of metaphysical transcendence resides in the very "title in which Levinas suspends the hierarchy of the attribute and the subject. . . . [T]he other-man is the subject."[26] This point is pursued in a well-known excursus in *Writing and Difference*,[27] where Derrida portrays Levinas as blind to the possibility of recognizing the other as an *alter ego*, and thereby mired in the very violence of transcendentalism that his gesture of care for the wholly other purports to overcome. Derrida writes that by refusing to acknowledge an intentional modification of the ego—which would be a violent and totalitarian act for him—[Levinas] deprives himself of the very foundation and possibility of his own language. What authorizes him to say 'infinitely other' if the other does not appear as such in the zone he calls the same, and which is the neutral level of transcendental description? . . . To refuse to see in it [the other] an ego in this sense is, within the ethical order, the very gesture of all violence.[28]

This is a trap that Husserl, for one, was careful to avoid, ceaselessly stressing, according to Derrida, that the other is "irreducible to *my* ego, precisely because it is an ego, because it has the form of the ego."[29] Thus, while Levinas is to be commended for situating the perspective of the other's otherness beyond the horizon of the Same, for opening it up to "surprises" and "eruptions" of thought foreclosed by the formal logic and elementary unity of the conceptual "totality," his approach ultimately founders on its own incapacity to acknowledge the standpoint of the symmetrically identical, on its inability to envisage the other's infinite alterity as always already imbricated in the "play of the Same." Derrida, in contrast, insists on the need for a "differential contamination" between the two perspectives such that ego's obligations vis-à-vis alter's radical alterity can be recognized at the level of ethics and politics in the first place. His idea is to ratchet up the implications of Levinas's (ultimately humanistic) effort to destabilize the encounter with the other. To this end, Derrida abjures the phenomenological foundation of Levinas's "face-to-face" meeting and fashions an unsettled association between the perspectives of symmetrical equality (law) and one-sided concern for the other's irreducible alterity (goodness). "Dissymmetry," he argues, "itself would be impossible without this symmetry, which is not of the world, and which, having no real aspect, imposes no limit upon alterity and dissymmetry—makes them possible, on the contrary. This dissymmetry is an *economy* in a new sense: a sense which would probably be intolerable to Levinas."[30]

While Young, as we have noted, defends the viability of this proposed alliance between the symmetrical and asymmetrical moral standpoints, Honneth remains far less sanguine about Derrida's maneuver. To be sure, Honneth commends Derrida for positioning the gesture of unreserved care for the other's otherness beyond what can be countenanced within strictly Kantian principles of equal treatment and reciprocal respect. He nonetheless reproaches him for taking what is rightly diagnosed as an irresolvable and fruitful tension between the two orientations as license to effectively integrate them into a single framework, one in which the ethical gesture of care for a single unrepresentable individual is situated as a "self-correcting" moral guidepost for the implementation of an (always already deferred) ideal of reciprocal universal justice:[31]

> Derrida claims revealingly that a relation of violent, irresolvable, and yet productive conflict obtains between the two moral viewpoints distinguished in Levinas's ethics. This conflict is ultimately is irresolvable because the idea of equal treatment necessitates a restriction of the moral perspective from which the other person in his or her particularity can become the recipient of my care. My offer of boundless concern and my position of unlimited help would amount to a neglect of the moral duties that follow from the reciprocal recognition of human beings as equals. This conflict is productive inasmuch as the viewpoint of care continually provides a moral ideal from which the practical attempt to gradually realize equal treatment can take its orientation in a self-correcting manner.[32]

Whatever his efforts at conceptual alliance building, Derrida, in other words, has *privileged* the vantage point of the incalculably immeasurable over that of the quantifiably commensurable. For him there is "no responsibility, no ethicopolitical decision, that must not pass through the proofs of the incalculable or the undecidable. Otherwise everything would be reducible to calculation, program, causality, and, at best, 'hypothetical imperative.'"[33] In Honneth's view, Derrida situates the obligation to provide unlimited care for the other as a "central principle of morality" at the cost of opening up the prospect of a totalizing heterogeneity.[34]

Keen to avoid this outcome, Honneth, in accord with the tradition of Kant and Habermasian discourse ethics, argues that completely dissymmetrical, nonreciprocal relations of concern for the welfare of the other must ultimately be constrained by principles of equal treatment and universal justice. "[T]he moment," writes Honneth, "the other person is recognized as an equal being among others—in that he or she is capable of participating in practical discourses—the unilateral relation of care must come to an end, for an attitude of benevolence is not permissible toward subjects who are able to articulate their views and beliefs publicly."[35] This conclusion is consonant with the objectives of Honneth's broader recognition-theoretic framework, which I shall consider at length in chapter 5. Suffice it to say for the moment that a principal aim of Honneth's approach is to situate the attitude of affective sympathy as conceptually and genetically prior to our expressly public and impartial moral dealings with one another, but without undermining the architectonic primacy of the latter orientation. Put differently, Honneth attempts to position one-sided relations of care beyond the cognitivist moral standpoint of Habermasian discourse ethics, but without allowing the attitude of unilateral concern for the other's welfare to commandeer principles of universal justice and equal treatment in the manner suggested by Derrida.

Unburdened by deconstruction's limitless moral self-reflexivity, Honneth is at liberty to propose three distinct intersubjective criteria—i.e., bodily abuse, denial of rights, and esteem-diminishing acts of denigration—against which we can judge whether and on what terms moral selves have "forgotten" the antecedent recognitional stance and succumbed to the pathological tendency to misrecognize others as mere insensate objects. From this perspective, Derrida can be taken to task for allowing ego's obligation to care everlastingly for its untranslatable alter to overtake and forestall precisely the sorts of universalistic moral judgments that both Honneth's and Habermas's moral theories make possible.

In what follows, I shall endeavor to develop this argument against Derrida, underscoring the impasses that the deconstructive standpoint encounters when addressing the question of care, as well as the disparate, yet not wholly disassociated, problem of "terrorism."

CARE AND TERRORISM: ACHILLES' HEELS
OF DERRIDA'S ETHICS OF DIFFERENCE?

At first glance, events such as the 11 September 2001 attacks on the U.S. Pentagon and World Trade Center appear to bear little resemblance to unilateral expressions of concern for the singularly unique needs, goods, and affective attachments of the other. Indeed, insofar as they are aimed at the annihilation of the definitional identities of concrete singularities, such acts seem to be entirely at odds with gestures of empathetic concern for the other's existential welfare. These patent and undeniable disparities notwithstanding, terrorism and care share at least one distinguishing, and by no means merely semantic, feature: they are both *unilateral* actions unbound by regulative norms of reciprocation and equal exchange. If this is the case, then how precisely is one poised, from the standpoint of a deconstructive ethics of difference, to valorize nonuniversalizable expressions of care against similarly one-sided acts of terrorism? This is a question that animates the interchange between Habermas and Derrida in *Philosophy in a Time of Terror*. Here Derrida, for his part, is at pains to distinguish the moral standpoint of deconstruction from the discourse of terrorism, which is marked in his view by its thoroughgoing antipathy toward the posture of limitless concern for the untranslatable vocabularies of ego and alter. Terrorism, as Michel Rosenfeld observes, is beyond what Derrida recognizes as "the meaning-endowing discourse that allows for the development of ethical links between self and other."[36]

Yet the question to which we have just alluded remains: By what criteria are moral agents to adjudge the practice of terrorism in relation to other ideals, value orientations, and conceptions of the good? Derrida's approach poses formidable conceptual obstacles to answering this question, insofar as its "strong normative call for a common bond of identity between self and other" is raised, as Rosenfeld puts it, alongside a paramount "obligation to account for the full panoply of differences of the irreducible other."[37] The consequences of Derrida's radical disarticulation of Kantianism's intersubjectivity-theoretic resources are indeed considerable with respect to a problem like terrorism—a practice that agents are ill disposed to repudiate absent an appeal to an unambiguously universal moral standpoint. In envisaging—with Levinas's aid—an irreducible residue of violence attendant to the pursuit of justice itself, Derrida's framework places no *prima facie* onus upon the self to renounce the terrorist's attempt to eradicate the core identity of the other, and in fact seems to justify "violence necessary to prevent eradication of the self's identity"—even if it cannot countenance outright disregard for the other.[38] Accordingly, although the sincerity of Derrida's repudiation of terrorism is beyond question, one can justifiably wonder whether his pronouncements are simply expressions of personal distaste or a stance that the deconstructive ethics of difference has the categorical resources to defend. As Rosenfeld observes, in its bid to creative discursive room for all differences and singularities, deconstruction destabilizes the very intersubjective vantage point needed to valorize one form of ineradicable violence over and against another, leaving agents without

> a *sufficiently stable common identity* to sift through competing claims regarding what is required for self-preservation and for protection of the core identity of the self. In other words, as radical singularity precludes establishing a *common intersubjective criterion* to assess conflicting claims issuing from different perspectives, at least in the short run, each claim can only be evaluated from the standpoint of the subjective perspective from which it is made.[39]

As we noted in chapter 1, Seyla Benhabib has likewise drawn attention to the risks of allowing the care-ethical viewpoints of concrete subjectivities to proliferate absent oversight from an expressly universalistic moral framework. To illustrate her argument, Benhabib points to the intragroup consociative traditions of organized crime syndicates such as the Mafia, which are marked by an unmistakable ethos of care and affective concern for members of one's immediate clan or extended family. However, within the Mafia, "caring for the family" is often manifest as patent enmity and contempt for the dignity, autonomy, and indeed the very lives of those deemed to be in conflict with the claims and objectives of one's own group. The limitations of care ethics as a standpoint from which to critically evaluate the social practices and value orientations of the Mafia are precisely the same shortcomings that deconstruction faces when attempting to come to terms with the problem of terrorism. For Benhabib, the case of the Mafia shows that in failing to permit universalistic principles of equal treatment to "trump" the one-sided value convictions of the other, "[a] morality of care can revert simply to the position that what is morally good is what is best for those who are like me. Such a claim is no different than arguing that what is best morally is what pleases me most."[40] In *this* sense, Mafia care morality is no different from the care morality manifest in primary loving relationships, where, as Honneth observes, "the singular identity of our beloved cannot play any part in justifying the love we feel, and we reduced to repeatedly insisting that we just love this person."[41] In both instances, agents are under no onus to abstract from particulars and give universally defensible reasons for the actions that they take in relation to or on behalf of the beloved other. The deconstructive ethics of radical singularity likewise demotes the duty of egalitarian reciprocation at the cost of stripping moral discussants of a common intersubjective standpoint from which to repudiate the terrorist's instrumental, self-preservation–directed goal of annihilating the identity of the other. Indeed, as Thomas McCarthy notes, Derrida's approach succumbs to the romanticist belief that "uprooting and destabilizing universalist structures will of itself lead to letting the other be in respect and freedom rather than to intolerant and aggressive particularism."[42] It is in this sense beset with a self-generated normative deficit that undermines the very difference-ethical aims that it has set for itself. Viewed in this light, there appear to be good grounds for referring, with Rosenfeld, to a problem like terrorism as an "Achilles' heel" of the deconstructive ethics of difference.[43]

Habermas, as we have noted, offers a way around this difficulty: unencumbered by the limitless self-reservation of deconstructive care ethics, his discourse theory positions communicative agents to order and prioritize particular validity claims and value orientations from an expressly universalistic moral standpoint. It wrests Kant's categorical imperative from the purview of a solipsistic moral ego and enjoins full and equal participants in public life to reach uncoerced and rationally conceived agreements about competing ideals and value orientations, even if mutual cognitive dissonances are for the moment held in abeyance.[44] As Rosenfeld emphasizes, "Habermas allows all interests from all perspectives associated with all conceivable conceptions of the good to be considered in the determination of morally binding norms. However, because only universalizable claims can command consensus, Habermasian morals just as their Kantian counterpart must rise above all particular conceptions of the good."[45] From this vantage point, Habermas can portray terrorism as a grandiose "communicative pathology" precisely because it is carried forth in express contravention of the symmetrical norms of ideal role taking, universalizability, and perspectivity, absent which ego and alter remain estranged from one another and indifferent to the discursive negotiation of their respective validity claims.[46] Terrorist organizations, in other words, endow themselves with the authority to one-sidedly determine the boundaries of the moral "from the viewpoint of their own preferences and value-orientations,"[47] directly subverting the standpoint of egalitarian reciprocation to which the discourse-ethical model accords regulative primacy.

To the extent that it brings the subjective perceptions of the good/ethical within the orbit of the principle of universal justice, and indeed effectively eliminates the distinction between them, the ethics of radical singularity remains saddled with a troubling evaluative deficit that, according to Habermas, allows "the refuse heap of interpretations, which it wants to clear away in order to get at the buried foundations, mount ever higher."[48] To be sure, the latter claim overreaches considerably inasmuch as Derrida's aim is not to overthrow the standpoint of measurable equality *tout court* and therewith commend us to the nihilism of an ineliminably nonreciprocative *an-archē*. For Derrida, such a stance would amount, as Richard Bernstein astutely observes, to little more than "another fixed metaphysical position."[49] Rather than "simply dismiss or ignore those ethical and political principles that are constitutive of our traditions" Derrida's unsettled alliance between the measurably symmetrical and the immeasurably other invites us to remain "prepared to act decisively 'here and now'—where we do not hide in bad faith from the double binds that we always confront."[50] As Derrida himself insists, "Deconstruction always presupposes affirmation."[51] In *Writing and Difference*, he speaks indeed of a "joyous" affirmation, one that rejects the "*negative*, nostalgic, guilty" structuralist *topos* of broken immediacy in favor of an expressly Nietzschean emphasis on

> the play of the world and the innocence of becoming . . . a world of signs without fault, without truth, and without origin which is offered to an active interpretation. *This affirmation then determines the noncenter otherwise than as loss of center.* And it plays without security. For there is a *sure* play: that which is limited to the *substitution* of *given* and *existing, present,* pieces. In absolute chance, affirmation also surrenders itself to *genetic* indetermination, to the *seminal* adventure of trace.[52]

One is nonetheless hard pressed to ascertain what the substantive content, or at least the broad theoreticopractical contours, of such playful affirmation in the "here and now" might look like, given deconstruction's congenital allergy to anything resembling an ethicopolitical program or even an account of the institutional and political dynamics of modern societies. Bernstein notes that Habermas, for one, does not avoid the question, critique in the name of what? His quarrel with many so-called "postmodern" thinkers [including Derrida] is that they fail to confront this question, obscure it, or get caught in performative contradictions. One reason Habermas speaks to so many of "us" . . . is because however feeble and fragile this aspect of the Enlightenment legacy has become, and despite the attacks on this legacy, it nevertheless will not die—the demand for freedom and claim for dialogical reasonableness does have a "stubbornly transcending power."[53]

In the foregoing discussion, I have attempted to underscore the limitations of Derridean deconstruction as a vantage point from which to normatively evaluate competing *ethoi* of care. In the preceding chapter, I noted that while Habermas has been willing to position the asymmetrical perspective of care as a source of nourishment for the impartialist symmetricality of normative justification, his framework is not sufficiently equipped to defend itself against the criticisms of Derrida and other difference ethicists, who view his insistence upon a categorical demarcation between the good and the right as a structural encumbrance that gives rise to an unwarranted cognitive centric devaluation of the care attitude. I will endeavor to rectify this deficit by proposing a reconstruction of Habermas's model in chapter 5. In chapter 4, I will consider the prospects for an accord between Habermas's and Derrida's respective engagements with the problem of care morality. However, before embarking upon these interventions, the following chapter will examine the conceptual disparities between each thinker's approach to the question of "care for the other of nature"—discrepancies that are no less palpable than those that demarcate their perspectives on the problem of care for the human other, to which we have thus far confined ourselves.

NOTES

1. Jacques Derrida, *Given Time: Counterfeit Money*, trans. Peggy Kamuf (Chicago: The University of Chicago Press, 1992), 12.

2. Derrida, *Given Time*, 41.

3. Iris Marion Young, "Asymmetrical Reciprocity: On Moral Respect, Wonder, and Enlarged Thought," *Constellations* 3, no. 3 (1997): 356.

4. In chapter 4, I will examine this category in relation to Ernst Bloch's concept of noncontemporaneity and Benjamin's kindred notion of *Jetztzeit*.

5. Jacques Derrida, *On the Name*, ed. Thomas Dutoit, trans. David Wood et al. (Stanford: Stanford University Press, 1995), 124.

6. Chantal Mouffe, "Democracy, Power, and the Political," in *Democracy and Difference: Contesting the Boundaries of the Political*, ed. Seyla Benhabib (Princeton: Princeton University Press, 1996), 247.

7. Jacques Derrida, "Remarks on Deconstruction and Pragmatism," in *Deconstruction and Pragmatism*, ed. Chantal Mouffe (New York: Routledge, 1996), 83.

8. Derrida, "Remarks on Deconstruction and Pragmatism," 83, 84.

9. Derrida, "Remarks on Deconstruction and Pragmatism," 87.

10. Jacques Derrida, "Hospitality, Justice and Responsibility: A Dialogue with Jacques Derrida," in *Questioning Ethics: Contemporary Debates in Philosophy*, ed. Richard Kearny and Mark Dooley (New York: Routledge, 1999), 69.

11. Jacques Derrida, *Rogues: Two Essays on Reason*, trans. Pascale-Anne Brault and Michael Nass (Stanford: Stanford University Press, 2005), 52.

12. Jacques Derrida, "Deconstructing Terrorism," in *Philosophy in a Time of Terror: Dialogues with Jürgen Habermas and Jacques Derrida*, ed. Giovanna Borradori (Chicago: The University of Chicago Press, 2003), 169.

13. Derrida, *Rogues*, 52.

14. Jacques Derrida, "*Fichus*: Frankfurt Address," in *Paper Machine*, trans. Rachel Bowlby (Stanford: Stanford University Press, 2005), 171.

15. Jacques Derrida, *Politics of Friendship*, trans. George Collins (London: Verso, 1997), 22.

16. Jürgen Habermas, *Philosophical-Political Profiles*, trans. Frederick G. Lawrence (Cambridge, Mass.: The MIT Press, 1983), 139.

17. Richard J. Bernstein, "An Allegory of Modernity/Postmodernity: Habermas and Derrida," in *The Derrida-Habermas Reader*, ed. Lasse Thomassen (Chicago: The University of Chicago Press, 2006), 78.

18. Bill Martin, *Matrix and Line: Derrida and the Possibilities of Postmodern Social Theory* (New York: The State University of New York Press, 1992), 88–87.

19. Young, "Asymmetrical Reciprocity," 355; my emphasis.

20. Young, "Asymmetrical Reciprocity," 357.

21. Young, "Asymmetrical Reciprocity," 357.

22. Iris Marion Young, "Communication and the Other: Beyond Deliberative Democracy," in *Democracy and Difference: Contesting the Boundaries of the Political*, ed. Seyla Benhabib (Princeton: Princeton University Press, 1996), 130.

23. Axel Honneth, *Disrespect: The Normative Foundations of Critical Theory* (Cambridge, UK: Polity Press, 2007), 121.

24. Honneth, *Disrespect*, 120.

25. Steven Hendley, *From Communicative Action to the Face of the Other: Levinas and Habermas on Language, Obligation, and Community* (Lanham, Md.: Lexington Books, 2000), 49–50. To Hendley, it is precisely his emphasis on the role of reciprocity in self-other relations that links Levinas to an author like Habermas. This idea is affirmed by Simon Critchley, who likewise portrays the Levinasian third party as a conceptual bridge between Derrida and Habermas. (See chapter 4 for an elaboration of Critchley's argument.) These interpretations stand in marked contrast to that of George Trey. Trey sees Levinas's view of the irreducible difference between an "I" and "another" as resting on a relational view of ethical conduct that is unambiguously at odds with Habermas's

conception of communicative reciprocation. Unlike the latter, the former is one whose language "is pre-systematic, pre-rational, and operates solely on the basis of response-ability. I am in an ethical relation when I respond to the other qua his/her alterity." George Trey, "Communicative Ethics in the Face of Alterity: Habermas, Levinas and the Problem of Post-Conventional Universalism," *Praxis International* 11, no. 4 (1992): 412.

26. Derrida, *Rogues*, 279. On Derrida's contention that the Heideggerian *Dasein* is likewise burdened with a residual transcendentalism, see chapter 4 of this book.

27. Jacques Derrida, "Violence and Metaphysics: An Essay on the Thought of Emmanuel Levinas," in *Writing and Difference*, trans. Alan Bass (Chicago: The University of Chicago Press, 1978), 79–153.

28. Derrida, "Violence and Metaphysics," 125.

29. Derrida, "Violence and Metaphysics," 125.

30. Derrida, "Violence and Metaphysics," 126.

31. It should be noted that this reading is not without its critics. Simon Critchley, for one, rejects Honneth's contention Derrida has placed an ethics of care and an ethics of equal treatment in an uneasy relationship with one another. (Nor is there any such tension in Levinas, says Critchley, in apparent agreement with the interpretation advanced by Steven Hendley [see Hendley, *From Communicative Action to the Face of the Other*].) Critchley argues that for Derrida there is, in effect, "only one source of moral orientation, namely, justice." Because "the latter is not ethical but *political*," the "fundamental aporia" of deconstruction is thus "the relation between ethics and politics." Simon Critchley, "Habermas and Derrida Get Married," in *The Ethics of Deconstruction: Derrida and Levinas* (Edinburgh: Edinburgh University Press, 1999), 275.

32. Honneth, *Disrespect*, 121.

33. Derrida, *Rogues*, 273.

34. The claim that the moral standpoint of *différance* is ultimately encumbered by "a powerful principle of unity" is defended by Peter Dews in his *Logics of Disintegration: Post-structuralist Thought and the Claims of Critical Theory* (New York: Verso, 1987). To Dews, *différance* owes its totalizing character to Derrida's appropriation of the transcendental and speculative accounts of experience set forth in Husserl and Hegel. See chapter 4, note 26 for an elaboration of this point.

35. Honneth, *Disrespect*, 124.

36. Michel Rosenfeld, "Derrida's Ethical Turn and America: Looking Back from the Crossroads of Global Terrorism and the Enlightenment," *Cardozo Law Review* 27, no. 2 (2005): 824.

37. Rosenfeld, "Derrida's Ethical Turn and America," 821.

38. Rosenfeld, "Derrida's Ethical Turn and America," 823.

39. Rosenfeld, "Derrida's Ethical Turn and America," 834.

40. Seyla Benhabib, "The Debate over Moral Theory Revisited," in *Situating the Self: Gender, Community and Postmodernism in Contemporary Ethics* (New York: Routledge, 1992), 187.

41. Honneth, *Disrespect*, 170.

42. Thomas McCarthy, "The Politics of the Ineffable: Derrida's Deconstructionism," in *Hermeneutics and Critical Theory in Ethics and Politics*, ed. Michael Kelly (Cambridge, Mass.: The MIT Press, 1991), 158.

43. Rosenfeld, "Derrida's Ethical Turn and America," 823.

44. Jürgen Habermas, "Religious Tolerance—The Pacemaker of Cultural Rights," in *The Derrida-Habermas Reader*, ed. Lasse Thomassen (Chicago: The University of Chicago Press, 2006), 200.

45. Rosenfeld, "Derrida's Ethical Turn and America," 836.

46. Jürgen Habermas, "Reconstructing Terrorism," in *Philosophy in a Time of Terror: Dialogues with Jürgen Habermas and Jacques Derrida*, ed. Giovanna Borradori (Chicago: The University of Chicago Press, 2003), 64.

47. Jürgen Habermas and Giovanna Borradori, "Fundamentalism and Terror—A Dialogue with Jürgen Habermas," in *Philosophy in a Time of Terror: Dialogues with Jürgen Habermas and Jacques Derrida*, ed. Giovanna Borradori (Chicago: The University of Chicago Press, 2003), 41.

48. Jürgen Habermas, "Beyond a Temporalized Philosophy of Origins: Jacques Derrida's Critique of Phonocentrism," in *The Philosophical Discourse of Modernity: Twelve Lectures*, trans. Frederick G. Lawrence (Cambridge, Mass.: The MIT Press, 1990), 183.

49. Richard J. Bernstein, "An Allegory of Modernity/Postmodernity: Habermas and Derrida," in *The Derrida-Habermas Reader*, ed. Lasse Thomassen (Chicago: The University of Chicago Press, 2006), 85.

50. Bernstein, "An Allegory of Modernity/Postmodernity," 85.

51. Jacques Derrida and Richard Kearney, "Dialogue with Jacques Derrida," in Richard Kearney, *Dialogues with Contemporary Continental Thinkers: The Phenomenological Heritage* (Manchester: Manchester University Press, 1984), 118.

52. Jacques Derrida, *Writing and Difference*, 292; emphasis in original.

53. Bernstein, "An Allegory of Modernity/Postmodernity," 88.

Chapter Three

Caring for Nature in Habermas and Derrida: Reconciling the Speaking and Nonspeaking Worlds at the Cost of "Re-enchantment"?[1]

In the previous chapter, I examined Derrida's efforts to subsume the orientation of measurable reciprocation within a categorically preeminent principle of unconditional care for a single, immeasurably unrepresentable other. Deployed to the radically liminal register of trace, *an-archē*, and *différance*, ethicopolitical interventions such as hospitality, friendship, and gift giving were found to be positioned rather far outside the compass of Habermas's communications theory, which maintains an intractable categorical divide between an ethics of care and a morality of justice. This distinction between "the good/ethics" and "the just/moral" is in fact consonant with Habermas's overarching effort to avoid the antirationalist and contextualist implications of Derrida's language-theoretic subversion of reason, metaphysics, and the totalizing ideals of the European continental tradition, and thereby safeguard the dignity, autonomy, and relevance of the dialogic subject.

An associated Kantian demarcation between human and nonhuman nature is likewise essential to Habermas's discourse-ethical defense of Enlightenment modernity as an "unfinished" political and emancipatory project. From this vantage point, Habermas upholds the legitimacy and permanence of Galilean science's anthropocentric view of the natural world, and discounts the possibility of elevating "nature-in-itself" to the level of a moral-ethical subject. Here Habermas breaks with Frankfurt School predecessors such as Herbert Marcuse, who envisage "instrumental reason" as a category that has come to exert increasing control over the transformation of "external" nature (through science, technology, and industry) as well as the transformation of "internal" nature (through individuation and various forms of psychosocial domination). In positing a

63

distinction between strategic and communicative action and a related division between system and lifeworld, Habermas loosens the connection between the instrumental domination of internal and external nature considerably. In his account, "reification" is depicted as a possible pathological consequence of instrumental rationalization in contemporary societies, rather than as the ineluctable telos of a scientific rationality gone wild. Habermas is thus positioned to circumvent many of the aporias attendant to the earlier critical theory's attempt to theorize a way out of Weber's bureaucratic "iron cage" via "teleologized" prescriptions for both nature and the knowledge of nature.

Habermas's "disenchanted" view of modern science and technology raises the question of whether it is possible (or indeed desirable) to construct something like an "ecological ethics" from the standpoint of an anthropocentric theory that avoids all references to nature as an end-in-itself. In view of this problem, this chapter considers whether the difference-ethical standpoint of Derridean deconstruction might be mobilized to open up a certain moral access to the natural world that seems to be foreclosed by the thoroughgoing anthropocentrism of Habermas's discourse model. In this context, attention will be drawn to Derrida's argument against the idea of an originary nature—a nature construed as wholly independent of the social—and his associated criticism of Habermas's methodological dualism. The chapter also examines Steven Vogel's kindred "constructivist" critique of Habermas's account. Against both Derrida's and Vogel's efforts to undermine the dualistic epistemological standpoint of the discourse-ethical framework, I maintain that a viable ecological ethics can be forged only by formalistically linking the "good-for-nature" to the communicatively conceived "good-for-humanity." Such an ethics can in my view prevent what Habermas understands as humanity's "knowledge-constitutive interest" in the instrumentalization of the environment from being pressed forth as a project of limitless domination and mastery. Habermas is nonetheless rightly taken to task for keeping the attitude of "affective sympathy" at strict categorical remove from our dealings with the natural world. Here I find Axel Honneth's idea of a "derivative" recognitional orientation toward nature a useful intervention, in that it opens up the possibility of an ethics of felt concern for the domain of objects, but without obliging us to abandon Habermas's view of an eternally objectified, ahistorical nature-in-itself. It is my thesis that in rejecting dualism in favor of a monistic conception of the subjective and objective worlds, writers such as Derrida and Vogel lack the categorical resources needed to avert the slide toward a re-teleologized account of nature and the knowledge of nature.

THE PROBLEM OF NATURE IN LUKÁCS
AND THE EARLY FRANKFURT SCHOOL

In his groundbreaking *History and Class Consciousness*, Georg Lukács takes the epistemological convictions of Friedrich Engels's *Dialectics of Nature* to task. The latter book errs, insists Lukács, in following Hegel's lead and extending

> the method [of dialectics] to apply also to nature. However, the crucial determinants of dialectics—the interaction of the subject and object, the unity of theory and practice, the historical changes in the reality underlying the categories as the root cause of changes in thought, etc.—are absent from our knowledge of nature.[2]

In *Against Nature*—one of the most thoroughgoing assessments of the problem of nature in critical theory to date—Steven Vogel notes that "[w]ith this apparently simple remark (deceptively placed in a footnote), Lukács founds Western Marxism."[3] In a word, Lukács is here endeavoring to uphold the value neutrality of the methods of the mathematical sciences when confined to their own "proper" sphere—the world of objects—while at the same time underscoring the capacity of those methods to exert pathological effects upon extension to the domain of the social. "Reification," in other words, entails a situation in which laborers under capitalism fail to comprehend the social world as a product of their own transformative practices, convinced as they are of the scientistic account of that world set forth in modern "bourgeois thought." As a *social* theory, dialectics is poised to defetishize this worldview, revealing how the epistemological framework of modern science is deployed to further the expressly ideological objective of reproducing capitalist relations of production. *Contra* Engels, however, Lukács contends that when applied to the realm of nonhuman things, the methods of the natural sciences do indeed admit of the objectivity and benign value neutrality attributed to them: only when mobilized as a framework for explaining the social world do they provide ideological cover for capitalist conditions of domination and exploitation.

Significantly, this claim, which Vogel terms the "misapplication thesis," stands in sharp conceptual tension with the other major nature-theoretic strand of Lukács's account—namely, the contention that nature is a "societal category":

> whatever is held to be natural at any given stage of social development, however this nature is related to man and whatever form his involvement with it takes, i.e. nature's form, its content, its range and its objectivity are all socially conditioned.[4]

Lukács's portrayal of the natural world as always already socially mediated is set forth in express contravention of the methodological dualism upheld in his misapplication thesis and its attendant critique of Engelsian nature dialectics. According to Vogel, this aporia of Lukács's theory becomes nothing less than the "the central dilemma of the [subsequent] Western Marxist tradition, which wants to combine a Hegelian epistemology emphasizing the social character of knowledge with a materialist faith in the otherness and priority of nature over the human—an impossible combination that only generates the antinomies about nature that the tradition constantly confronts."[5]

In the writings of the early Frankfurt School, these antinomies are brought into bold relief. On the one hand, thinkers such as Max Horkheimer and Theodor Adorno evince due respect for the critical and indeed revolutionary trajectory of the Enlightenment sciences, which raise implicit methodological commitments to the pursuit of truth, clarity, and freedom of inquiry. On the other hand, Horkheimer and Adorno are at pains to show how the "rational kernel" of the sciences has been disfigured by the social conditions under which these discourses are produced and applied in advanced industrial society. Indeed, even if their aim is not to reject modern science and technology *tout court*, the two authors single out the framework of instrumental rationality that undergirds them for severe criticism, underlining the terms in which it has become both constitutive of late capitalism's hegemonic structures and complicit in their legitimation. In *Dialectic of Enlightenment*, Horkheimer and Adorno argue that as "the agency of calculating thought," instrumental reason has turned out

> to be the interest of industrial society. Being is apprehended in terms of manipulation and administration. Everything—including the individual human being, not to mention the animal—becomes a repeatable, replaceable process, a mere example of the conceptual models of the system. Conflict between administrative, reifying science, between the public mind and the experience of the individual, is precluded by the prevailing circumstances.[6]

On this view, modern science is said to adopt precisely the same objectivating stance toward nature and people that actuarial theory assumes toward life and death: in both instances, "[i]t is the law of large numbers, not the particular case, which recurs in the formula."[7]

In a world in which both internal and external nature are increasingly subject to processes of instrumental-technical administration and control, Horkheimer and Adorno are intuitively drawn to the prospect of a return to nature prior to "disenchantment," a nature imitated in mimesis and disencumbered of all Enlightenment demands for renunciation. Here the two Frankfurt School authors place themselves on the tip of a philosophical arc that extends from Swabian Pietism to Friedrich Schelling to the early Karl Marx to Ernst Bloch—a trajectory that champions the "resurrection of fallen nature"[8] as an avenue for resolving the conflict between the human and nonhuman worlds. Yet whatever their affinities with this tradition of romantic nature specula-tion, Horkheimer and Adorno distance themselves from certain of its strands—notably, Nazism and other right-wing ideologies, which vest their efforts to construct the utopian social order in appeals to the transhistorical ideal of "nature worship." In contrast, the two writers emphasize the ex-pressly historical, social, and *nonconceptual* character of the natural world. For them, it is precisely a conceptual "memory" of nature's intrinsic noncon-ceptualness that can provide the basis for a defetishizing critique of modern identifying thought and the reified conditions it legitimates. Indeed, as Vogel notes, nature as nonconcept "points at immediacy, hints at . . . some mode of representation that is different than the ordinary one, showing what cannot be said instead of vainly trying despite everything to say it."[9] This anamnestic gesture toward the nonconcept of nature is beset by a stubborn aporia, how-ever, inasmuch as it seems to structurally constrain the two authors from specifying what precisely is to be "remembered."

Horkheimer and Adorno's tendency to view nature as amenable to "lib-eration" from the fetters of instrumental rationalization is carried forth in the work of Herbert Marcuse, albeit on rather different terms. A principal point of demarcation is Marcuse's far more distrustful view of modern sci-ence and technics *as such*. On the conviction that "[s]cience, *by virtue of its own method* and concepts, has projected and promoted a universe in which the domination of nature has remained linked to the domination of man," Marcuse holds open the possibility that the conditions of a new, "pacified" world would issue forth a new type of science, one that "would arrive at essentially different concepts of nature and establish essentially different facts."[10] To Marcuse, such a new science and its associated technology would shatter the epistemological foundations of their present-day counter-parts, eschewing their orientation toward instrumental domination in favor of a "liberatory mastery" of nature. Significantly, this new epistemological and technical vantage point would present itself as a fundamentally "aes-thetic" or "erotic" attitude, with the capacity to accord full respect to nature-in-itself. "The things of nature," writes Marcuse, "become free to be what they are. But to be what they are they *depend* on the erotic attitude: they receive their *telos* only in it."[11] Marcuse's plea for a new eroticized science and technology aimed at liberating the natural world from instrumental-technical repression and establishing different facts about it revives "with a vengeance," as Vogel puts it, Lukács's conviction that na-ture is a social category.[12]

HABERMAS'S CONCEPTION OF
THE "MISAPPLICATION THESIS"

It is of course precisely such a "re-enchanted" view of nature and the knowledge of nature that Habermas is keen to contest. Despite various modifications in terminology, Habermas's thinking on this score has not veered fundamentally from the argument set forth in *Knowledge and Human Interests* in 1968. Then as now, Habermas's objective is not to disparage the achievements of modern science as such, but rather to criticize "*scientism*, i.e., the grandiose claims made for the specialized form of rationality embodied in modern science."[13] To this end, he reconstructs the account of reification advanced by Lukács and developed by the early critical theorists. In his revised view, reification does not describe a situation in which scientific reason fulfills its presumed epistemological mission to bring both internal and external nature under the yoke of instrumental-technical rationalization. Instead, Habermas portrays reification, or "technocratic consciousness," as a sort of "border violation," in which the purposive rationality of modern science strays from its "proper" realm and subjects the communicative reason of the lifeworld to the kind of instrumental-technical manipulation that is appropriate only in relation to the nonspeaking world. "The reified models of the sciences," Habermas writes, "migrate into the sociocultural life-world and gain objective power over the latter's self-understanding. The ideological nucleus of this consciousness is *the elimination of the distinction between the practical and the technical*."[14]

Here we are presented with a version of the misapplication argument, but with a crucial language-theoretic twist: unlike Lukács, Habermas maintains that the methodological dualism of such a thesis can be sustained only if it includes an account of the natural sciences that is independent of that set forth in the standard positivist model. To provide such an explanation, he advances his theory of "knowledge-constitutive interests." As initially fleshed out in *Knowledge and Human Interests*, this framework identifies two key realms of human action: "work" and "communicative interaction." Work, or "instrumental action," is associated with the specifically human interest in the purposive-rational control of the external world; at the level of epistemology, such action is tied to the "empirical-analytic" methods of the natural sciences. In contrast, communicative interaction retains the *telos* of mutual understanding through argument, an objective consistent epistemologically with the "historical-hermeneutic" orientation of the *Geisteswissenschaften*. On this move, Habermas presents a language-theoretic transfiguration of Kant's partition of theoretical and practical reason and the associated split between humans and nature. In Habermas's innovative framework, the domains of communicative interaction and labor, and the corresponding human interests in mutual understanding and technical control of the environment, are portrayed as irreducibly distinct and "equiprimordial," constitutive of our anthropological endowment as language-speaking beings. As such, both modes of human action and interests retain unique "quasi-transcendental" epistemological functions that "arise from actual structures of human life."[15]

A major advantage of Habermas's account of knowledge-constitutive interests is its ability to mount a critique of positivism while clarifying the status of the *Naturwissenschaften* and their investigatory domain, which is left epistemologically ambiguous in Lukács. As Vogel observes, Habermas's methodological dualism is more robust and fruitful than that of Lukács, insofar as it underscores that the natural sciences

> do not investigate "reality as such," but rather that segment of the world constituted by the human interest in prediction and control of the environment—just as the *Geisteswissenschaften*, marked not by empirical methods but by hermeneutic ones, investigate a different segment, constituted by the human interest in achieving mutual understanding.[16]

Since he locates the epistemological roots of modern science and technology in the transsocial "species-interest" in the purposive-rational mastery of nature and in the very structure of instrumental action itself, Habermas has good grounds for rejecting Marcuse's call for a new eroticized science and technics aimed at fundamentally transforming nature and setting it free to be what it truly is. Convinced that the human species will always need to "achieve self-preservation through social labor and with the aid of means that substitute for work," Habermas is disabused entirely of Marcuse's vision of a "fraternal relationship"[17] with nature and his related demand that we renounce "*our* technology, in favor of a qualitatively different one."[18] For him, nature remains ineliminably reified, ahistorical, and asocial, a domain that communicative agents have a deep-seated knowledge-constitutive interest in predicting and controlling with the assistance of the mathematical sciences and their allied technologies. The latter are in fact "irreversible" achievements of modern societies, in whose wake all demands for the resurrection of fallen nature become little more than vestiges of an obsolete "heritage of mysticism."[19] Indeed, the tradition of romantic nature speculation is one that Habermas, "situated as he is between Marx and Kant, cannot recognize, much less accept."[20]

HABERMAS AND THE QUESTION OF ENVIRONMENTAL ETHICS

Redirected away from an attack on scientific reason *per se* and toward a critique of the illicit encroachment of instrumental rationality upon the norms of communicative interaction, it would seem that we are well positioned to construct an ethics of the environment that links the "good-for-nature" to the communicatively conceived "good-for-humanity." This is in fact the approach of Habermas's colleague Karl-Otto Apel, who argues that communicative ethics has a legitimate and indeed urgent interest in defending the lifeworld from the environmental crisis that is presently threatening to destroy the natural habit upon which all flourishing forms of communicative sociation depend. "In the context of the present ecological crisis of scientific-technological civilization," writes Apel, "the preservation of a just social order meeting the standard of the ideal communication community must be linked on an international scale with the system-theoretical requirements for securing the preservation of the ecosphere."[21]

Yet whatever its possible advantages over the early critical theory's teleologized prescriptions for nature, science, and technology, nagging doubts remain about the viability of an ecological ethics in which the good-for-nature is conceived in strictly formalistic terms—that is, *in relation* to communicatively adjudicated conceptions of the human good. Such misgivings date back to the 1970s, when the environmental crisis became a pressing concern for a growing number of authors. Henning Ottmann, for one, noted that while it is not advisable to reject the modern type of instrumental mastery of nature *tout court* or revert to the "mythical" ideal of transfiguring nature into a cosubject, "the present-day experience with an increasingly disrupted environment . . . sets a limit to the boundless will-to-control which could result in the destruction of external nature as the foundation of society."[22] For Ottmann, it is therefore imperative to view nature not only, with Habermas, as a "purpose-for-us" (insofar as it must be mastered to ensure our survival), but also as a "purpose-in-itself" (in light of the objective restrictions that it imposes on our ability to control it).

A more thoroughgoing set of criticisms has been raised in connection with the alleged "psychosocial" deficit of Habermas's unreservedly anthropocentric view of humanity's relationship to the natural world. In 1979, Joel Whitebook underscored the difficulty of resolving the conflict between society and nature "without a major transformation in our social consciousness of the natural world—e.g., a renewed reverence for life."[23] More recently, this line of argument has been taken up by writers such as Joel Kovel. Against Habermas, Kovel contends that nature must no longer be seen as "an inert object outside ourselves, [but] rather as an entity from which we draw our own being and re-create in the act of production."[24] Kovel concedes that our capacity for signification renders us fundamentally distinct from nonspeaking nature—which will always remain an object of transformation for us—but insists that the Newtonian understanding of nature as a purposeless, thoroughly mechanized domain must be eschewed in favor of an orientation that accords it due "respect, wonder, and reverence."[25] From the perspective of deep ecology, Warwick Fox goes even further: expressing an unequivocal distaste for the "firm ontological divide" in the field of existence posited by the modern scientific-technical worldview, Fox refuses to allow for any distinctions between the human and nonhuman realms. "To the extent that we perceive boundaries," he avers, "we fall short of a deep ecological consciousness."[26]

From the vantage point of social ecology, Murray Bookchin likewise defends a version of the Lukácsian nature as a social category thesis over and against the argument on behalf of methodological dualism. Bookchin pins his hopes for a radically transformed relationship with nature on the science of ecology, a discipline that overcomes the limitations of modern instrumental reason and reveals nature in "all its aspects, cycles, and interrelationships," in all its "diversity in unity."[27] To Bookchin this decidedly holistic, nonanthropocentric perspective cancels out all human aspirations to master and control the planet, and thereby denude it of any intrinsic purpose or value. In fact, ecological science commends us to see that nature is host to "a kind of intentionality, . . . a graded development of self-organization that yields subjectivity and, finally, self-reflexivity in its highly developed human form."[28]

As might be expected, Habermas has no use for such "ecological science as new science" arguments: to him, they amount to little more than warmed-over Engelsian nature dialectics, accounts "loaded with ontological assumptions of an objective teleology set in nature itself."[29] Indeed, as the foregoing discussion has underscored, for Habermas a return to a teleologized conceptualization of the natural world is precisely the risk of all endeavors to undermine the inviolable rift between the natural and the social established in the epistemological framework of Kantianism.

STEVEN VOGEL'S CONSTRUCTIVIST CRITIQUE

Perhaps the most formidable obstacle for any environmental ethics constructed on strictly Habermasian terms is the verdict that postempiricism has leveled over the past forty years against the presumed objectivity and value neutrality of the Galilean model of science. The postempiricist cudgel has been taken up, in one form or another, by many contemporary critics of Habermas's nature-theoretic maneuvers. One of the most ambitious endeavors to wield postempiricism against the dualistic scaffolding of Habermas's framework is mounted by Vogel. In *Against Nature*, Vogel observes that contrary to Habermas's initial efforts to portray the natural world as presocial and immutable, and the perspective of the scientific investigator as objectivating and monologic, the critique of empiricism initiated by thinkers such as Thomas Kuhn and Paul Feyerabend shows that the natural sciences are in fact constitutively connected to discourses of the hermeneutic-historical type.

Granting a certain legitimacy to such objections, Habermas eventually broke with the account of scientific reason that he advanced in his early writings. This shift begins in the early 1970s with "A Postscript to *Knowledge and Human Interests*."[30] These later formulations acknowledge that in addition to its monologic framework of purposive-rational action, the mathematical sciences do indeed admit of a discursive and social dimension. Agreeing with Friedrich Schleiermacher, Habermas was forced to concede that however much a scientific researcher "might seem to work alone in the library, at his desk, or in the laboratory, his learning processes are inevitably embedded in a public communication community of researchers. Because the enterprise of the cooperative search for truth refers back to the structures of public argumentation, truth . . . can never become the mere steering medium of a self-regulating subsystem."[31] In this modified account, the structure of scientific discourse is located expressly in the communicative reason of the lifeworld, an etiology that is especially evident during periods of crises in scientific thinking, which are marked by "bursts" of hermeneutic-historical reflection. Be this as it may, Habermas does not distance himself from his earlier conviction that "*normal* science is characterized by routines and by an objectivism that shields the everyday practice of research from problematizations"; in fact, he maintains that even when crises arise, "the suppression of degenerating paradigms by new ones takes place quasinaturally rather than through a reflective process."[32]

The basic problem with this revision, according to Vogel, is its retention within the natural sciences of a formalizable, prediscursive framework of instrumental action alongside a (rightly acknowledged) hermeneutic-historical one. In insisting on both of these components, Habermas fails to grasp the full thrust and significance of the postempiricist argument, which rejects resolutely the idea that the natural sciences are host to an independent nonsocial, value-neutral epistemological foundation "uncorrupted by the messiness of ordinary language."[33] Eager to steel his theory of knowledge-constitutive interests against the temptations of "Lysenkoism," or the politicization of science, Habermas upholds dualism at the cost of being unaccountably dismissive of the crucial postempiricist claim that the natural sciences, no less than the social sciences, are normative and hermeneutic *through and through*, "marked by an unavoidable, and nonvicious, circularity in the relation between interpretive scheme (theory) and data, [and] by a constitutive role for discourse among investigators."[34]

To Vogel, Habermas's revised assessment is in fact little more than a "complex double game," which nods knowingly, with postempiricism, at the discursive aspect of natural-scientific inquiry while at the same time denying its expressly *social* character. It presents us with an antinomical scenario in which scientists engage "in some strange kind of practice which is scarcely practice at all, a 'discourse' in which experimentation takes on an other-worldly purity and bears little or no connection to the practices of ordinary people under ordinary circumstances or to the objects with which they interact."[35] In a desperate bid to salvage the distinction between the instrumental framework of knowledge and the communicative one, Habermas glosses over what postempiricism has shown to be the constitutively social character of natural-scientific discourse, revealing "the extent to which [he] himself remains in thrall to positivist assumptions."[36]

There are therefore good grounds, contends Vogel, for returning to the Lukácsian nature as a social category thesis, rather than cling, with Habermas, to the outmoded dualistic epistemology of Kantianism. Indeed, Habermas's effort to depict the natural sciences as both discursively hermeneutic *and* oriented toward "objective" inquiry into a realm wholly independent of the social presents itself as oxymoronic and unsustainable in the wake of the postempiricist critique, whose lesson is precisely that

> [t]here is no "nature in itself," or at least none that we can say anything about or that it does the slightest good for our epistemology to assume. The nature we encounter has no noumenal status nor even any noumenal correlate: it is something we constitute—in our actions, our theories, our poetry, our metaphysics and religion, our social institutions—and so it changes as we do. . . . [I]t is constituted subject to interests. But these interests are real social interests, which arise historically and also pass away. Thus nature turns out to be social from the very beginning.[37]

By adopting a constructivist approach to the problem of nature and the natural sciences, Vogel hopes to avoid the aporias into which Habermas's account lapses in its defense of dualism. The constructivist view, he suggests, is indeed a logical extension of the communicative-theoretic program, one that Habermas himself might have adopted had he been able to overcome his deep-seated fears about the "Lysenkoist" and "relativist" consequences of a full-blown embrace of postempiricism. Unencumbered by such reservations, Vogel insists that everything that Habermas associates with the framework of "instrumental action" is in fact always already social and historical, that there is "a fundamentally and irreducibly hermeneutic and indeed normative aspect to our relations to and knowledge of nature (and a fortiori to natural science)."[38]

From this vantage point, we are situated to return, with Marcuse, to the prospect of establishing a "new science" relieved of the Enlightenment's misguided convictions about the transsocial and transhistorical character of the natural world. Indeed, to recognize nature's inherent sociality and historicity is to accede to the expressly Marcusean hope of establishing "essentially different facts and concepts of nature" under changed sociohistorical conditions. Vogel is nonetheless critical of Marcuse, inasmuch as he, no less than Habermas, can be faulted for embracing the idea of a natural realm prior to and independent of society and history. That Marcuse mobilizes the notion of nature-in-itself not in the interests of dualism, but rather as the foundation of a naturalistic social critique that "perversely" enjoins us to "change nature first in order to make it possible for it in turn to change us" does little to recommend his approach over Habermas's.[39] Yet, as he is also little enamored of Habermas's effort to sever nature entirely from the realm of the social, Vogel recommends a third path, one that is capable, in his view, of affirming nature's intrinsically sociohistorical constitution without falling prey to the romantic aporias that plague the Marcusean program of transforming nature into a cosubject. On Vogel's alternative account, nature presents itself as the *Umwelt*, or built environment, a domain always already marked and produced by our prior social practices, and constantly changing in accord with shifts in those same practices. It is revealed, in other words, as the world *"for which we are responsible*, in both the causal and the moral sense of that word, and hence . . . as possessing a normative significance of just the kind that Habermas thinks discourse ethics has trouble explaining."[40]

Such a constructivist view of our relationship to nature is to Vogel precisely the standpoint from which a "truly" environmental ethics becomes possible, and precisely the position to which the discourse-ethical model might have led had Habermas not felt the need to encumber it with an unwarranted epistemological dualism. Indeed, in Vogel's view, the constructivist approach to environmental ethics has the distinct advantage of abandoning the attempt to read a solution to the problem of nature's domination of nature-in-itself (*à la*, for example, Marcusean naturalism) in favor of the "justifiably anthropocentric" conviction "that questions about the environment have to be seen as *social* questions"—that is, as questions that "can only be answered in a discourse of the sort to which Habermas believes that all normative claims implicitly appeal."[41]

IN DEFENSE OF DUALISM

Whatever its innovations, Vogel's effort to ground an environmental ethics in a constructivist version of Lukács's monistic thesis on nature and society is ultimately unconvincing. The fundamental defect of Vogel's argument arises from what I believe is his misreading of the implications of the postempiricist critique of the Galilean model of scientific reason. Vogel is certainly correct to portray postempiricism as emphasizing the hermeneutic and historical character of the natural sciences, and thereby breaking with an older understanding of these discourses as predominately monologic and nonsocial. However, there is simply no justification for his claim that postempiricism has construed the *domain* of natural-scientific inquiry—the nonspeaking world—as likewise historically mutable and social. Indeed, while the technological achievements of the *Naturwissenschaften* (flat-screen televisions, skyscrapers, mobile phones, nuclear waste—in short, the *built*, or *transformed*, environment) are no doubt endowed with socially mediated meanings that shift alongside the changing framework of concepts and assertions of these same natural sciences, there is no reason to believe that such sociality and historicity can be ascribed to nature as unmediated substrate.

To support this claim, a closer examination of the arguments of Kuhn and Feyerabend is in order. As is well known, to Kuhn prevailing regimes of scientific inquiry are susceptible to "paradigm shifts" the moment they push beyond and can no longer accommodate a certain threshold of the conceptual anomalies that they themselves have generated in the normal course of scientific investigation. The orientation of scientific investigators is on this view exposed as expressly value laden, insofar as it is always guided by ascendant normative assumptions about the appropriate ways to conduct scientific research. Feyerabend does not dispute this basic contention, but goes a step further than Kuhn, rejecting the latter's notion of a hierarchy of scientific adequacy and his attendant retention of the concept of scientific "truth." Feyerabend's aim is to demonstrate "the arbitrary character of hegemonic scientific law, and, in turn, to challenge, the substantive norms that guide its certification by the scientific community."[42] Yet, crucially, neither Kuhn nor Feyerabend are inclined to envisage their critiques of the supposed ahistoricity and asociality of the natural sciences as having concomitant ramifications for nature itself. Although he is no more enamored of the empiricist model of science than Vogel, Stanley Aronowitz underscores this point well: "both Kuhn and Feyerabend," he notes, "remain bound by a realist theory of science to the extent that *the object of knowledge remains fixed; only understanding varies.*"[43] In line with this observation, I maintain that the notion of nature-in-itself is by no means inimical to the postulates of either Kuhnian or Feyerabendian postempiricism. However, *contra* both Aronowitz and Vogel, I see no reason to move beyond the argument for the historicization of the sciences to the demand for an associated historicization of "the material object."[44]

Indeed, in my view Habermas is correct to retain the idea of an eternally reified, ahistorical natural world via the strategy of dualism. In rejecting this approach in favor of the coextensive historicization of nature and the knowledge of nature, monistic perspectives such as Vogel's are vulnerable to what Habermas describes as the "dangerous bewitchments" of Lysenkoism.[45] Vogel, for one, acknowledges such risks as real, but argues that they can be corralled by "careful and principled reflection by methodologically self-aware scientists about science's true epistemological status."[46] He insists, in fact, that such a "self-reflective science that knew its own rootedness in the social would be *less*, not more likely" to succumb to enticements of Lysenkoism than one that did not.[47] This claim strikes me as rather specious, however, since it is hard to imagine how a heightened level of self-reflection would render scientists more attuned to the "true epistemological status" of their discourses in a world in which *the very facticity of nature* is constantly in flux, tethered irreducibly to changes in human social practices.

In view of this formidable difficulty, it is indeed remarkable that the demand for the historicization of nature continues to hold sway over a number of authors. In line with both Vogel and Andrew Feenberg, Eduardo Mendieta, for example, disputes Habermas's portrayal of instrumental action as a framework of species-based learning. To Mendieta the "weak naturalism" of the latter perspective is incompatible with Habermas's own commitment to the "detranscendentalization of all knowledge and rationality claims."[48] Rather than fully come to terms with the implications of the postempiricist, postrepresentational, postpositivist standpoint, Habermas has in Mendieta's view essentialized both science and technology and succumbed to "a 'naïve instrumentalism' that conceives science as a neutral and always advancing species project"; from the latter vantage point, it is impossible to see that the "very 'objects' of science are socially and historically constituted."[49]

One may nevertheless wish to consider whether such conclusions have been drawn too hastily. In this context, it is useful to recall the case of the scientists who operated under the flag of the Third Reich. Against the understandings of their predecessors in the Weimer Republic, these scientists were keen to demonstrate the "superiority" of the "Aryan" genetic constitution over that of its "non-Aryan" counterpart. Consonant with this revised conviction, advances were made in the field of biochemical engineering that were of service to the Reich's program of genocide against those deemed to be "genetically inferior." While the science and technology produced and applied under Nazism were no doubt coextensive with a new understanding of the *Umwelt*, it is quite a leap from this insight to the claim that the laws of physicochemistry that underlie elements of the natural world—be they human liver cells, birch bark, or bovine pancreatic acid—were themselves subject to historical transformation under the auspices of Third Reich science. Such a position is by no means substantiated from the standpoint of the postempiricist critique, whose crucial contribution is precisely its demonstration that the *discourses and techniques* of the natural sciences admit of a social and historically mutable orientation, not nature-in-itself.

The preference for a reconstructed version of Lukács's nature-theoretic monism over and against Habermas's competing framework of methodological dualism can be attributed in my view to the apparent conviction—of Vogel and others—that the objectivating attitude of the natural sciences labors under the weight of its own "false consciousness."[50] In fact, consonant with the claims of *Dialectic of Enlightenment*, Vogel portrays the framework of instrumental action as constitutively incapable of recognizing its putative asociality and value neutrality as an *illusion*, a mask that obscures its underlying *telos* of dominative mastery. His approach is thus at bottom an *ideology critique*, an argument aimed at laying bare the "falseness" of modern science's belief in the eternal facticity of nature and in the objectivism of its own methods. This position is well summarized and affirmed by Aronowitz, who also refutes the suggestion that the methodological imperatives of prediction, control, and measurability are the only viable routes to verification and falsification within the natural sciences. "The concept of [such scientific] normalcy," writes Aronowitz, "is an illusion of philosophers, including Marxist philosophers. Science is precisely characterized by its lack of normalcy; in fact, the notion of normalcy itself, the notion of neutrality, is ideologically reactionary."[51]

Having likewise disabused himself of the "myth" of the value neutrality and objectivity of the *Naturwissenschaften*, Vogel is now positioned to plea for a "truly" environmental ethics, one that remains fully cognizant of the need to replace the present "ideological" framework of scientific reason with a "radically different" one:

> No longer in thrall to the objectivist myths about the possibility of a pure description of external reality (myths that themselves simply reflect the prevailing reification), such a science would finally know itself to be social, to be historical, to be "interested," and hence would know its own connection to the world it has helped create. It is that very knowledge that breaks the link between science and domination.[52]

Of course the claim that such a link exists to be broken—which Vogel takes as axiological—can itself be criticized for being fraught with ideological assumptions. With Habermas, I see no evidence for a constitutive connection between instrumental rationality and the domination of the social world, and maintain that all efforts to undermine the epistemological foundations of modern science and technics invite the possibility of regression to prerational epistemological traditions. In fact, it is my contention that the categorical resources needed to avert the slide toward a re-teleologization of nature and the knowledge of nature are dissolved precisely at the moment when one opts for some iteration of Lukács's nature-theoretic monism—be it that of Vogel, early critical theory, or, as we shall soon see, Derrida—over and against the contrary argument on behalf of methodological dualism. With his discourse-ethical spin on Lukács's dualistic misapplication thesis, Habermas rightly redirects critical theory away from an attack on scientific reason *per se* and toward a critique of scientism—a situation in which the framework of instrumental rationalization strays from its proper realm (of things) and pathologizes norms of communicative interaction in the lifeworld. From his perspective, we are no longer obliged to equate (with, say, Horkheimer and Adorno) the goal-directed aspect of human reason with rationalization as such. Instead, as Richard Bernstein observes, in Habermas a distinction is drawn between purposive-rational action—whose two different aspects include "the empirical efficiency of technical means and the consistency of choice between suitable means"—and the drastically different type of rationalization characteristic of the sphere of communicative action.[53] In the latter domain, insists Habermas, rationalization "means extirpating those relations of force that are inconspicuously set in the very structures of communication and that prevent conscious settlement of conflicts."[54]

Habermas's proposed division between communicative and purposive-rational action types means, of course, that any "ethics of the environment" must ultimately be constructed as an "ethics by association," a framework in which the well-being of the natural world can be acknowledged only *in relation* to the knowledge-constitutive interests of humanity. Human agents are herewith precluded at the level of categorization from adopting toward the natural world the perspectives on both sides of the "razor-sharp" moral-ethical divide that we examined in chapter 1—that is, the orientation of egalitarian reciprocation and the asymmetrical attitude of care. All hopes of entering into a noninstrumental relationship with nature-in-itself or establishing a fundamentally different kind of science and technology are on these terms firmly extinguished.

ANIMALS AS "LIMIT CONCEPT"

Whatever its advantages over approaches such as Vogel's, which attempt to hold on to the basic ethical impulse of the Lukácsian idea of socialized nature, the Habermasian variant of environmental ethics is not without its stumbling blocks. Perhaps the most salient such difficulty arises in connection with the question of humanity's relationship with animals. Given their incapacity for speech, animals would seem to be excluded *prima facie* from assuming the status of coequal "communication partners." Exiled from the field of moral-ethical deliberation, they appear destined to take their place alongside the rest of the nonspeaking world as mere transsocial, transhistorical objects amenable to instrumental-technical control. Clearly, such an appraisal runs counter to our everyday moral intuitions about our "nonobjectivated" dealings with animals—particularly "higher-order" creatures such as cats, dogs, and horses, with whom we often establish deep and long-lasting emotional bonds.

Habermas's efforts to address this problem date back to his 1982 essay, "A Reply to My Critics." Here he concedes that insofar as animals can be classed as "quasi-teleological," an ethics that merely associates human and nonhuman interests formalistically is inadequate, since it holds no place for the

impulse to provide assistance to wounded and debased creatures, to have solidarity with them, the compassion for their torments, the abhorrence of the naked instrumentalization of nature for purposes which are ours but not its, in short the institutions which ethics of compassion place with undeniable right in the foreground, cannot be anthropocentrically blended out.[55]

To redress this flaw, Habermas argues that animals unable to "take up the role of *participants* in practical discourses" must be recognized as a "limit concept" to our interest in predicting and controlling the nonspeaking world.[56] In fact, such limit cases enjoin us to extend the neo-Aristotelian orientation of *Fürsorge* ("caring-for") toward nonhuman beings, such that we might gain a certain "quasi-moral" access to them.[57]

This concession to Adorno's desire to move the expressive attitude of "compassion" and "solidarity" within the orbit of sentient nature notwithstanding, Habermas is adamant that the "yawning gap" between a naturalistic ethic and a discourse ethic cannot be bridged. Although it is certainly possible for humans to evince "feelings analogous to moral feelings" toward (at least some) animals, our dealings with them must remain *quasi*moral: insofar as animals, unlike us, do not address one another in accord with intersubjectively binding norms, the discourse ethic's "norm-conformative attitude" can no more be adopted toward them than toward other entities within nonspeaking nature. Indeed, for Habermas the natural world, including nonhuman animals, yields no "problems that could be stylised to questions of justice from the standpoint of normative validity"[58] and remains forever closed off from consideration as a moral end-in-itself. It is only humans—language-speaking beings endowed with knowledge-constitutive interests in both mutual understanding and instrumental-technical control of the environment—who have been released into "autonomy and responsibility."[59]

DERRIDA AND THE PROBLEM OF "CARING" FOR NATURE

As it is encumbered by none of Habermasianism's self-reservations about destabilizing the dualistic epistemology of the Kantian tradition, it is worth considering whether Derrida's deconstructive ethics of radical singularity is poised to open up a certain hitherto foreclosed moral access to what might be called "nature."

Although Derrida does not lay claim to the term, it is fair to say that something like a "critique of nature" resides at the core of his project. Indeed, Derrida's effort to demolish the link between language and representation, to deny that the signifier has any "'natural attachment' to the signified within reality"[60] seems to return us to *Dialectic of Enlightenment*'s view of nature as irreducibly nonconceptual. However, the radical antifoundationalism of the deconstructive maneuver ratchets up the implications of the early Frankfurt School's critique of modern identifying thought, pointing not just to the non-conceptualness of nature but to its very *nonexistence*. After all, if everything that is taken to be original and foundational is revealed by deconstruction as mere *appearance*, as constituted not by a priori essences but by complex, shifting, and unpredictable sociolinguistic processes, the very idea of "nature" or "naturalness" is likewise demythologized. This point is duly underscored by Vogel, who notes that in Derrida

> that which is supposed to be foundational is always discovered to be not what it was "meant" to be, and so the arrival of the origin is always, as Derrida famously puts it, deferred. With this, the promise that there is indeed something original, something out of which everything else is built but that was not itself built, becomes harder and harder to believe.[61]

If one of the implications to be drawn from the exposure of the "myth of foundation" is that nature—at least as conceived from the vantage point of *logos*—does not in fact exist, it would seem, at first glance, that we are left rather ill positioned to set forth something like a deconstructive "ethics of the environment": What basis do we have for favoring one type of natural habitat over another if the very notion of an originary nature is discounted from the outset? As suggested in the preceding chapter, the ethicopolitical framework of irreducible singularity elaborated in Derrida's later texts appears to be aimed at staving off charges that its relentless endeavors to disarticulate the modern *ratio* lead inexorably to the blind alley of "anything goes" perspectivism. The question in the present context is whether Derridean overtures such as incalculably unconditional hospitality, friendship, and gift giving—in short, the asymmetrically reciprocal orientation of "care"—could be deployed not only with respect to our dealings with the human other but with the *non-human other* as well.

While Derrida does not elaborate a systematic framework of environmental ethics, indications of his thinking on this question are scattered throughout his text. Consider, for example, his "*Fichus*: Frankfurt Address," which he delivered in 2001 upon being awarded the Adorno Prize. Here Derrida underlines a number of important conceptual affinities between the Adornian and deconstructive approaches to the question of humanity's relationship to the nonhuman.[62] He notes that both vantage points commend nothing less than a new "critical ecology" that sets "itself against two formidable forces, often opposed to one another, sometimes allied"—namely, the idealist/humanist tradition of Kantianism and the nature worship tradition of fascism.[63] To Derrida, the former is to be taken to task for securing the "dignity" and "autonomy" of the human at the cost of disqualifying all attempts to extend the attitude of affective sympathy toward nonhuman beings. As a passage entitled "Man and Beast" in *Dialectic of Enlightenment* notes,

> In this world liberated from appearance—in which human beings, having forfeited reflection, have become once more the cleverest animals, which subjugate the rest of the universe when they happen not to be tearing themselves apart—to show compassion for animals is considered no longer merely sentimental but a betrayal of progress.[64]

Derrida upholds this portrait of Kantian man, for whom there is

> [n]othing more odious . . . than remembering a resemblance or affinity between man and animality . . . for an idealist system, animals play a role virtually the same as the Jews in a fascist system. . . . Authentic idealism (*echter Idealismus*) consists in *insulting* the animal in man or in treating man like an animal.[65]

Yet while idealism inveighs against animality, refusing it any and all impulses of compassion or felt concern, Nazism's ideology of nature worship evinces a contrary but no less troubling *interest in animals*, such that "[f]ascism begins when you insult an animal, including the animal in man."[66] For Horkheimer and Adorno, it was precisely on this conviction that Göring was able to link "animal protection to racial hatred, the Lutheran-Germanic joys of the happy murderer with the genteel fair play of the aristocratic hunter."[67] In accord with this critique of both Kantianism's anthropocentric verdict against animals and Nazism's opposing but nevertheless kindred orientation of animal worship, Derrida calls for a "revolution in our dwellings together with these other living things that we call animals"[68]—a revolution that would presumably allow the expressive attitude of *Fürsorge* to be extended toward nonspeaking nature—or at least the sentient portion thereof.

The terms of such a proposed revolution remain rather ambiguous, however, as one is never entirely certain to what extent Derrida is prepared to dissolve the boundary between the speaking and nonspeaking worlds. In an essay entitled "The Animal That I Therefore Am," he expressly denies that his intention is to ignore or efface "everything that separates humankind from the other animals, creating a single large set, a single great fundamentally homogeneous and continuous family tree going from the *animot* to the *homo* (*faber*, *sapiens*, or whatever else)."[69] In fact, any such effort to collapse the distinction between the two realms is deemed nothing less than an "*asinanity*." Yet in other places, Derrida seems to overcome his erstwhile reservations about radically smudging the line between the human and the nonhuman. In the final essay of *Rogues*, for instance, he appears rather amenable to the idea, insisting that

> the stakes are becoming more urgent—that none of the conventionally accepted limits between the so-called human living being and the so-called animal one, none of the oppositions, none of the supposedly linear and indivisible boundaries, resist a rational deconstruction—whether we are talking about language, culture, social symbolic networks, technicity or work, even the relationship to death and to mourning, and even the prohibition against and avoidance of incest—so many "capacities" of which the "animal" (a general singular noun!) is said so dogmatically to be bereft, impoverished.[70]

Such flirtations with the idea of entering into a noncalculative relationship with the nonhuman realm begin to sound, on a certain reading, vaguely Marcusean.

Witness the interview with Jean-Luc Nancy entitled "Eating Well, or the Calculation of the Subject," where Derrida expressly allies deconstruction with a critique of the "carno-phallogocentrism" that inflects the subject-object model of knowledge. Here he argues that displaced from the epistemological confines of the latter framework and reinscribed in the register of the trace, iterability, and *différance*, the possibilities or necessities of language reveal themselves as marked by "irreducibility from the inside," such that they must be understood as *not in themselves strictly human*. Indeed, according to Derrida, the deconstructive standpoint suggests precisely that there is no "single, linear, indivisible, oppositional limit, to a binary opposition between the human and the infra-human."[71] Still, this gesture toward boundary blurring aside, Derrida cannot quite bring himself to obliterate the distinction outright. Recalling the proviso raised in "The Animal That I Therefore Am," he cautions that the critique of carnophallogocentrism is "not a question of covering up ruptures or heterogeneities [between the human and the nonhuman]."[72] The point is rather to expose the canonized discourses of the Western ontotheological tradition as undergirded by a *sacrificial structure* that divests humanity of any and all responsibilities toward animals. In so doing, this structure constructs the subject as a self-present, virile carnivore whose flourishing is linked not only to the slaughter of actual animals but to the symbolic cannibalistic sacrifice of other human beings. Yet rather than "start a support group for vegetarianism, ecologism, or for the societies for the protection of animals," the task for deconstruction is to discern whether there is "a place left open, in the very structure of these [hegemonic] discourses (which are also 'cultures') for a *noncriminal* putting to death [of animals]"—a task, concedes Derrida, that is marked by its essential "enormity" and "excessiveness."[73] Ultimately, it would appear that Derrida wishes to contest the violence or "a lack of respect toward what we still so confusedly call the animal"[74]—to which the tradition of metaphysicoanthropocentrism enjoins us—but without going so far as to embrace the prospect of a full-blown merger of the two spheres.

However the question, it seems to me, is whether or not Derrida's resistance to the idea of a complete dissolution of boundaries is a stance that can be defended through an appeal to the philosophical resources of deconstruction itself. This difficulty is highlighted if we consider one of the implications of his framework's radical disarticulation of the objectivating attitude of the mathematical sciences—namely, the opening up of these sciences to the indeterminate orientation of *play* and the *mythopoetic*. In *Writing and Difference*, Derrida entertains precisely this prospect in his critique of Claude Lévi-Straus's distinction between the scientistic perspective of the "engineer" and the contrasting disposition of *bricolage*. To Derrida, Lévi-Straus's engineer commits the grave blunder of assuming that "the totality of his language, syntax, and lexicon" can be constructed "out of whole cloth," "out of nothing," thereby making him "the creator of the verb, the verb itself."[75] This outlook stands in marked distinction to that of the *bricoleur*, who is fully aware of "the necessity of borrowing one's concepts from the text of a heritage which is more or less coherent or ruined."[76] A scientific engineer endowed with the capacity to dispense with all forms of *bricolage* is in Derrida's view an illusory, indeed a *theological*, notion. "As soon as we cease to believe in such an engineer . . . we admit that every finite discourse is bound by a certain *bricolage* and that the engineer and the scientist are also species of *bricoleurs*."[77] Derrida's aim is thus to extend what Lévi-Straus underscores as the "mythopoetic nature of *bricolage*"—marked precisely by its lack of a center, a subject, and a privileged reference to an originary foundation—to the discursive field as a whole, including the standpoint of the so-called empirical technician. Stripped of its totalizing aspirations and its concept of finitude, the *epistēmē* of the empirical sciences is radically disfigured: unbound from "the absolute requirement that we go back to the source, to the center, to the founding basis, to the principle," its calculative discourses are released into the perspective of the *bricoleur*—the infinitely incalculable vantage point of "supplementarity," play, trace, and the mythopoetic.[78]

Bristle as Derrida might at their proposals, many contemporary writers concerned with the problem of environmental ethics have read his deconstructive attack on the totalizing epistemological pretensions of the mathematical and human sciences as removing all categorical barriers against dismantling outright the boundary that the modern *ratio* has drawn between the human and nonhuman.[79] No less than the human other, the "other of nature," they have argued, is exposed by the deconstructive maneuver as shot through with ineliminable incalculability, immeasurability, unpredictability, and unknowability. From this vantage point, the logocentric conception of the nonspeaking world as irreducibly distinct, reified, and conquerable is radically disfigured, such that it too can be approached ethically only through the injunction to care without conditions or calculations.

Vogel, for one, affirms that the demand for an ethics of care for all that *logos* aims to reify as "nature" does indeed issue from the deconstructive critique of nature as an originary "Thing, present and available for inspection and fully open to conceptual understanding."[80] He is quick to stress, however, that in its attempt to "honor" and "respect" nature, such an ethics must resist the "strong temptation to re-reify it, to turn it into some particular object"[81] remanded to our custodial care—a danger that would presumably adhere to a formalistic environmental ethics such as Apel's as well as to a naturalistic ethic like Marcuse's, in which the solution to the problem of nature's domination is read off nature itself. Satisfied with neither of these options, Vogel, as we noted earlier, maintains that our ongoing involvement in the transformation of the environment entangles us in nature irremediably, thereby enjoining us to adopt a decidedly *anthropocentric* orientation of responsibility and care toward it.

This effort to cobble together an environmental ethics that upholds both the deconstructive disfiguration of the distinction between the nonhuman and human worlds *and* an anthropocentric critique of naturalism and its attendant romanticist aporias is in my view conceptually illicit. Nature, after all, cannot be both a non-thing (in the deconstructive sense) as well as an entity for whose care humans—on account of their continual involvement in its alteration—are accorded special responsibility. Vogel cannot have it both ways. I would submit that in embracing deconstruction's radical antidualism and its attendant disarticulation of the objectivating orientation of the natural sciences, he, no less than Derrida, remains defenseless against the prospect of a re-teleologized natural world. Indeed, in demolishing the divide between value-laden subject and value-neutral object, the deconstructive critique of nature removes all categorical prohibitions against extending recognitional gestures like unreserved gift giving, hospitality, and friendship toward nonhuman others—be they fir trees, snow leopards, or woolen tapestries.

While this outcome is rightly resisted by the communicative turn in critical theory, it must be acknowledged that an environmental ethics that categorically bars the attitude of affective sympathy from being extended toward all but a few politely exempted "quasi-teleological" segments of the natural world remains highly unsatisfactory at the level of social psychology, as Whitebook, Kovel, and many other critics have emphasized. On this score, it simply won't do, they have argued, to abide by Habermas's injunction to confine the expressive attitude to our dealings with these designated "limit concepts" to the human interest in the prediction and control of the environment, while leaving other elements of the natural world (the Himalayan Mountains, the Great Barrier Reef, a starlit evening sky) entirely off limits to affective orientations such as "respect, wonder, and reverence."[82]

AXEL HONNETH'S RECOGNITION-THEORETIC SOLUTION TO HABERMAS'S "PSYCHOSOCIAL" DEFICIT

A highly innovative effort to equip critical social theory with categorical resources that would allow it to accommodate the ethical impulse of care toward nature but without at the same time eschewing, with romanticism, humanity's knowledge-constitutive interest in adopting an objectivating stance toward the objective world is undertaken by Honneth in his recent book, *Reification: A New Look at an Old Idea*. Here Honneth's aim is to show that even in the face of the reifying socioeconomic conditions of capitalism, "the elementary structures of the human form of life characterized by 'care' [in Heidegger's terms] and existential interestedness [in Lukács's] are always already there."[83] Reification, that is to say, arises precisely when the "conceptually and genetically prior" moral orientations of care and existential interestedness are "forgotten" and the tendency to "misrecognize" other persons as "mere insensate objects" becomes characteristic of self-other relations. This portrait of reification as a pathological forgetting of the recognitional stance that precedes the orientation of cognitive understanding is of course Honneth's interpretation of what we referred to earlier in this chapter as the misapplication thesis.

I will examine Honneth's attempt to reconstruct the Frankfurt School's analysis of reification from a recognition-theoretic perspective more closely in chapter 5. Of interest in the present context is what the Honnethian account of reification portends with respect to the question of humanity's relationship to the natural world. In approaching this problem, Honneth is at pains to avoid the conclusion—drawn by Martin Heidegger and John Dewey, for example—that the qualitative significance of objects in the natural environment must first be disclosed to human agents before they can regard them in a theoretical manner.[84] He is keen, in other words, to distance himself from the conviction that adopting an objectivating attitude toward nature is in itself a violation of the normative foundations of our social practices. "We may regard the possibility of interactive, recognitional dealings with animals, plants, and even things to be ethically desirable," he writes, "but this normative preference cannot provide any sound arguments for claiming that society cannot go beyond these forms of interaction."[85] Here Honneth's aim is to reject the monistic trajectory of Lukács's nature as a social category thesis—and the romantic nature speculations toward which it is all too readily led—and to uphold a version of epistemological dualism consistent with the idea that relations of care are conceptually and genetically prior to the attitude of detached cognition. In chapter 5, I argue that Honneth's effort to conceptualize the objectifying attitude from the vantage point of recognition theory is not entirely successful; in fact, it appears to come at the cost of a certain ambiguity regarding the epistemological status of this orientation.

However at present, I will confine the discussion to Honneth's appropriation of Adorno's psychoanalytic idea of "primordial imitation," an account that appears well situated to redress the psychosocial deficit that we have identified in Habermas's nature theory. According to Adorno, the world of objects becomes available to us cognitively only upon a "libidinal cathexis" of a significant figure of attachment in early childhood. Honneth observes that "[t]his act of imitating a concrete second person, which draws upon libidinal energies, becomes transmitted, so to speak, onto the object by endowing it with additional components of meaning that the loved figure of attachment perceives in the object."[86] Our subjective feelings for and conceptions of nonhuman entities are seen, on this view, as originating in the attitudes that other persons have already displayed toward given objects, whose very existence is then bound up with these previously ascribed meanings.

To Honneth, Adorno's notion of primordial imitation has profound implications for the conceptualization of the human relationship with the natural world: it positions us to entertain not only the prospect of adopting a recognitional orientation toward nonhuman objects but also the related possibility of a pathological forgetting of this stance: our relations to nature become "reified" the moment that we forget that animals, plants, and insensate objects "possess a multiplicity of existential meanings for the people around us."[87] Honneth is quick to stress, however, that we can "misrecognize" objects in the natural world only in an "indirect" or "derivative" sense. In contrast to the "direct" reification of the social world—which entails losing sight of our antecedent recognition of other persons *in and of themselves*—in the case of nature, it is the *meanings* that other persons have ascribed to nonhuman entities that are in danger of being overlooked. The Adornian idea of primordial imitation thus commends us to respect the constellation of attributes and significations that others have accorded to the world of objects. Yet at the same time we are by no means obliged to forgo the possibility of cognitively disclosing this realm by adopting a reifying stance toward it. Indeed, it is Honneth's contention that "the 'reification' of objects or nonhuman sentient beings does not constitute a violation of a practical prerequisite of our social lifeworld, [although] this certainly is the case whenever we take up a reifying stance toward other persons."[88]

CONCLUSION

Honneth's account of a derivative recognitional orientation toward the objective world is in my view an attractive solution to the psychosocial deficit that plagues Habermas's uncompromisingly anthropocentric conception of discourse ethics. This perspective urges us to "recognize," "respect," and "care" for nonhuman entities on terms consistent with the sorts of ethical gestures (gift giving, friendship, hospitality) that Derrida's text opens up toward the world of objects. Yet because the recognitional stance that we adopt toward objects is indirect—originating from and linked to human-ascribed meanings—we are not required to locate a solution to the conflict between nature and society within nature itself, such that we now face the prospect of elevating the non-speaking world to the level of a cosubject. Rather, from the standpoint of Honneth's Adornian object attachment proposal, we can defend the methodological dualism of the Kantian tradition against antifoundationalist critiques such as Derrida's while upholding humanity's knowledge-constitutive interest in the objectification of the environment (even if Honneth, for one, would not invoke such Habermasian terminology in this context). The framework of instrumental action is in this manner preserved, along with the cognate idea of a historically immutable, asocial, and instrumentalizable "nature-in-itself." Such a move is initiated, moreover, without any of the self-contradiction that besets an argument like Vogel's, which seeks to eviscerate the idea of an originary nature while smuggling in, as it were, an anthropocentric claim for humanity's special responsibility for the custodial care of the natural world.

We can on these terms construct an ecological ethics aimed not at eschewing the reified sciences and their associated technologies *per se*, but at criticizing the *sociohistorical conditions* under which they are presently being mobilized—specifically, the "self-propelling" mechanisms of limitless economic growth[89] that are steering modern societies to degrade the natural habit upon which the very possibility of communicative sociation depends. The assumption here is that modern science and technology can be effectively decoupled from the value-expansion imperatives of the capitalist market,[90] thereby opening up the prospect of public discussion and debate about their appropriate uses and the social arrangements under which they are deployed: any shifts in our relationship with the natural world will pertain, as Whitebook puts it, *"to the socioeconomic context within which nature is objectified and not to the way in which nature is objectified."*[91] The aim here would be to create a heightened level of oversight over scientific research and its technical applications on the part of lifeworld actors, such that the former are to at least some extent loosed from the grip of the strategic organizing directives of the administrative and economic subsystems. In the "dimension of scientific self-reflection," claims Habermas, "it would be possible to make the connections of research processes transparent in terms of those processes themselves, and not only their connections to the application of scientific and scholarly information [*Wissenschaft*] but also and especially their connection to culture as a whole, to general processes of socialization, to the continuation of traditions, and to the enlightenment of the political public sphere."[92]

An environmental ethics constructed from this vantage point is poised to formalistically link the well-being of nature to the communicatively conceived good-for-humanity while guarding against the possibility of our knowledge-constitutive interest in the instrumentalization of the environment being pressed forth as a project of inexhaustible domination and mastery. Such an ethics is also readily and well advisedly supplemented with Honneth's idea of an indirect recognitional attitude toward the world of objects, which accommodates the impulse of care for nature but without succumbing to the aporias of a naturalistic ethic. The result is an environmental-ethical framework in which the Enlightenment account of the natural world as a realm of eternally reified facticity emerges not so much as a callous accusation but rather as a sober and well counseled diagnosis.

In the foregoing discussion, I have attempted to redress a significant "Derridean" objection to Habermas's thinking without at the same time destabilizing, with deconstruction, the basic philosophical objectives of the theory of communicative action. This intervention raises the question of a possible "reconciliation" of the broader deconstructive and discourse-ethical projects—an idea to which a number of writers have been drawn in recent years. In the following chapter, I shall consider the prospects for such a rapprochement in greater detail.

NOTES

1. This chapter is a somewhat modified and expanded version of my "Caring for Nature in Habermas, Vogel, and Derrida: Reconciling the Speaking and Nonspeaking Worlds at the Cost of 'Re-enchantment'?," *Radical Philosophy Review* 13, no. 2 (2010), in press.

2. Georg Lukács, *History and Class Consciousness*, trans. Rodney Livingstone (Cambridge, Mass.: The MIT Press, 1971), 24n.

3. Steven Vogel, *Against Nature: The Concept of Nature in Critical Theory* (New York: State University of New York Press, 1996), 12.

4. Lukács, *History and Class Consciousness*, 234.

5. Vogel, *Against Nature*, 84.

6. Max Horkheimer and Theodor W. Adorno, *Dialectic of Enlightenment: Philosophical Fragments*, trans. Edmund Jephcott (Stanford: Stanford University Press, 2002), 65.

7. Horkheimer and Adorno, *Dialectic of Enlightenment*, 66.

8. Marx's version of this desideratum is set forth in his *Economic and Philosophic Manuscripts*, where he describes the emancipated society as one in which nature exists only "as the foundation of [man's] own human existence. Only here has what is to him his natural existence become his human existence, and nature become man for him. Thus society is the complete unity of man with nature—the true resurrection of nature—the consistent naturalism of man and the consistent humanism of nature." Karl Marx, *Economic and Philosophic Manuscripts*, in *Marx and Engels: Collected Works,* vol. 3 (New York: International Publishers, 1975), 297–98; my emphasis. Bloch's speculative philosophy of nature will be discussed in connection with Derrida's idea of *khôra* in chapter 4.

9. Vogel, *Against Nature*, 85.

10. Herbert Marcuse, *One-Dimensional Man: Studies in the Ideology of Advanced Industrial Society* (Boston: Beacon Press, 1964), 166–67; emphasis in original.

11. Herbert Marcuse, *Eros and Civilization* (New York: Vintage Books, 1962), 151.

12. Vogel, *Against Nature*, 105.

13. Joel Whitebook, "The Problem of Nature in Habermas," *Telos* 40 (Summer 1979): 52.

14. Jürgen Habermas, *Toward a Rational Society: Student Protest, Science, and Politics*, trans. Jeremy J. Shapiro (Boston: Beacon Press, 1970), 113; emphasis in original.

15. Jürgen Habermas, *Knowledge and Human Interests*, trans. Jeremy J. Shapiro (Cambridge, UK: Polity Press, 1987), 194.

16. Vogel, *Against Nature*, 108.

17. While Habermas employs the term "fraternal relationship" to describe Marcuse's view of an altered mode of association between humans and nature, the phrase is not invoked by Marcuse himself. According to Andrew Feenberg, Habermas's appellation is in fact a misnomer, since Marcuse's proposal has less to do with "fraternity" with nature than with liberating nature's own repressed capacities and relocating them within the methods and structures of technical reason. "Marcuse does advocate relating to nature as to another subject," Feenberg writes, "but the concept of subjectivity implied here owes more to Aristotelian substance than to the idea of personhood. Marcuse does not recommend chatting with nature but, rather, recognizing it as possessing potentialities of its own with a certain inherent legitimacy. That recognition should be incorporated into the very structure of technical rationality." Andrew Feenberg, "Marcuse or Habermas: Two Critiques of Technology," *Inquiry* 39 (1996): 45–70. www-rohan.sdsu.edu/faculty/feenberg/marhab.html (14 July 2010).

18. Habermas, *Toward a Rational Society*, 87.

19. Habermas, *Knowledge and Human Interests*, 33.

20. Bill Martin, *Matrix and Line: Derrida and the Possibilities of Postmodern Social Theory* (New York: The State University of New York Press, 1992), 122.

21. Karl-Otto Apel, "The Conflicts of Our Time and the Problem of Political Ethics," in *From Contract to Community: Political Theory at the Crossroads*, ed. Fred R. Dallmayr (New York: Marcel Dekker, 1978), 83.

22. Henning Ottman, "Cognitive Interests and Self-Reflection: The Status and Systematic Connection of the Cognitive Interests in Habermas's *Knowledge and Human Interests*," in *Habermas: Critical Debates*, ed. John B. Thompson and David Held (Cambridge, Mass.: The MIT Press, 1982), 88.

23. Whitebook, "The Problem of Nature in Habermas," 64.

24. Joel Kovel, "The Dialectic of Radical Ecologies," *Capitalism, Nature, Socialism* 14, no. 1 (2003): 82–83.

25. Kovel, "The Dialectic of Radical Ecologies," 82.

26. Warwick Fox, "Deep Ecology: A New Philosophy of Our Time?," in *Philosophical Dialogues: Arne Naess and the Progress of Ecophilosophy*, eds. Nina Witoszek and Andrew Brennan (Lanham, MD: Rowman & Littlefield, 1999), 157.

27. Murray Bookchin, *Post-Scarcity Anarchism* (Berkeley: Ramparts Press, 1971), 59.

28. Murray Bookchin, *The Ecology of Freedom* (Palo Alto: Cheshire Books, 1982), 353–54.

29. Jürgen Habermas, "A Reply to My Critics," in *Habermas: Critical Debates*, ed. John B. Thompson and David Held (Cambridge, Mass.: The MIT Press), 243.

30. Jürgen Habermas, "A Postscript to *Knowledge and Human Interests*," *Philosophy of the Social Sciences* 3 (1973): 157–89.

31. Jürgen Habermas, "The Idea of the University: Learning Processes," in *The New Conservatism: Cultural Criticism and the Historians' Debate*, trans. and ed. Shierry Weber Nicholsen (Cambridge, UK: Polity Press, 1989), 124.

32. Habermas, "The Idea of the University," 119.

33. Vogel, *Against Nature*, 116.

34. Vogel, *Against Nature*, 116.

35. Vogel, *Against Nature*, 130.

36. Vogel, *Against Nature*, 119.

37. Vogel, *Against Nature*, 123.

38. Vogel, *Against Nature*, 133.

39. Vogel, *Against Nature*, 140.

40. Vogel, *Against Nature*, 167.

41. Vogel, *Against Nature*, 165.

42. Stanley Aronowitz, "The Production of Scientific Knowledge: Science, Ideology, and Marxism," in *Marxism and the Interpretation of Culture*, ed. Cary Nelson and Lawrence Grossberg (Chicago: University of Illinois Press, 1988), 529.

43. Aronowitz, "The Production of Scientific Knowledge," 529; my emphasis.

44. Aronowitz, "The Production of Scientific Knowledge," 533.

45. Habermas, "Appendix," in *Knowledge and Human Interests*, 315.

46. Vogel, *Against Nature*, 124.

47. Vogel, *Against Nature*, 142; emphasis in original.

48. Eduardo Mendieta, "Globalizing Critical Theory of Science," in *Globalizing Critical Theory*, ed. Max Pensky (Oxford: Rowman & Littlefield, 2005), 200.

49. Mendieta, "Globalizing Critical Theory of Science," 199, 203.

50. To bolster his argument on this score, Vogel highlights a passage from the "Appendix" to *Knowledge and Human Interests*, in which Habermas himself acknowledges that in order to carry out their epistemological aims, the natural sciences must relieve themselves of the responsibilities of hermeneutic-historical self-reflection and remain hoodwinked by a "false" belief in the objectivity of their own methods. (See Habermas, "Appendix," in *Knowledge and Human Interests*," 315.) This language (which Habermas has wisely steered clear of in ensuing writings) is indeed unfortunate and does appear to leave Habermas vulnerable to Vogel's charge that he would just as soon immunize the natural sciences against the Enlightenment ideal of subjecting all truth claims to unfettered interrogation. This, however, is in my view a misreading of the ultimate aims of Habermas's effort to distinguish between empirical-analytic and hermeneutic-historical problem-solving languages, a division whose viability this chapter attempts to defend.

51. Aronowitz, "The Production of Scientific Knowledge," 532.

52. Vogel, *Against Nature*, 143.

53. Richard J. Bernstein, "An Allegory of Modernity/Postmodernity: Habermas and Derrida," in *The Derrida-Habermas Reader*, ed. Lasse Thomassen (Chicago: The University of Chicago Press, 2006), 76.

54. Habermas, *Communication and the Evolution of Society*, trans. Thomas McCarthy (Boston: Beacon Press, 1979), 117, in Bernstein, "An Allegory of Modernity/Postmodernity," 76.

55. Jürgen Habermas, "A Reply to My Critics," in *Habermas: Critical Debates*, ed. John B. Thompson and David Held (Cambridge, Mass.: The MIT Press, 1982), 245.

56. Habermas, "A Reply to My Critics," 247.

57. I will return to this proposal in the following section, which considers the affinities between Horkheimer and Adorno's nature-theoretic overtures and those of Derrida.

58. Habermas, "A Reply to My Critics," 248–49.

59. In *The Future of Human Nature* (Cambridge, UK: Polity Press, 2003), 33, Habermas upholds as sacrosanct the partition between animals (who "do not belong to the universe of members who address intersubjectively accepted rules and orders *to one another*") and humans (whose "dignity" and "autonomy" derives from the fact that they do). This conviction is at the root of his arguments against the adulteration of the species boundary between humans and nonhumans, a risk that is becoming increasingly pronounced in the wake of recent advancements in the field of biotechnology.

60. Jacques Derrida, *Of Grammatology*, trans. Gayatri Spivak (Baltimore: Johns Hopkins University Press, 1997), 46.

61. Steven Vogel, "Nature as Origin and Difference: On Environmental Philosophy and Continental Thought," *Philosophy Today, SPEP Supplement* (1998): 170.

62. Well before Derrida's "*Fichus*" speech, Peter Dews weighed Adorno's approach to the question of the subject-object distinction against that of deconstruction. His conclusions suggest that the two perspectives may have less in common than Derrida imagines. Dews argues that Adorno, in distinction to Derrida, "does not wish to abolish mediation altogether, to collapse the subject into the object, but rather to establish an emphasis which is the opposite of that maintained by the philosophical tradition." Indeed, "[i]n his evocations of '*différance*,' 'arche-writing,' the 'trace,' Derrida has still not escaped the 'idea of the first,' even though this first cannot take the form of 'presence.' In this respect, Adorno's characterization of the vapidity of *Ursprungsphilosophie* well captures the weakness of the thought of *différance*." Dews, *Logics of Disintegration: Post-structuralist Thought and the Claims of Critical Theory* (New York: Verso, 1987), 48, 49. On Dews's accusation that *différance* is ultimately circumscribed and subsumed by the principle of unity, see chapter 4, note 26.

63. Jacques Derrida, "*Fichus*: Frankfurt Address," in *Paper Machine*, trans. Rachel Bowlby (Stanford: Stanford University Press, 2005), 180.

64. Horkheimer and Adorno, *Dialectic of Enlightenment*, 211.

65. Derrida, "*Fichus*: Frankfurt Address," 180–81.

66. Derrida, "*Fichus*: Frankfurt Address," 181.

67. Horkheimer and Adorno, *Dialectic of Enlightenment*, 211.

68. Derrida, "*Fichus*: Frankfurt Address," 180.

69. Jacques Derrida, "The Animal That I Therefore Am," in *Animal Philosophy*, ed. Matthew Calarco and Peter Atterton (New York: Continuum, 2004), 125.

70. Jacques Derrida, "To Arrive—At the Ends of the State (and of War, and of World War)," in *Rogues: Two Essays on Reason*, trans. Pascale-Anne Brault and Michael Nass (Stanford: Stanford University Press, 2005), 151.

71. Jacques Derrida, "Eating Well, or the Calculation of the Subject," in *Points . . . Interviews, 1974–1994*, trans. Peggy Kamuf et al. (Stanford: Stanford University Press, 1995), 285.

72. Derrida, "Eating Well," 285.

73. Derrida, "Eating Well," 278; my emphasis. In this context, see Matthew Calarco, "Deconstruction Is Not Vegetarianism: Humanism, Subjectivity, and Animal Ethics," in *Continental Philosophy Review* 37, no. 2 (2004): 175–201.

74. Jacques Derrida, "Force of Law," in *Acts of Religion*, ed. Gil Anidjar (New York: Routledge, 2002), 247.

75. Jacques Derrida, "Structure, Sign, and Play in the Discourse of the Human Sciences," in *Writing and Difference*, trans. Alan Bass (Chicago: The University of Chicago Press, 1978), 285.

76. Derrida, "Structure, Sign, and Play," 285.

77. Derrida, "Structure, Sign, and Play," 285.

78. Derrida, "Structure, Sign, and Play," 286, 289.

79. See, for example, Verena Andermatt Conley, *Ecopolitics: The Environment in Poststructuralist Thought* (London: Routledge, 1997); Arran E. Gare, *Postmodernism and the Environmental Crisis* (London: Routledge, 1995); and Max Oelschlaeger, ed., *Postmodern Environmental Ethics* (Albany: SUNY Press, 1995).

80. Vogel, "Nature as Origin and Difference," 173.

81. Vogel, "Nature as Origin and Difference," 173.

82. Kovel, "The Dialectic of Radical Ecologies," 82. See also Whitebook, "The Problem of Nature in Habermas," 64.

83. Axel Honneth, *Reification: A New Look at an Old Idea* (Oxford: Oxford University Press, 2008), 32.

84. John Dewey puts the matter this way: "The *intrinsic* nature of events is revealed in *the immediately felt qualities of things*. The intimate coordination and even fusion of these qualities with the regularities that form the objects of knowledge, in the proper sense of the word 'knowledge,' characterizes intelligently directed experience, as distinct from mere casual and uncritical experience." Dewey, *Experience and Nature* (Whitefish, Mt.: Kessinger Publishing, 2003), v; second emphasis mine.

85. Honneth, *Reification*, 61–62.

86. Honneth, *Reification*, 62.

87. Honneth, *Reification*, 63.

88. Honneth, *Reification*, 64.

89. Habermas, *Toward a Rational Society*, 95.

90. In contrast to received Marxist precepts, Habermas maintains that the strategic organizing principles of the present economic and political subsystems (which are undergirded by the "delinguistified" steering media of money and administrative power, respectively) are requisite for the coordination of complex, large-scale processes in modern societies. Thus, for him "[t]he goal is no longer to supersede an economic system having a capitalist life of its own and a system of domination having a bureaucratic life of its own but to erect a democratic dam against the colonizing encroachment of system imperatives on areas of the life-world." Habermas, "Further Reflections on the Public Sphere," in *Habermas and the Public Sphere*, ed. Craig Calhoun (Cambridge, Mass.: The MIT Press, 1992), 444. Habermas's system/life-world model has of course been criticized from a number of perspectives. Honneth's objection to this paradigm is discussed in chapter 5.

91. Whitebook, "The Problem of Nature in Habermas," 63–64; emphasis in original.

92. Habermas, "The Idea of the University," 118.

Chapter Four

"Habermasian Care" versus "Derridean Care": Asymmetry or Accord?

The preceding chapter has underscored a number of substantial categorical discrepancies between the respective frameworks of Habermas and Derrida in relation to the problem of "care for nature." At the same time, in chapters 1 and 2, I drew attention to the work of several writers—Seyla Benhabib, for example—who have endeavored to in some sense "strike a balance" between Derrida's ontology of radical singularity and Habermas's framework of moral universalism. The present chapter will consider whether the conceptual rifts that we have encountered are irresolvable or if something like an "accord" between the two approaches to care morality is in fact possible. The salient question in this regard has been posed succinctly by Simon Critchley: Are Derrida's and Habermas's views of the relation between symmetrical and asymmetrical intersubjectivity "mutually exclusive, or do they supplement each other in an unexpected way?"[1]

Before exploring the prospects for such an unexpected reconciliation of their respective projects, this chapter calls attention to Habermas's and Derrida's contrasting receptions of Heidegger's account of care, a dispute that in my view marks a key point of conceptual demarcation between the two philosophers. I then consider the arguments of several commentators who likewise see the categorical gulf separating Habermas and Derrida as formidable if not insurmountable. While I concur with this general assessment, I demur from the tendency of critics who share it to weigh in on Derrida's side of the philosophical divide. Instead, I maintain that the Habermasian paradigm offers a more promising framework through which to approach the question of care morality, albeit one that must be retooled structurally so that it can better fend off the accusations of cognitive centrism that Derrida and other commentators have brought against it (see chapter 5 for an outline of my proposed contribution to such a reconstruction). To further underscore some of the weaknesses of Derrida's approach as well as its fundamental incompatibility with Habermas's, this chapter examines the two thinkers' dispute over the legacy of Ernst Bloch and Walter Benjamin. Like their disagreements over the work of Heidegger, I argue that Derrida's and Habermas's divergent receptions of Bloch and Benjamin do not bode well for a possible rapprochement between deconstruction and discourse ethics—notwithstanding a number of recent attempts to forge precisely such a reconciliation.

THE CONTESTED LEGACY OF HEIDEGGER

The suggestion that the basic categories and aims of the Derridean and Habermasian frameworks are rigorously at odds with one another is by no means novel or even especially controversial. The diagnosis of conceptual incompatibility is in fact drawn by Habermas himself. As we have noted elsewhere (see the introduction), Habermas early on depicted deconstruction's attempt to radically disaggregate the scientific, the moral-practical, and the aesthetic as distinct problem-solving languages as being carried forth at the cost of undermining the politiconormative potentials for human emancipation unleashed by the modern bourgeois democratic revolutions. On this reading, deconstruction is said to remain ensnared in a "performative contradiction": to fulfill its aim of persistently destabilizing *logos*, it consigns itself to the register of the "poetic," thereby divesting itself of the rationalist criteria of defensibility needed to uphold the normative principles in the name of which it speaks. The consequences of this move are dire, insofar as philosophy is therewith robbed of its critical illocutionary force—indeed, of its "seriousness." "Whoever transposes the radical critique of reason into the domain of rhetoric in order to blunt the paradox of self-referentiality," says Habermas, "also dulls the sword of the critique of reason itself."[2]

In later years, Habermas would of course strike a more conciliatory tone toward his colleague, even going so far as to coauthor with Derrida a plea for a common foreign policy in Europe in 2003 (see the following section).[3] This warming in their working relationship aside, Habermas has been careful to underscore what to his mind are the intractable philosophical disparities between his perspective and Derrida's. In an interview published shortly before Derrida's death in October 2004, for instance, he notes that if one can speak of a common link between them at all, it is "the philosophical reference to an author like Kant."[4] However, this tenuous point of resonance does little to diminish the towering shadow of "antirationalist" figures such as the later Heidegger in Derrida's thought, an inheritance that Habermas construes as an inviolable barrier to something like a rapprochement between deconstruction and communicative ethics. To Habermas the philosophical benefits of consorting with a thinker like Heidegger are few and far between, insofar as the latter is guilty of committing nothing less than

> treason against that caesura which is marked, in various ways, by the prophetic-awakening Word from Mount Sinai, and by the Enlightenment of a Socrates. When Derrida and I mutually understand our so different background motives, a difference of interpretation must not be taken as a difference in the thing being interpreted. Be that as it may, "truce" or "reconciliation" are not really the proper expressions for a friendly and open-minded interchange.[5]

For our purposes, it is especially important to highlight Habermas's and Derrida's divergent receptions of the Heideggerian account of care. Habermas develops his views on this aspect of Heidegger's thinking in several early essays.[6] These writings indict *Being and Time*'s existential analysis of *Dasein* for turning away from the rationalist effort to conceive acts of knowing and doing in terms of subject-object relationships. In so doing, *Dasein*, Habermas argues, reimagines such acts as "derivatives from the basic modes of standing within a lifeworld, within a world intuitively understood as context and background. Heidegger characterizes these modes of being in the lifeworld, in view of their temporal structure, as having so many modes of caring, of having concern for something."[7] Yet the price that Heidegger pays for this so-called *Kehre* [reversal] is quite substantial: he relieves thought of the effort to solve problems through intersubjective dialogue and hands it over to "the objective event of an anonymous overcoming of metaphysics staged by Being itself."[8]

To shed light on Derrida's far more sympathetic reception of the Heideggerian account of care, it will be useful to draw attention to *Interpretation and Difference*, Alan Bass's psychoanalytic excursus on the "strangeness of care."[9] This book enlists a number of key Heideggerian *topoi* to criticize Freud's tendency to base his model of the psychic apparatus on objective, mechanical principles. According to Bass, this orientation at times leads Freud to conceive of the patient's self-preservative need for analytic care as a problem of "helplessness" or "empirical finitude." Heidegger's aim, in contrast, is to understand care—along with time and interpretation—in relation to *Angst*, uncanniness, and stress. From Heidegger's alternative standpoint of "differentiating finitude," argues Bass, we are positioned to shatter the mechanistic biases of Freud's account of the psychic apparatus and rethink the unconscious dynamics of interpretive care, and indeed the analytic setting itself, along the model of an "uncanny living machine."[10]

While he sees the orientation of uncanniness as primary in both Heidegger's and Freud's view of interpretive care (despite the latter's own unexamined logocentrism), Bass maintains that neither author "can remain in the out-of-joint time-space of disruptive spectrality of which both give glimpses."[11] Derrida, however, gestures precisely toward such an extension of their respective projects. In proposing a new metrics of time, a spectral messianicity that is not in itself messianic, Derrida repositions analytic care as "the 'promise' of *revenance*, the promise of a repetition poised on the tip of the opening and closure of the time-space of interpretation."[12] Intrinsically "uncanny and uncontrollable," the promise of disruptive spectrality threatens "to usurp the [dedifferentiating] mastery sought in opposition, presence, and tension reduction," resituating the unconscious as a nondeterministic "surface apparatus" shot through with the differential traces of what Freud calls "primary narcissism."[13] With respect to the problem of interpretive care, Bass contends, with Derrida, that there are in fact two "Freuds" to be considered: the Freud who remained convinced of the "inevitable progress in understanding according to the principle of reason," and an opposing Freud, who resisted the metaphysics of presence, discovered the irreducibility of the effect of deferral, and ultimately revealed the "*necessary* non-interpretation at the heart of the interpretable."[14]

Although he is not referenced in this context, Bass would presumably affiliate Habermas with the standpoint of the first of these two Freuds—that is, with an *Aufklärung* tradition that remains constitutively foreclosed to the radical reimagining of the care perspective to which Heidegger and, more radically still, Derrida commend us. Such is indeed the accusation of a writer like Lawrence Vogel. To Vogel, frameworks such as Habermasian discourse ethics are incapable of drawing the crucial lessons on care that emerge, perhaps most notably, in Heidegger's phenomenological account of *Dasein*. Rather than depict individuals as thinking and acting in isolated, solipsistic, and wholly arbitrary ways—as Habermas alleges—Vogel sees Heidegger's text as pointing toward an ethics of "attunement to the particularity of others, to the other as truly other, stemming from an awareness of the singularity of one's own existence."[15] In fact, according to Vogel, Heidegger's analysis of *Dasein* suggests "an *interpersonal* orientation motivated by one's desire not to incorporate others into 'the universal' but, rather, to 'let others be' in their freedom for their own possibilities and to allow one's own self-understanding to be informed by theirs."[16] In distinction to Derrida, authors like Habermas are in no position to read Heidegger's care ethic in such affirmative terms, given their philosophical commitment to the priority of impersonal, abstract rules and categories of moral reason, under which persons and situations are ultimately, as Vogel sees it, subsumed.

Habermas's and Derrida's conflicting receptions of the Heideggerian account of care can be further underscored if we shift the focus to the latter's attendant *critique of measure*. Perhaps the most salient category to consider in this context is that of *Ereignis* (typically translated as "event" or "concern"), which is developed in Heidegger's later writings. In his comprehensive account of the problem of measure in Heidegger, *Speaking Against Number*, Stuart Elden notes that *Ereignis,* like "Dasein, that simultaneously most common and yet most resistant to translation of Heideggerian words, is inherently tied to [the] refusal of measure and the politics of calculation."[17] Indeed, as Elden elaborates,

> *Ereignis* does not allow itself to be measured in conventional ways: "Immeasurable [*Unausmeßbar*] are the riches . . . the fullness of *Ereignis*."[18] This is no mere suggestion that riches are immeasurable, or that love is incalculable, but something that goes to the very heart of the matter. Indeed, it helps to bring together many of the key ideas of his thought as a whole. Heidegger suggests that overflow, or excess of measure [*Das Über-maß*], "is no mere abundance of quantity, but the self-withdrawing of all estimating and measuring" [*Schätzung und Ausmessung*].[19]

In this brief summation of *Ereignis*, the links to Derrida are already becoming apparent. Like Heidegger, Derrida sees any politics or ethics founded upon principles of enumeration, measurement, and aggregation as constitutively closed off to the very incalculability it aims to appropriate. Heideggerian categories such as *Ereignis* are of use to Derrida to the extent that they contribute to the ethicopolitical work of shielding the incalculably unconditional example from the threat of epistemic effacement that adheres to the very firmament of calculative thought. As Heidegger puts it,

> Calculative thinking . . . is unable to foresee that everything calculable by calculation [*Berechenbare der Rechnung*]—prior to the sum-totals and products that it produces by calculation in each case—is already a whole whose unity indeed belongs to the incalculable [*Unberechenbaren*] that withdraws itself and its uncanniness from the claws of calculation.[20]

Although he likewise wishes to situate irreducible incalculability and nonprogrammability under the sign of *Ereignis*, Derrida breaks with Heidegger on a number of important counts. It is well beyond the scope of the present discussion to reconstruct all of these objections here, but it is worth noting that one of Derrida's principal aims is to contest Heidegger's effort to *destroy* the history of metaphysics, ontotheology, and the determination of Being as presence. To this end, Derrida maintains, against Heidegger, that "[t]here is no sense in doing without the concepts of metaphysics in order to shake metaphysics. We have no language—no syntax and no lexicon—which is foreign to this history; we can pronounce not a single deductive proposition which has not already had to slip into the form, the logic, and the implicit postulations of precisely what it seeks to contest."[21] Here, in a double gesture of the sort that should by now be familiar to us, Derrida takes *Being and Time*'s crucial category of *Dasein* to task for remaining enmeshed in the very philosophy of the subject that it endeavors to annihilate. "In spite of everything it opens up and encourages us to think, to question, and to redistribute, *Dasein* occupies a place analogous to the transcendental subject. And its concept . . . is determined . . . on the basis of oppositions that remain insufficiently interrogated."[22] On this argument, Derrida's objective is not to wholly repudiate *Dasein* and the attendant network of metaphors that permeate the later Heidegger's thought. Rather, as Bill Martin observes, Derrida seeks to rigorously *disrupt* Heidegger's category, such that an "essential estrangement within the house of Being" is no longer poised to destroy "real human possibilities." For Derrida we are instead faced with a situation in which humanity has no "home" or "Being" to return to. Indeed, to him humanity must "forever live in an 'uncanny' (the typical translation of *unheimlich*) condition."[23]

As we have seen, Habermas has his own quarrels with Heidegger. However, *contra* Derrida, Habermas's objection is by no means couched as an attack on *Dasein*'s insufficient openness to "processes of differance, trace, iterability, exappropriation, and so on."[24] Instead, Habermas finds the Heideggerian *Dasein*, along with the residue of this concept that inflects Derridean deconstruction, to be guilty of entanglement in an expressly *transcendental* framework of subjectivity. So encumbered, the perspectives of both Heidegger and Derrida remain precariously estranged from the principle of dialogical reasonableness and its cognate standpoint of egalitarian measurement [*Ausmessung*]. As David Ingram notes, on Habermas's account, Derrida's thought distances itself from Heidegger's fate of Being even as it continues to retreat, with the latter, "from public communication to an arbitrary play of signifiers, in which interpretation remains ultimately arcane, an act of private revelation, or at most, an esoteric discourse with a hidden God."[25] On this contention, Habermas has little use for Derrida's belated attempts to forge a reckoning between the principle of measurable equality and the attitude of unconditional care for the other's incalculable singularity: inasmuch as deconstruction continues to accord categorical preeminence to the latter standpoint, it remains, in Habermas's estimation, weighted down with Heidegger's impulse to relieve moral discourse of the effort to solve problems through intersubjective dialogue, and thereby burdened with the very residue of transcendentalism that it seeks to subvert. Peter Dews makes much the same point. In setting forth "an essential *logical priority* of nonidentity over identity," Dews argues, the strategy that Derrida mobilizes to "outflank"

Heidegger, "the strategy of suggesting that the ontological difference and the history of Being are themselves subordinate to *différance*," ironically allows *différance* itself to emerge as "a powerful principle of unity."[26]

Although they do not concur with Dews and Habermas on this count, a number of contemporary commentators have been just as hard pressed to discern grounds for a possible concordance between deconstruction and discourse ethics. It is to these criticisms of Habermas's model and their attendant arguments on behalf of conceptual incongruity that I shall now turn.

DISSYMMETRY AND DISCORD? HABERMAS'S CRITICS THINK AGAINST MEASURE[27]

I begin with an overview of the arguments of Martin Morris, who has authored a number of careful albeit highly critical appraisals of Habermas's perspective, including *Rethinking the Communicative Turn*.[28] In sympathy with the standpoint of Derrida, Morris contends that try as it may to accommodate a plurality of human differences and distance itself from all metalinguistic enticements, the Habermasian discourse ethic is oblivious to his own effort to achieve, as Derrida puts it, "the effects of metalanguage."[29] As such, it remains mired in what Drucilla Cornell has called the "philosophy of the limit."[30] Habermas's difference-theoretic blind spot persists, argues Morris, notwithstanding his attempt to account for the "porosity" of communicative intersubjectivity. In this context, Morris calls attention to a passage from *Postmetaphysical Thinking*, in which Habermas insists that

> [t]he intersubjectivity of linguistically achieved understanding is by nature porous, and linguistically attained consensus does not eradicate from the accord the differences in speaker perspectives but rather presupposes them as ineliminable. . . . The grammatical role of personal pronouns forces the speaker and the hearer to adopt a performative attitude in which one confronts the other as *alter ego*: only with a consciousness of their absolute difference and irreplaceability can one recognize himself in the other.[31]

While Habermas may well attempt to acknowledge the "absolute difference and irreplaceability" of the self and its other, Morris maintains that the overarching discourse-ethical requirement of self-other *identification* renders his model constitutively incapable of appreciating the "radical non-identity" at the heart of intersubjective recognition. Nonidentity, observes Morris, emerges—in Adorno's negative-dialectical sense—as a concept that is always already entwined with difference such that it "reaches beyond itself without ever being able to grasp its subject matter"; marked by "an absence not a presence," the content of nonidentity eludes "capturing" by theories of moral universalism such as Habermas's.[32]

Accordingly, against the communicative idealizations and orientation toward universalistic problem-solving of Habermas's discourse ethic, Morris petitions, with Derrida, for a new, generatively paradoxical encounter with the other, in which the irreducible nonidenticalness and untranslatablity of ego and alter are always already imbricated in processes of articulation in the public sphere. From this "non-identical condition of all identities" he seeks to retrieve, *pace* Habermas, an expressly *aesthetic* "mode of democratic inclusion of the other and of acknowledgement of difference"—even as he concedes that Habermas is right to warn of the antidemocratic risks of an "utterly unconstrained desublimation of aesthetic energy."[33] With Adorno, Morris views the aesthetic sphere as poised to perform such ethicopolitical work inasmuch as art—in stark contrast to the moral argumentation norms prioritized in Habermas's framework—engages not simply "the unrepresentability of the unrepresentable": it is "most eloquent in speaking to us of this darkness it alone is privy to. Thus there must be more to be expected from the appeal to the aesthetic . . . than a contemplative letting be, or simply a liberal respect of difference."[34]

In joining what Habermas views as the philosophical effort—begun at the close of the eighteenth century—to redress "the deformations of a one-sided everyday praxis," ethicopolitical standpoints like Morris's rest not on appeals to the unforced forced of dialogical argumentation but on "the mythopoetic power of an art that is supposed to form the focal point of a regenerated public life."[35] From this vantage point, Morris reads Derrida's deconstructive maneuver as consonant with Adorno's dialectics of nonidentity, inasmuch as it likewise affords entrée into the aestheticized dimension of philosophical critique that alone seems capable of "outsmarting" the subject-object model of knowledge and its tyrannical Concept. In clinging to the latter, Habermas, observes Morris, has no choice but to envisage that which lies beyond consensus as mere deception and violence.[36] Derrida, in contrast, has much higher hopes for the space beyond identity. To him it is precisely the aporetic, liminal, formless, endless, bottomless, "shuddering" in-between chasm or abyss of *khôra* (see chapters 2 and 4) that allows the gesture of care for the other's irreducible nonidenticalness to emerge as an expressly ethical and political intervention. The unrevealable presence of *khôra*—marked by "the paradoxical absence of things as the condition for their appearance in space"—is in fact "just what calls us to democracy, to the passion for critique and engagement."[37] According to Morris, Habermas is powerless to appreciate the political implications of this radically asymmetrical and aestheticized spatiotemporal plane of self-other relations. Ensconced as he is in the subject-object model of epistemology, Habermas devalues the orientation of nonidentity (consigning it, as we have seen, to the realm of the "ethical") only to thereby enfeeble his framework's very status as a *critical* theory. "One does not get critical theory by coordinating epistemology (social theory) with normative philosophy," claims Morris; "one gets mainstream theories that moralize."[38]

Bonnie Honig is also eager to take discourse ethics to task for excising the asymmetrical moral standpoint from the terrain of the political. To this end, Honig focuses on Habermas's effort to portray constitutionalism and democracy as internally related elements of a "self-correcting" and indeed "teleological" learning process. The deficiency of this "co-originality" thesis, claims Honig, lies precisely in its portrayal of law as a "calm" center, and its related depiction of rights as "dead instruments" rather than "live practices." In Habermas, the hoped-for democratic future emerges as a *ground*, a fixed Archimedean point from which one fails to appreciate the importance of *a*constitutional democratic activism and the "wild," "dangerously unscripted futures" that it calls forth. One is insensible, that is, to the crucial Derridean insight that "[t]he perpetual production of new textual bodies points to something that exceeds the economy of constitutional democracy and even haunts it."[39] To Honig, Habermas's framework accords architectonic primacy to the universalistic norms of moral argumentation such that the radical asymmetricality of the self-other relation—indispensible for any conception of a vibrant democratic polity—is logocentrically blended out.

In his comments on the Derrida-Habermas interchange, Lasse Thomassen shows some sympathy for this view, but criticizes Honig for not developing her argument in a sufficiently "Derridean" direction. She, like Habermas, is too invested, he contends, in trying to "strike a balance" between constitutionalism and democracy. With Derrida, Thomassen insists that the relationship between these two concepts is radically irreconcilable and undecidable, that constitutional democracy is, in fact, temporally and constitutively "out of joint." He notes that on Habermasian premises one remains anesthetized to Derrida's critical observation that it is exactly this "simultaneous lack and lag" that makes constitutional democratic practices "meaningful." Indeed, in Habermas the discourse-ethical *telos* of agreement enjoins a *reconciliation* between the addressees of the constitution and its authors, "a final and rational consensus eliminating all disagreement."[40] The effort to construe constitutionalism and democracy as ultimately congruent moments of a rational, self-correcting learning process is for Thomassen a *structural* failing of Habermas's theory. Unlike Derrida, Habermas sees the gap between the two arenas not as constitutive and always already deferred but as something to be "overcome" and "recuperated." He is thus unable to recognize that constitutional democracy is a "worthwhile enterprise" precisely insofar as it is shot through with infinitely irresolvable disagreement, contingency, vicious circularity, imperfectability, and textual and temporal disjointedness.

It would seem, then, that for critics like Thomassen and Morris, Habermas's model tethers itself to the dualistic scaffolding of the Kantian *ratio* only to remain structurally incapable of apprehending the asymmetrical gesture of care for a single unrepresentable individual as coimbricated with an always already deferred promise of universal justice-to-come. On this reading, the conceptual splits between the two thinkers vis-à-vis the problem of care for the human other are as formidable as the divisions we encountered in the preceding chapter in relation to the question of care for the nonhuman other.

ESPRIT DE FINESSE VERSUS *ESPRIT DE GÉOMÉTRIE*?: THE DISPUTE OVER BLOCH AND BENJAMIN

Consistent with this diagnosis of conceptual incompatibility, Giovanna Borradori has invoked Blaise Pascal's distinction between *esprit de finesse* and *esprit de géométrie* to characterize the disparate philosophical registers in which the Derridean and Habermasian projects are respectively articulated. To Borradori, the term *esprit de finesse* signifies Derrida's "extreme sensitivity for subtle facts of language . . . [and] his unmatched ability to combine inventiveness and rigor, circumvention and affirmation," whereas *esprit de géométrie* reflects the "rather Spartan," "very compact, and elegantly traditional" nature of Habermas's philosophical dialogue.[41] Here Borradori appears to valorize Derrida's highly sophisticated and nuanced interrogation of the liminal text over and against Habermas's blunt, old-world logocentrism. Borradori's characterization is useful for our purposes in that it underscores the objections to the alleged cognitive-centric disposition of Habermas's discourse ethic that we have highlighted in the foregoing chapters. Nevertheless, her stylization of the divide between Derrida and Habermas seems to gloss over the possibility that the deconstructive maneuver may be beset with deficits of its own. In the preceding chapter, I suggested that the deconstructive critique of the idea of nature-in-itself carries with it the prospect of a re-teleologized orientation toward the nonspeaking world. In chapter 2, I argued that in prioritizing the standpoint of the incommensurably singular, Derrida effectively strips moral agents of a common intersubjective framework for evaluating the competing value orientations of concrete singularities. In an effort to further scrutinize the limitations of the deconstructive approach—and its incompatibility with that of Habermas—it will be helpful to think Derrida's portrayal of the radically liminal ethicopolitical time-space of *khôra* alongside Ernst Bloch's idea of nonsimultaneity and Walter Benjamin's notion of *Jetztzeit*. While there are important conceptual differences between these various interventions, each seems to claim much more for the perspective of the immeasurably singular than can be countenanced from the universalistic moral standpoint of Habermasian discourse ethics.

Let us begin with Bloch's nonsimultaneity concept. Developed in his *Heritage of Our Times*, this idea reads against the grain of the dialectics of capitalist synchronicity, or totality—as elaborated, notably, in Lukács—to advance the rather paradoxical claim that "[n]ot all people exist in the same Now."[42] On this move, the contemporary social field is reimagined as a complex, heterogeneous matrix of multitemporal and multispatial contradictions, a diverse, and rather muddled, assemblage of coexisting sociocultural arrangements and economic structures from assorted epochs.[43] Reframing the remarks on precapitalist social formations in Marx's *Grundrisse*, Bloch thus allows for the possibility that there are phenomena that stand "completely outside" the modern *ratio*; consigned to the "catalogue of the omitted," these "unincorporated" spheres remain undefined or underdefined in bourgeois terms. To be sure, even from the standpoint of a Hegelian dialectical totality, one must concede that there are no terms that are not, in a sense, "drunk"; nevertheless, for Bloch such a totality remains a monadic mode of remembrance wherein each term is obliged "to sober up on the spot as it were, because it [is] 'endowed with the complete wealth of mind.'"[44] For Bloch, then, dialectics is neither a unity of contradictions (as in Schelling)[45] nor a unity of the unity of contradictions (as in Hegel). Instead, the point of Bloch's nonsimultaneity theory is to read history as an unfinished text—an unresolved, disjointed patchwork of past, present, and future contradictions unfolding along discontinuous, fragmented, and unpredictable temporal and spatial axes. Moreover, because it accords cultural products the capacity to "jut beyond" the historical circumstances in which they emerge, Bloch's idea of noncontemporaneity rearticulates the dialectical relation between immanence and transcendence inscribed in Marx's emancipatory promise, transforming it into something like a "waking dream" that draws its sustenance precisely from that which has been overlooked. In Bloch, observes Stephen Eric Bronner, "[u]nacknowledged works by the most diverse cultures, 'traces' (*Spurren*) of forgotten lives, fragments of historical production, retain untapped perspectives on the 'best life,' which never simply 'vanish' (Hegel) into immediate forms of practice."[46]

In this sense, Bloch's idea of noncontemporaneity reverberates importantly with Derrida's portrayal of *khôra* as a spatially and temporally out-of-joint abyss in which the ethicopolitical gesture toward a democracy-to-come can be executed. There is a crucial distinction between the two concepts, however: against Derrida's effort to think the disjointed spatiotemporality of *khôra* as *a*messianically messianic—oriented toward an always already deferred promise of democracy—Bloch subjects the disjointed present to what Habermas calls the "utopian treatment," endowing it with an eschatological *telos* of ideal finality. Indeed in Bloch, the forgotten, anachronistic traces of mythical ciphers, symbols, dreams, visions, poetry, and philosophy are interpreted as emblems of an expressly utopian "not-yet": "What is most genuinely real in this world is still outstanding; it waits, 'in the fear of getting stalled and in the hope of getting achieved,' for its realization by means of the labor of humans in society. . . . Bloch [thus] gives Schelling's doctrine of the potencies a Marxist interpretation."[47] In fact, in Bloch, Schelling's romantic *Naturphilosophie* is appropriated to summon forth a vision of "a utopian projected harmony of the unreified object with the manifest subject, and of the unreified subject with the manifest object"—a vision in which "the echo of an ancient identity" is deciphered.[48] From this standpoint, Bloch inherits Schelling's concomitant disbelief in the "innocence" of the modern sciences and their technological applications; subject to the latter's "mechanical mode of treatment," nature becomes "estranged," "lost," and "in need of a homecoming."[49] To Bloch, such a resurrection of fallen nature is to be realized under the aegis of a new "technology without violence," a "broader physics" that would "exclude mathematical calculation, at least of the type made so far."[50]

Formulations such as these lead Habermas to stylize Bloch's thought as permeated with a "heritage of Jewish mysticism," which in his view also inflects the philosophy of history and nature speculations of Walter Benjamin. Consonant with Bloch's noncontemporaneity thesis, Benjamin posits a present in which glimpses of the "best life" are already in play. He portrays these asynchronous moments of "messianic time" as shooting through the homogeneous *Jetztzeit* (now time) of capital, threatening it with collapse.[51] To Benjamin, it is precisely the "mimetic capacity" of messianic time that promises to dislocate *Jetztzeit* from its own emptiness. Signified by a linkage between the animalistic and expressly human properties of language, this mimetic capacity finds expression, as Habermas puts it, "in magical practices, lives on in the primal anxiety of animistic world views, and is preserved in myth."[52] On this conviction, Benjamin rejects the method of *Ideologiekritik* favored by Adorno and other Marxists, who approach "cultural tradition methodologically as a part of social evolution . . . making it accessible to a materialist explanation."[53] Instead, he gravitates toward a "conservative-revolutionary" philosophy of history that locates in the sphere of aesthetics precisely those exoteric, indeed "divine," mythopoetic forces that at once preserve and emancipate.

This perspective positions Benjamin to reimagine the vocation of the human species as a quest to retrieve the secular content of the messianic promise—that is, as an effort to eradicate the mimetic capacity's primordial subservience to the repressive forces of nature, but "without sealing off the powers of mimesis and the streams of semantic energies, for that would be to lose the poetic capacity to interpret the world in light of human needs."[54] Significantly, notwithstanding his wish to move beyond both the materialist limitations of the *Ideologiekritik* of an Adorno and the utopian idealizations of a Bloch, Benjamin shares with such thinkers the thesis that the project of human emancipation must take its cues from exoteric elements of the present that somehow stand outside the identarian *ratio* of subject-object epistemology. Indeed, the *Jetztzeit* of capital encounters its encirclement by messianic time's mimetic capacity as a *catastrophe*: it must now contend with experiences of aesthetic expressivity that are antinomical to its own efforts to bring both subject and object under the pernicious fetters of instrumental-technical control. As Habermas observes, Benjamin's attempt to rescue "the messianic moments" and "endangered semantic potential" of the history of art expresses itself "not as reflection on a process of self-formation but as identification and *retrieval* of emphatic experiences and utopian contents."[55] Like Adorno, Benjamin herewith defends of a version of Lukács's nature-theoretic monism (see chapter 3) that in turn counsels a view of the aesthetic as a terrain whose semantic potentials are alone poised to elude the orbit of modern identifying thought and liberate both the human and the nonhuman from the empty homogeneity of *Jetztzeit*. According to Habermas, Benjamin pleas, in fact, for "a condition in which the esoteric experiences of happiness have become public and universal, for only in a context of communication into which nature is integrated in a brotherly fashion, as if it were set upright once again, can human subjects open up their eyes to look in return."[56]

Derrida's radically liminal time-space of *khôra* evinces significant affinities with the proposals of Bloch and Benjamin. In accord with these writers, his effort to dislocate the present out of contemporaneity with itself is coterminous with an endeavor to undermine the foundational precepts of the subject-object framework of knowledge, such that the idea of nature-in-itself is no longer tenable. The argument that I have already advanced vis-à-vis this move (see chapter 3) bears reemphasizing here: Derrida's radical antifoundationalism does not unburden itself of what Alfred Schmidt calls the "basically magical and animistic"[57] imprint of romantic nature speculation (be it that of a Schelling, a Bloch, or a Benjamin), inasmuch as it likewise removes all categorical barriers against the re-teleologization of the natural world.

Further points of resonance between Derrida and Benjamin emerge in relation to their respective engagements with the question of law. These parallels are drawn by Derrida himself in "Force of Law," which includes a lengthy excursus on Benjamin's "Critique of Violence."[58] Here Derrida notes that deconstruction shares with Benjamin the conviction that "something is 'rotten' at the heart of law."[59] According to Derrida, Benjamin locates this "rotten-ness" in the two kinds of violence of which law admits—namely, the *founding* violence that sets forth and implements law (*die rechtsetzende Gewalt*) and the *preserving* violence that ensures law's durability and enforceability (*die rechtserhaltende Gewalt*). In contrast to its conserving aspect, the founding violence of law is at its core "mystical," in that it is not, and does not need to be, justified in reference to any preexisting legality: the sufferings, tortures, and crimes that accompany it suspend established law in the interest of forging another legal regime. There is in this sense a founding moment of violent, revolutionary nonlaw at the heart of all law. Accordingly, for a critique of vio-lence to be meaningful, it must acknowledge that violence "is not an accident arriving from the outside of law. That which threatens law already belongs to it, the right to law [*au droit au droit*], to the origin of law."[60]

Benjamin has on this view identified a "differential contamination" (Der-rida's term) between the mystical violence that establishes law and the itera-tive, self-preserving violence at the heart of the originary. "Perseveration in turn refounds, so that it can claim to preserve what it claims to found."[61] To Benjamin, annihilating the mythic violence that founds law as well as the iter-ability that conserves the irruptive instant of foundation necessitates an ap-peal to the expiative principle of "divine" justice—a principle that stands in sharp contrast to the merely retributive standpoint of the Greek *mythos*: "In-stead of founding law, [the violence of God] destroys it; instead of setting limits and boundaries, it annihilates them; instead of leading to fault and ex-piation, it causes to expiate; instead of threatening, it strikes;[62] above all—and this is the essential issue—instead of killing with blood, it kills and annihi-lates *without bloodshed*."[63]

As an avenue through which to contest the violence that both founds and preserves law, Benjamin's secular appropriation of Jewish messianism has much to recommend it, in Derrida's view. Indeed, whatever the discrepancies between their respective vernaculars, Derrida sees a certain kinship between the Benjaminian idea of divine justice and the deconstructive perspective of the incalculable decision. In their respective endeavors to attend to the wound to the nonidentical for which the violence of law and its ideal of selfhood as ipseity are responsible, both orientations rise "above reason and universality, beyond a sort of *Aufklärung* of law, [which] is nothing other . . . than a refer-ence to the irreducible singularity of each situation."[64] While decidability is, to be sure, "on the side" of Benjamin's idea of divine violence, such violence—in contrast to the mythic violence that founds law—"does not lend itself to any human determination, to any knowledge or decidable 'certainty' on our part. It is never known in itself, 'as such,' but only in its 'effects' and its effects are 'incomparable.' They do not lend themselves to conceptual generalization."[65]

This affinity aside, a crucial point of emphasis distinguishes the two critiques of law: in contrast to Benjamin's divine justice, Derrida aims not to *destroy* the inescapably violent measurability at the spine of law but to subordinate it to the radically incalculable standpoint of the unsubsumable example, a perspective from which the always already deferred effort to achieve universal justice must take its moral bearings. Indeed, Derrida's deconstructive discourses do not seek to annihilate law *simpliciter* but are rather "both regulated and without regulation"; they break with law's principle of calculative equality but also confirm it in pursuit of a universal justice-to-come. In their irreducible plurality, they "participate in an impure, contaminating, negotiated, bastard and violent fashion" in both the decision and the undecidable.[66]

The foregoing reflections suggest that consonant with various interventions by both Bloch and Benjamin, deconstruction reads against the grain of modern identifying thought in a bid to bring the perspective of the spatiotemporally disjointed trace to the fore of social critique. In so doing, Derrida's approach presents itself, in my view, as fundamentally at odds with the basic categorical suppositions of Habermas's project. Indeed, far from following deconstruction in according conceptual primacy to the perspective of the incalculable decision, Habermasian discourse ethics enjoin moral agents to reach universalizable agreements about contested validity claims of truth, rightness, and sincerity. The unforced force of communicative reason is herewith valorized as a framework for the achievement of universal justice, placing Habermas's model unequivocally and irretrievably on the side of what Derrida views as the violence of decidable knowledge and certainty that both founds and preserves law. However, it should be noted that many readers would demur from my efforts to portray the theoretical disparities between Derrida and Habermas as unbridgeable. It is to these more conciliatory appraisals that I shall now turn.

WEIGHING THE PROSPECTS FOR RAPPROCHEMENT

I begin with a consideration of the arguments Richard Rorty, a writer who is far more sanguine about a possible reconciliation between communicative ethics and deconstruction, even if he finds Habermas, for one, ill disposed to appreciate the complementarity of the two perspectives. Rorty attributes this recalcitrance to Habermas's profound apprehension about the antirationalist implications of contextualism and his concomitant quest for "universal validity." He takes Habermas's orientation to be symptomatic of a craving common to all iterations of "radical" politics—namely, the desire "for a sublime Otherness, something to which the everyday predicates in terms of which we describe the difference between the beautiful and the ugly, the pleasant and the painful, do not apply."[67] To the extent that discourse ethics retains such a Marxian division between freedom and ideology as well as a "residual acceptance" of Kant's nature-freedom distinction, it is guilty of being not so much critical of "the philosophy of subjectivity" as enmeshed in it. This is by no means to deny that Habermas's "liberal" emphasis on public problem solving can contribute importantly to pragmatic efforts to redress social injustice, pain, and humiliation: it is only to upbraid him for assigning "some sort of epistemic priority" to his own communicative-theoretic reconstruction of Enlightenment rationalism over and against the nonfoundationalist plea for an "ironic" distance between the incommensurate vocabularies of self and other set forth in the Nietzsche-Heidegger-Derrida tradition. For Rorty, this bias ultimately prevents Habermas from seeing that the activities of liberalism and irony "can coexist peacefully. There is no reason why philosophy should have to choose between them."[68]

Rorty's suspicion that the conceptual incongruities between the two philosophers are in some sense complementary is shared by Richard Bernstein. To Bernstein, both Derrida and Habermas contribute vitally to our understanding of the dynamic, transmutational "force-field" known as "modernity/postmodernity." Indeed, for him their frameworks must be considered not as mutually exclusive "Either/Ors" but as indispensable "Both/And" theorizations of this complex constellation.[69] While he sees no possibility of an *Aufhebung*—a reconciliation "without gaps, fissures, and ruptures"—Bernstein maintains that *together* the perspectives of Derrida and Habermas form a "juxtaposed rather than an integrated cluster of changing elements that resist reduction to a common denominator, essential core, or generative first principle."[70] Notably, other writers have been willing to push Rorty's and Bernstein's claims further, finding grounds (particularly in their respective post-2001 writings) for something approximating an outright rapprochement. Martin Matuštík, for instance, suggests that Habermas's "fallibilist," "self-limiting" critique of Enlightenment modernity can be fruitfully merged with Derrida's "intensified" deconstruction of the identity logic of cultural and economic domination, such that one is better situated to engage questions of multiculturalism and "postsecular hope." Matuštík ventures that in recent years, Derrida's deconstructive operation has found a "home in Habermas's procedural institutions, thereby curbing the dangers of idealist unreality and political ineffectiveness. Intensifying the promise of democracy, deconstruction [assists] Habermas to bring the exiled otherness back to the very ideal of communication community."[71]

To Matuštík, nowhere is this synergistic link between the two writers more conspicuous than in their coauthored plea for a vital and flourishing public sphere in Europe, where, in the wake of the U.S.-led invasion of Iraq in 2003, demands were being raised for increased international cooperation and the formation of a common European foreign policy in opposition to Washington's unilateral interventions. In this letter—entitled "February 15, or What Binds Europeans Together: A Plea for a Common Foreign Policy, Beginning in the Core of Europe"—Habermas and Derrida jointly commend the regulative notions of communicative pluralism and deliberative democracy, but allow them to "tremble," as Matuštík puts it, flinging "open the shutters of the European club to its other."[72] The two colleagues affirm that the continent's variegated sociocultural terrain, beleaguered for centuries by antagonisms between town and country, faith and knowledge, and states and classes, "has had to painfully learn how differences can be communicated, contradictions institutionalized, and tensions stabilized. The acknowledgement of differences—the reciprocal acknowledgement of the Other in his otherness—can also become a feature of a common identity."[73] For Matuštík, such proposals signal an unmistakably productive alliance between the self-limiting sovereignty of Habermas's world cosmopolitanism and Derrida's accentuated deconstruction of justice as a "trans-political" political principle. They gesture, indeed, toward a chimeric, radically pluralist, postsecular philosophical overture disencumbered of many of the paralytic stylizations of modernity and postmodernity set forth in the polarizing debates of the 1980s and 1990s.

This is also the intuition of Michel Rosenfeld. To Rosenfeld, the limitations of both approaches can be successfully transcended from the vantage point of "a strong version of pluralist ethics." He argues that such a comprehensive pluralism has the advantage of striking "the best possible balance" between Derrida's difference-theoretic ethics and Habermas's ethics of identity. With Derrida, Rosenfeld's idea of strong pluralism aims to guarantee "a non-trivial *ex ante* equal hearing to all perspectives and conceptions of the good," while also refusing, with Habermas, "to treat irreducible singularity as an absolute."[74] According to Rosenfeld, such a pluralism pleas for the freedom of all individuals to adopt and express their own ideals and goods, and refrains from privileging the substance of any one ethical conviction over and against another. To the extent that it entertains the notion at all, "*the* good" for strong pluralism is precisely the freedom of each to give voice to his or her own value convictions on free and equal terms. So far Rosenfeld's perspective is consistent with the deontological aims of Habermas's program. Rosenfeld breaks with Habermas, however, in arguing that a viable comprehensive pluralism requires and is indeed *parasitic* upon conceptions of the good that are indifferent or even opposed to its own core normative commitment to the open and unconstrained play of subjective viewpoints. Without such contrary "conceptions to incorporate or accommodate," Rosenfeld maintains, "pluralism itself becomes meaningless."[75]

This posture of openness toward perspectives that abjure strong pluralism's own effort to cast all views of the good as *prima facie* worthy of recognition and fortification is, to Rosenfeld, more accommodative of difference than the moral standpoint of Habermasian discourse ethics. Strong pluralism, he claims, can freely admit moral and ethical claims that run counter to its own basic tenets—for example, those voiced by certain variants of religious fundamentalism—into a pluralist society, an allowance that is not readily made on strictly Habermasian premises.[76] This greater openness toward singularity aside, Rosenfeld demurs from pushing his perspective in a direction wholly in sync with Derrida's proposals. For Rosenfeld, comprehensive pluralism must desist from its difference-ethical objective to "accommodate as much diversity as possible" the moment a given conception of the good threatens the functional unity of an open and inclusive society. Inasmuch as it is aimed at disaggregating the polity and annihilating those who do not share its particular idea of the good, a practice like terrorism can be readily shown to have crossed the threshold of what strong pluralism can accommodate in relation to the free play of differences. In proposing the "unity of the relevant sociopolitical unit"[77] as an unambiguous universalistic constraint upon the difference-ethical claims of moral agents, Rosenfeld has squarely distanced his standpoint from the asymmetrical moral counterpoint prioritized in Derrida, which (as noted in chapter 2) is ill situated to unequivocally exclude and condemn a practice like terrorism. Rosenfeld contends, indeed, that "in its insistence that the practical need for unity limit the extent of recognition ultimately accorded to difference, comprehensive pluralism embraces an ethics that is inconsistent with Derrida's conception of an unbreakable bond between the ethics of difference and the ontology of singularity."[78]

Although well intentioned, Rosenfeld's appeal to the "unity of the polity" as a universalistic bulwark against the potentially destabilizing consequences of a wholly unconstrained free play of differences suffers from a basic flaw: it is conceptually limited in its ability to subject state-administered actions aimed at solidifying political unity—the American invasion and occupation of Iraq, for example—to the same type of moral scrutiny that it extends toward nonstate actors who endeavor to undermine that unity. After taking pains to broaden the moral compass of the immeasurably singular beyond what can be countenanced by Habermas, it is in fact rather ironic that Rosenfeld ultimately falls back on a notion of political sovereignty that is in a sense "pre-Habermasian." Indeed Rosenfeld's proposed universalistic constraint on the proliferation of differences does not seem to take us very far beyond what Michael Hardt and Antonio Negri identify as the basic principle of the tradition of political theory—namely, that "only 'the one' can rule, whether that be conceived of the monarch, the state, or the party"; these categories of political subjectivity, they argue, absorb "the plural singularities of the multitude . . . [into the] undifferentiated unity of the people."[79]

Such dedifferentiation is precisely the outcome that Rosenfeld wishes to avoid, so one can only wonder why he does not make better use of Habermas's more difference-accommodative notion of constitutional patriotism in this context. According to Habermas, the modern democratic constitution is certainly a check on the ability of concrete singularities to pursue their unilateral agendas *ad libitum*. However, in contrast to traditional notions of sovereignty, the aim here is not to anchor the affective allegiance[80] of communicative actors in the firmament of a specific polity or state, but to associate it with constitutional-democratic principles, institutions, and practices that enable agents to adjudicate contested convictions and ideals and reach mutual understanding. Habermas's constitutional patriotism is therefore far better equipped to both constrain and accommodate difference than Rosenfeld's "unity of the polity." In fact, as noted in the introduction to this study, Habermas sees the democratic constitution as endowed with the capacity to countenance actions and beliefs that overstep its existing normative boundaries. It is poised, as he puts it, to self-reflexively "tolerate resistance from dissidents who, after exhausting all legal avenues, nonetheless oppose legitimately reached decisions."[81] The only stipulation imposed upon such noncompliant actions is that they must be carried forth in a manner that does not undermine the democratic principles and practices upheld in the constitution itself. Here Habermas demurs—rightly in my view—from Rosenfeld's contention that the viability of a pluralistic polity is vouchsafed by its tolerance of public discourses that are anathema to its own normative commitment to the unconstrained exchange of subjective viewpoints. His notion of constitutional patriotism nevertheless justifies not only the legitimacy of civilly disobedient actions; it also guards against the ossification of democratic-constitutional arrangements, and against their retrenchment into fixed ontotheological programs, as Derrida and his defenders might put it. Indeed, Habermas's standpoint enjoins precisely

> a *dynamic understanding* of the constitution as an unfinished project. From this long-term perspective, the constitutional state does not represent a finished structure but a delicate and sensitive—above all fallible and revisable—enterprise, whose purpose is to realize the system of rights *anew* in changing circumstances, that is, to interpret the system of rights better, to institutionalize it more appropriately, and to draw out its contents more radically.[82]

In light of the intractable conceptual disparities to which we have drawn attention, Simon Critchley is justifiably cautious about the possibility of a successful alliance between Habermas and Derrida, even if he, like other commentators we have considered, does discern grounds for a fertile theoretical collaboration. Critchley notes that in tune with communicative ethics, Derrida's later writings—*Politics of Friendship*, *Specters of Marx*, "Force of Law," for example—are "oriented around the quasi-normative axis of an emancipatory, democratic politics, based in the undeconstructible, context-transcendent, formal universality of justice."[83] In others words, in Critchley's view echoes of something like a Habermasian discourse norm can be found in the later Derrida's view of deconstructive justice and responsibility, "which can [likewise] be qualified as undeconstructible, unconditional, a priori, and universal."[84] Yet however warranted one may be in portraying formal universality and context-transcendent unconditionality as a common overlay to their respective approaches to the problem of justice, Critchley cautions that the obstacles to a thoroughgoing accord between the two thinkers must not be underestimated: the theoretical discrepancies between the discourse ethic's decidedly impartial, universalistic procedures of normative justification and the deconstructive effort to unbind the self's encounter with the other from regulative constraints of equalitarian reciprocation and exchange cannot be easily wished away. In an effort to move beyond the limitations of the moral proceduralism of the discourse ethic as well as deconstruction's privileged standpoint of radical asymmetricality, Critchley leans on Levinas's idea of the "third party,"[85] which is developed in the latter's *Totality and Infinity*.[86] To Critchley, greater emphasis on Levinas's third other on Derrida's part would go a long way toward fleshing out the underdetermined politiconormative dimensions of deconstruction's quasiphenomenological standpoint of difference-ethical asymmetry. Indeed, he contends that by looking at ego through the eyes of alter, the Levinasian third party assures

> that my ethical obligations to the other always take place in a political context, within a public realm where the question of justice for others and for humanity as a whole can be raised. Thus, the introduction of the third introduces the dimension of universality, and the ethical asymmetry of the relation of the other is supplemented by the symmetry of relations among equals. In short the moment of the third in Levinas is the moment when the principle of equal treatment and universality presupposed in discourse ethics can be grafted on to the asymmetry of the ethics of care. It is the third party that marries Derrida and Habermas.[87]

In this sense, Critchley is proposing the Levinasian third party as a moment of intersubjective sociation that is poised to bridge the gap between the discourse ethic's procedures for adjudicating moral validity claims and rendering them universally binding (politics), and deconstruction's moral counterpoint of unconditional care for the wholly unrepresentable and incalculable alterity of the other (ethics). His aim here is to redress both the "ethical overload" of the latter perspective (about which Habermas has complained) and the former's emphasis on communicative idealizations and universalistic problem-solving (to which Derrida has objected).

For Critchley, the frameworks of both Derrida and Habermas lack the categorical resources needed to resolve their respective deficits from, as it were, the inside: ameliorating these conceptual shortcomings will therefore necessitate supplementation from without. While Critchley's interventions are a noteworthy overture in this direction, they are much less ambitious and rigorous than the negotiation of the Derrida-Habermas exchange undertaken by Axel Honneth, a writer to whom Critchley himself devotes a considerable amount of attention. Honneth's recognition-theoretic paradigm is not so much an attempt to reconcile the two thinkers but rather an effort to *reconstruct* the Habermasian model on terms that render it better equipped to attend to the deconstructive perspective of ethical asymmetricality. Thus, as Critchley notes, a crucial aim for Honneth is to grant relations of care a place in moral discourse such that the goal of solidarity is no longer in danger of becoming an "empty abstraction."[88] Yet at the same time, Honneth insists that any endeavor to accommodate relationships of affective sympathy within moral theory must not be undertaken at the price of subverting the norms of equal treatment and mutual respect to which the tradition of Kant and Habermasian discourse ethics have extended categorical primacy. Honneth's expansive recognition-theoretic project is in fact critical for any future research program aimed at reconstructing the Habermasian model along such lines. His arguments will therefore figure significantly in the contribution to such a reconstruction that I shall attempt to offer in the following chapter.

NOTES

1. Simon Critchley, "Frankfurt Impromptu—Remarks on Derrida and Habermas," in *The Derrida-Habermas Reader*, ed. Lasse Thomassen (Chicago: The University of Chicago Press, 2006), 103.

2. Jürgen Habermas, "Excursus on Leveling the Genre Distinction between Philosophy and Literature," in *The Philosophical Discourse of Modernity: Twelve Lectures*, trans. Frederick G. Lawrence (Cambridge, Mass.: The MIT Press, 1990), 210.

3. Jürgen Habermas and Jacques Derrida, "February 15, or What Binds Europeans Together: A Plea for a Common Foreign Policy, Beginning in the Core of Europe," in *The Derrida-Habermas Reader*, ed. Lasse Thomassen (Chicago: The University of Chicago Press, 2006), 270–77.

4. Jürgen Habermas and Eduardo Mendieta, "America and the World: A Conversation with Jürgen Habermas," *Logos: A Journal of Modern Society and Culture* 3, no. 3 (Summer 2004): 104, www.logosjournal.com/issue_3.3.pdf (14 July 2010).

5. Habermas and Mendieta, "America and the World," 104.

6. See Jürgen Habermas, "Martin Heidegger: The Great Influence," in *Philosophical-Political Profiles*, trans. Frederick G. Lawrence (Cambridge, Mass.: The MIT Press, 1983), 53–60, and "The Undermining of Western Rationalism through the Critique of Rationalism: Martin Heidegger," in *The Philosophical Discourse of Modernity: Twelve Lectures*, trans. Frederick G. Lawrence (Cambridge, Mass.: The MIT Press, 1990), 131–60.

7. Habermas, "The Undermining of Western Rationalism," 147–48.

8. Habermas, "The Undermining of Western Rationalism," 156.

9. The following discussion draws on my "Interpretative Care and the Postmetaphysical Tradition: The Legacy of Two Freuds." Review of Alan Bass, *Interpretation and Difference: The Strangeness of Care*, H-Ideas, H-Net Reviews, February 2009, www.h-net.org/reviews/showrev.php?id=22980 (15 July 2010).

10. Alan Bass, *Interpretation and Difference: The Strangeness of Care* (Stanford: Stanford University Press, 2006), 68.

11. Bass, *Interpretation and Difference*, 134.

12. Bass, *Interpretation and Difference*, 168.

13. Bass, *Interpretation and Difference*, 161.

14. Bass, *Interpretation and Difference*, 179.

15. Lawrence Vogel, *The Fragile "We": Ethical Implications of Martin Heidegger's* Being and Time (Chicago: Northwestern University Press, 1994), 70.

16. Vogel, *The Fragile "We,"* 71; emphasis in original.

17. Stuart Elden, *Speaking Against Number: Heidegger, Language and the Politics of Calculation* (Edinburgh: Edinburgh University Press, 2006), 175.

18. Martin Heidegger, *Contributions to Philosophy: From Enowning*, trans. Parvis Emad and Kenneth Maly (Bloomington: Indiana University Press, 1999), 7.

19. Elden, *Speaking Against Number*, 174–75.

20. Martin Heidegger, *Pathmarks*, ed. William McNeil (Cambridge, UK: Cambridge University Press, 1998), 235, in Elden, *Speaking Against Number*, 174.

21. Jacques Derrida, "Structure, Sign, and Play in the Discourse of the Human Sciences," in *Writing and Difference*, trans. Alan Bass (Chicago: The University of Chicago Press, 1978), 280–81.

22. Jacques Derrida, "Eating Well, or the Calculation of the Subject," in *Points . . . Interviews, 1974–1994*, trans. Peggy Kamuf et al. (Stanford: Stanford University Press, 1995), 273. According to Derrida, an unexamined residue of transcendentalism leaves both the Heideggerian *Dasein* and the Levinasian subject ill positioned to destabilize the carno-phallogocentrism of the Western ontotheological tradition (see chapter 2). For the latter, the flourishing of the subject is tied to the slaughter of actual animals as well as to the symbolic cannibalistic sacrifice of other human beings (see chapter 3). Both Levinas's subject and Heidegger's *Dasein*, in other words, neglect to "*sacrifice sacrifice.* The subject (in Levinas's sense) and the *Dasein* are 'men' in a world where sacrifice is possible and where it is not forbidden to make an attempt on

life in general, but only on human life, on the neighbor's life, on the other's life as Dasein." Derrida, "Eating Well," 279.

23. Bill Martin, *Matrix and Line: Derrida and the Possibilities of Postmodern Social Theory* (New York: The State University of New York Press, 1992), 120, 121.

24. Derrida, "Eating Well," 274.

25. David Ingram, *Habermas and the Dialectic of Reason* (New Haven: Yale University Press, 1987), 91.

26. Peter Dews, *Logics of Disintegration: Post-structuralist Thought and the Claims of Critical Theory* (New York: Verso, 1987), 33, 52. To Dews, Derrida opens himself to this outcome insofar as he "fails to question the transcendental and speculative interpretations of experience which he inherits from Husserl and Hegel, and is therefore obliged to jettison the concept altogether as tainted with presence." Paradoxically, having herewith shunned all immediacy, *différance* becomes guilty of becoming, "as Manfred Frank remarks . . . totalitarian and destructive of meaning (*totalitär und sinnerzersetzend*)." Manfred Frank, *Was ist Neostrukturalismus?* Frankfurt: Suhrkamp-Verlag), 550, in Dews, *Logics of Disintegration*, 50. Dews is in my view correct, up to a point: the totalization of difference is indeed a danger of the Derridean standpoint. However, my inclination would be to credit Derrida—as I have done throughout this study—with attempting to *ally* the perspectives of the identical and the non-identical, even if his *prioritization* of the latter orientation does indeed lead in the direction that Dews suggests.

27. The discussions in the second and fourth sections of this chapter draw on my "Derrida and Habermas: Asymmetry and Accord. Review of *The Derrida-Habermas Reader*," *Radical Philosophy Review* 10, no. 2 (2007): 197–203.

28. Martin Morris, *Rethinking the Communicative Turn: Adorno, Habermas, and the Problem of Communicative Freedom* (New York: The State University of New York Press, 2001).

29. Jacques Derrida, *The Other Heading: Reflections on Today's Europe*, ed. Pascale-Ann Brault, trans. Michael B. Naas (Bloomington: Indiana University Press, 1992), 51.

30. Drucilla Cornell, *The Philosophy of the Limit* (London: Routledge, 1992).

31. Jürgen Habermas, *Postmetaphysical Thinking: Philosophical Essays*, trans. William Mark Hohengarten (Cambridge, Mass.: The MIT Press, 1992), 48, in Morris, *Rethinking the Communicative Turn*, 155.

32. Morris, *Rethinking the Communicative Turn*, 155.

33. Morris, *Rethinking the Communicative Turn*, 246.

34. Morris, *Rethinking the Communicative Turn*, 174.

35. Jürgen Habermas, "The Undermining of Western Rationalism through the Critique of Rationalism: Martin Heidegger," in *The Philosophical Discourse of Modernity: Twelve Lectures*, trans. Frederick G. Lawrence (Cambridge, Mass.: The MIT Press, 1990), 139.

36. Morris, *Rethinking the Communicative Turn*, 242.

37. Morris, *Rethinking the Communicative Turn*, 245.

38. Morris, *Rethinking the Communicative Turn*, 204n. Morris levels this particular charge against the work of Seyla Benhabib, but he would presumably extend it just

as readily toward Habermas's kindred framework. In the following chapter, I revisit and reject Morris's claim that "moralizing" is the upshot of the discourse-ethical effort to link normative philosophy with a theory of knowledge-constitutive interests (see chapter 5).

39. Bonnie Honig, "Dead Rights, Live Futures: On Habermas's Attempt to Reconcile Constitutionalism and Democracy," in *The Derrida-Habermas Reader*, ed. Lasse Thomassen (Chicago: The University of Chicago Press, 2006), 169.

40. Lasse Thomassen, "'A Bizarre, Even Opaque Practice': Habermas on Constitutionalism and Democracy," in *The Derrida-Habermas Reader*, ed. Lasse Thomassen (Chicago: The University of Chicago Press, 2006), 185. This view suggests an affinity between Habermas's perspective and that of Jean-Jacques Rousseau. As is well known, Rousseau portrays the will of a legitimate sovereign as *identical* to the general will of the citizens who have entered into the social contract. Rousseau's thinking is in this sense at odds with the arguments of Thomas Hobbes and John Locke, inasmuch as the citizens in the latter two versions of the social contract "alienate" their wills—i.e., give over their law-making authority to a sovereign who then governs on their behalf.

41. Giovanna Borradori, ed., *Philosophy in a Time of Terror: Dialogues with Jürgen Habermas and Jacques Derrida* (Chicago: The University of Chicago Press, 2003), xii.

42. Ernst Bloch, *Heritage of Our Times*, trans. Neville Plaice and Stephen Plaice (Cambridge, UK: Polity Press, 1991), 97.

43. David C. Durst, "Ernst Bloch's Theory of Nonsimultaneity," *The Germanic Review* 77, no. 3 (2002): 171.

44. Bloch, *Heritage of Our Times*, 115.

45. Peter Dews draws an interesting parallel between Schelling and Derrida in this context. He notes that for the former, "[n]o stability can be found within the subject-object relation itself, but only by transcending this relation toward absolute identity. It is for this reason that Schelling can write that it is the very concepts of subject and object which are the 'guarantors' of the absolute. . . . Consequently, like Schelling, Derrida is only able to characterize what he terms '*différance*,' 'arche-writing,' or the 'trace,' through a sequence of fundamental negations." Dews, *Logics of Disintegration*, 29. To avoid the charge of metaphysical dogmatism (which Fichte leveled against Schelling) and to transcend the standpoint of finite consciousness, Derrida invokes the idea of a "track in the text." Yet, according to Dews, "this track can only be the mark of speculation. Derrida, in other words, is offering us a philosophy of the absolute." Dews, *Logics of Disintegration*, 30. See also Dews's complementary claim that *différance* fails to extricate from the principle of unity (outlined in note 26 of this chapter).

46. Stephen Eric Bronner, "Utopian Projections: In Memory of Ernst Bloch," in *Not Yet: Reconsidering Ernst Bloch*, ed. Jamie Owen Daniel and Tom Moylan (New York: Verso, 1997), 168.

47. Jürgen Habermas, "Ernst Bloch: A Marxist Schelling," in *Philosophical-Political Profiles*, trans. Frederick G. Lawrence (Cambridge, Mass.: The MIT Press, 1983), 69, 70.

48. Habermas, "Ernst Bloch: A Marxist Schelling," 70.

49. Habermas, "Ernst Bloch: A Marxist Schelling," 70.

50. Ernst Bloch, *Subjekt-Objekt: Erlauterung zu Hegel* (Berlin: Suhrkamp, 1952), 195, translation in Alfred Schmidt, *The Concept of Nature in Marx* (London: New Left Books, 1971), 233n.

51. See Walter Benjamin, "Theses on the Philosophy of History," in *Illuminations*, ed. Hannah Arendt (New York: Schocken, 1969), 253–64.

52. Jürgen Habermas, "Walter Benjamin: Consciousness-Raising or Rescuing Critique," in *Philosophical-Political Profiles*, 148.

53. Habermas, "Walter Benjamin," 149.

54. Habermas, "Walter Benjamin," 148.

55. Habermas, "Walter Benjamin," 149.

56. Habermas, "Walter Benjamin," 145–46.

57. Schmidt, *The Concept of Nature in Marx*, 161.

58. Walter Benjamin, "The Critique of Violence," in *Reflections: Essays, Aphorisms, Autobiographical Writings*, ed. Peter Dements, trans. Edmund Jephcott (New York: Schocken, 1986).

59. Jacques Derrida, "Force of Law," in *Acts of Religion*, ed. Gil Anidjar (New York: Routledge, 2002), 276.

60. Derrida, "Force of Law," 269.

61. Derrida, "Force of Law," 272.

62. In this context, the term *strike* signifies for Benjamin an association between divine justice and the general *proletarian* strike, which endeavors to abolish the juridicosymbolic violence of the state. This is in contrast to the general *political* strike, which is directed at little more than replacing the founding violence of one state with that of another. Derrida, "Force of Law," 271.

63. Derrida, "Force of Law," 287–88.

64. Derrida, "Force of Law," 286.

65. Derrida, "Force of Law," 291.

66. Derrida, "Force of Law," 291–92.

67. Richard Rorty, "Habermas, Derrida and the Functions of Philosophy," in *The Derrida-Habermas Reader*, ed. Lasse Thomassen (Chicago: The University of Chicago Press), 61.

68. Rorty, "Habermas, Derrida and the Functions of Philosophy," 55.

69. Richard J. Bernstein, "An Allegory of Modernity/Postmodernity: Habermas and Derrida," in *The Derrida-Habermas Reader*, ed. Lasse Thomassen (Chicago: The University of Chicago Press, 2006), 93–94.

70. Bernstein, "An Allegory of Modernity/Postmodernity," 94.

71. Martin Matuštík, "Between Hope and Terror: Habermas and Derrida Plead for the Im/Possible," in *The Derrida-Habermas Reader*, ed. Lasse Thomassen (Chicago: The University of Chicago Press, 2006), 280.

72. Matuštík, "Between Hope and Terror," 280.

73. Habermas and Derrida, "February 15, or What Binds Europeans Together," 274–75.

74. Michel Rosenfeld, "Derrida's Ethical Turn and America: Looking Back from the Crossroads of Global Terrorism and the Enlightenment," *Cardozo Law Review* 27, no. 2 (2005): 838.

75. Rosenfeld, "Derrida's Ethical Turn and America," 839.

76. See Jürgen Habermas, "On the Relation between the Secular Liberal State and Religion," in *The Frankfurt School on Religion: Key Writings by the Major Thinkers*, ed. Eduardo Mendieta (New York: Routledge, 2005), 327–38, and "Religious Tolerance—The Pacemaker of Cultural Rights," in *The Derrida-Habermas Reader*, ed. Lasse Thomassen (Chicago: The University of Chicago Press, 2006), 115–27. Note that whatever his efforts to position himself as more accommodative of fundamentalist religions than Habermas, Rosenfeld must likewise extend his overture to such worldviews within the strictly Kantian idiom of toleration. For a stance on religious fundamentalism more in tune with Foucauldian genealogy and Derridean difference ethics, see Saba Mahmood, *Politics of Piety: The Islamic Revival and the Feminist Subject* (Princeton: Princeton University Press, 2005). Here Mahmood counsels both Western and non-Western thinkers to parochialize their assumptions about matters such as piety, resistance, agency, self, and authority prior to forming judgments about "illiberal" traditions such as Islamism.

77. Rosenfeld, "Derrida's Ethical Turn and America," 841.

78. Rosenfeld, "Derrida's Ethical Turn and America," 841.

79. Michael Hardt and Antonio Negri, *Multitude: War and Democracy in the Age of Empire* (New York: The Penguin Press, 2004), 238, 99.

80. See chapter 1 for a discussion of Habermas's effort to associate the cognitivist perspective of justice with the affectivity that customarily animates the actions of constitutionally patriotic moral actors.

81. Jürgen Habermas and Giovanna Borradori, "Fundamentalism and Terror—A Dialogue with Jürgen Habermas," in *Philosophy in a Time of Terror: Dialogues with Jürgen Habermas and Jacques Derrida*, ed. Giovanna Borradori (Chicago: The University of Chicago Press, 2003), 41.

82. Jürgen Habermas, *Between Facts and Norms: Contributions to a Discourse Theory of Law and Democracy*, trans. William Rehg (Cambridge, Mass.: The MIT Press, 1996), 384; emphasis in original.

83. Critchley, "Frankfurt Impromptu," 100.

84. Critchley, "Frankfurt Impromptu," 103.

85. See also in this context the discussion of Steven Hendley in chapter 2. Like Critchley, Hendley underlines the conceptual affinities between the Levinasian third party and Habermas's conception of communicative reciprocity.

86. Emmanuel Levinas, *Totality and Infinity: An Essay on Exteriority*, trans. Alphonso Lingis (Pittsburgh: Duquesne University Press, 1969).

87. Simon Critchley, "Habermas and Derrida Get Married," in *The Ethics of Deconstruction: Derrida and Levinas* (Edinburgh: Edinburgh University Press, 1999), 273–74.

88. Critchley, "Frankfurt Impromptu," 104.

Chapter Five

Taking the Measure of Care

Throughout this study, I have drawn attention to a number of fundamental conceptual disparities between Habermas's and Derrida's respective efforts to theorize the moral perspective of care for the other. These discrepancies, I have argued, are an outgrowth of their divergent approaches to the question of measurability. To Derrida, the impulse to measure, to calculate, to count carries with it an ineliminable residue of violence, inasmuch as it threatens the irreducible alterity of the other with subsumption under the *logos* of identity and sameness. The danger of this wound aside, Derrida is keen to bring the unsubsumable and incalculable example into an intrinsically unsettled alliance with the principle of equal measurement, such that a deconstructive ethics of universal justice can be thought. However from a deconstructive standpoint, an association between the two perspectives can be attempted only if the standpoint of care for the other's immeasurable otherness emerges as an architectonically preeminent moral guidepost from which the (always already deferred) quest for calculable equality takes its bearings.

To Habermas, Derrida's privileging of the orientation of asymmetrical care is wholly unwarranted, in that it divests moral agents of a common intersubjective vantage point from which to sift through competing validity claims and arrive at unforced agreements about questions of universal justice (see chapter 2). In addition, in line with writers like Adorno and Marcuse, Derrida mistakenly detects an irreducible core of violence at the heart of *measure itself*, leading him to favor the perspective of the incalculably singular at the cost of removing all categorical barriers to a re-teleologization of both nature and the knowledge of nature (see chapter 3). Yet whatever the advantages of its decidedly "disenchanted" perspective of moral universalism, I have argued that Habermas's framework is in need of reconstruction, such that it can continue to privilege the moral standpoint of egalitarian reciprocation, but on terms that render it better equipped to defend itself against the charge of cognitive centrism leveled by Derrida and other critics. Accordingly, I turn now to an overview of some of the key theoretical overtures of Axel Honneth. While a number of conceptual difficulties beleaguer Honneth's account, his interventions are to my mind the most promising launching point for such a reconstruction of Habermas's program.

HONNETH'S RECOGNITION-THEORETIC APPROACH

Over the last several decades, Axel Honneth has examined the relationship between the moral standpoints of measurable equality and unconditional care in terms that are somewhat different from those that we have considered thus far. While he evinces an unmistakable kinship with Habermas's language-theoretic reconstruction of first-generation critical theory, Honneth breaks with and extends Habermas's model, drawing out its "recognition-theoretic" implications at the level of moral psychology, sociological analysis, and philosophical categorization. In line with objections that have already been entertained, Honneth contends that Habermas's valorization of impartial, universalizable, and symmetrical argumentation procedures imposes clear limitations on his ability to reconcile the ethical attitude of benevolent care with moral obligations of equal treatment. However, *pace* critics such as Stella Gaon, Honneth sees these constraints not as obstacles to be overcome but as problems to be explicated and fleshed out. For him, a principal question is how to theorize relationships of care, love, friendship, and so forth as intersubjective orientations extending beyond, but not subsuming, the Kantian requirement of reciprocal respect. The difficulty, in other words, is how, proceeding "from a universalistic morality of respect in the Kantian tradition . . . to concede a certain centrality to [such relationships], without thereby endangering the architectonic primacy of the obligation to impartiality."[1]

At the level of moral psychology, this problem can be solved, Honneth argues, by taking note of the "genetic sequence of love and morality," that is, "the genetic manner in which the bridge between affective ties and the universalistic morality of respect is forged."[2] Honneth pursues the question of a genetic derivation of the moral standpoint in his highly influential study, *The Struggle for Recognition*. Here he identifies the writings of thinkers such as Ernst Tugendhat as propaedeutic for any such endeavor, insofar as they demonstrate that the capacity for participation in mature moral discourse is dependent upon the formation of mutual bonds of respect between a child and its early figures of attachment. These bonds assure that each comes to recognize the other as an independent, self-directed moral agent. Indeed, it is precisely "this symbiotically nourished bond, which emerges through mutually desired demarcation, that produces the degree of basic individual self-confidence indispensable for autonomous participation in public life."[3] Thus, while Honneth does not deny that unwavering, expressly partial expressions of affective sympathy, care, and love contradict the moral "command of impartiality," he does insist that the child's early experiences of unlimited care and the "spontaneous feelings and affections" that it displays toward its primary caregivers are prerequisite, indeed "conceptually and genetically prior," to the emergence of an independent moral sphere based on symmetrical norms of equal treatment. He notes that the child's affective responses "during its first years of life to the constant loving care of its guardians eventually results, under the social demand that this love be generalized, in a willingness to respect all other persons in a manner appropriate to the requirements of the categorical imperative."[4] This genetic point of view allows Honneth to locate the "structural core of ethical life" [*Sittlichkeit*] in the antecedent "element of moral particularism" that attends to expressions of loving care.[5]

To explicate the genetic sequence of loving care and universalistic morality, Honneth draws from numerous quarters—for example, the object-relations theories of Donald Winnicott and Jessica Benjamin, and recent work in moral and developmental psychology. In this context, the perspective of an author like Stanley Cavell is of particular interest insofar as it underscores both the temporal and conceptual priority of the recognitional orientation of care in relation to all other modes of linguistic sociation. Cavell's research, notes Honneth, shows that the meaning of any given class of linguistic propositions becomes apparent only from the standpoint of "affective acknowledgement." "To put it briefly, the acknowledgement of the other constitutes a nonepistemic prerequisite for linguistic understanding."[6] For present purposes, the specific psychosocial and developmental postulates undergirding Honneth's account of the genetic sequence of care and morality are of no pressing concern. The preceding overview should be sufficient to situate this conception within Honneth's broader typology of three discrete "forms of recognition," a fuller explication of which is now in order.

In constructing his model, Honneth embarks upon a lengthy and rigorous examination of the portrait of ethical life set forth in Hegel's Jena-period *Realphilosophie*, together with the modification of this view found in George Herbert Mead's naturalistic theory of intersubjectivity. Revising and extending these analyses, Honneth identifies three divergent but interconnected domains of interaction, which in his view originate in three correspondingly different patterns of mutual recognition: affective expressions of love, care, friendship, and so on (manifest as emotional support in primary relationships); rights (expressed as cognitive respect in legal relations); and solidarity (articulated as social esteem in specific communities of value). Each of these spheres corresponds, moreover, "to a particular potential for moral development and to distinct types of individual-relations-to-self."[7]

Let us consider, firstly, the interrelationship between loving care and legal rights as conceived in Honneth's tripartite schematic. In accord with the genetic derivation of moral discourse that we have just sketched, Honneth maintains that mature, primary loving relationships—constituted by strong, affective bonds of support among a limited number of persons—can be mapped back to early experiences of continuous care, which accord children "the basic self-confidence to assert their needs in an unforced manner."[8] The experience of legal recognition is likewise said to have its conceptual and genetic origins in a child's early encounters with affective care; however, within the domain of legal rights, the crucial individual-relation-to-self fostered is not self-confidence but self-respect:

> The idea that self-respect is for legal relations what basic self-confidence [is] for the love relationship is already suggested by the conceptual appropriateness of viewing rights as depersonalized symbols of social respect in just the way that love can be conceived as the affectional expression of care retained over distance. Whereas the latter generates, in every human being, the psychological foundation for trusting one's own sense of one's needs and urges, the former gives rise to the form of consciousness in which one is able to respect oneself because one deserves the respect of everyone else.[9]

On this view, legal rights are understood to empower individuals to view themselves as sharing with all other members of their community the competencies necessary to engage in public moral discourses. Legal rights, that is to say, position us to gain universal recognition from our interaction partners as autonomous, morally responsible persons and to develop a commensurate sense of self-respect—i.e., an affirmative attitude toward our own capacities to participate in processes of discursive will-formation.

In addition to the spheres of affective and legal recognition, Honneth contends that the attainment of "an undistorted relation-to-self"—a self that relates positively to its own concrete abilities and traits—is dependent upon a third recognitional pattern, whose conceptual and genetic antecedents likewise lie in the child's early experiences of unlimited care. He names this final domain of recognition social esteem, which can be properly accounted for, in his estimation, only within the context of the intersubjectively shared value horizon of a given community. "For self and other can mutually esteem each other as individualized persons only on the condition that they share an orientation to those values and goals that indicate to each other the significance or contribution of their qualities for the life of the other."[10] Because it is oriented toward and conditioned by a community's prevailing ethical conceptions and objectives, social esteem admits of a context-dependent character that places it at odds with the pattern of recognition conveyed through the domain of legal rights, which, as we have just seen, is "a medium that expresses the universal features of human subjects."[11]

These differences aside, Honneth stresses that the forms of social esteem and relations of legality familiar to us today owe their specifically *modern* character to the conceptual and sociostructural transformations marking the transition from corporative societies to those of the present capitalist era. With regard to social esteem, the key movement is from concepts of social honor to categories of social "standing" or "prestige." According to Honneth, the idea of honor was deployed in traditional societies as a subjectively defined measure of the moral qualities ascribed to one's personality and to the collective identity of his or her group or social class. In modern societies, in contrast, patterns of social esteem are no longer tethered to substantive value-hierarchies, legal privileges, or class-specific proscriptions for an individual's moral conduct. Loosed from their metaphysical foundations, concepts of honor are gradually "watered down" into notions of prestige or standing, which take an individual's unique accomplishments and abilities to be the principal criteria for socially according esteem. Indeed, because the orientation is no longer "towards collective traits but towards the capacities developed by the individual in the course of his or her life," the modern view of esteem "signifies only the degree of social recognition the individual earns for his or her form of self-realization by thus contributing, to a certain extent, to the practical realization of society's abstractly defined goals."[12]

For present purposes, Honneth's account of the modern pattern of social esteem is of interest insofar as it is bound up with a conception of "solidarity," which can be fruitfully contrasted with Habermas's portrait of the same category (see chapter 1). For Honneth, social esteem can be said to take on a solidaristic character only in association with forms of recognition wherein the relationship between biographically individuated subjects is symmetrical, rather than asymmetrical. In other words, esteem may be adjudged as "modern" only if it breaks with asymmetrical ideals such as honor and reorganizes itself around symmetrical patterns of interaction "that allow the abilities and traits of the other to appear significant for shared praxis."[13] This expressly symmetrical reorientation notwithstanding, the modern esteem-based form of recognition continues to be drawn in relation to what individuals "can accomplish for society within the context of their *particular* forms of self-realization"[14]—the chief distinction being that unlike its historical antecedent, modern esteem is no longer *constitutively* linked to group status and collective identity.

Because it envisages the consociates of a shared form of life as possessing some level of concern for their mutual well-being, ideals, and value-orientations, Honneth's idea of solidaristic esteem can attend to the criticisms of Habermasian discourse ethics advanced by thinkers like Seyla Benhabib and Stella Gaon. Like them, he pleas for a concept of solidarity situated beyond the limited moral purview of autonomous, unambiguously rational Kantian subjects. Solidaristic relationships, argues Honneth, "inspire *not just passive tolerance but felt concern* for what is individual and particular about the other person. For only to the degree that I actively *care* about the development of the other's characteristics (which seem foreign to me) can our shared goals be realized."[15]

Note, however, that while Honneth's recognition-theoretic view of solidarity does allow for a degree of mutual concern for the welfare of others over and above that which can be accommodated within a strictly Kantian ideal of measurable equality, his effort to reserve a place for the empathetic dimension of social esteem is ultimately pulled short by the universalistic moral obligations of reciprocal respect that he is unwilling to destabilize. Thus, while he endeavors to go "beyond the bounds of the cognitive moment of ethical knowledge" and include an "emotional element" of sympathy within reciprocative solidarity,[16] Honneth can pursue this gesture in a universalistic direction only at the cost of a category mistake. For Honneth, then, solidarity

> cannot be conceived of without that element of particularism inherent in the development of every social community, insofar as members agree on particular, ethically defined goals and thus share the experience of specific burdens. . . . Hence, in contrast to the universalist idea of equal treatment, there is something abstractly utopian about the notion of a solidarity that encompasses all humanity; this makes it all the more implausible as a universalist representative of that moral principle which in the form of unilateral care and benevolence has always constituted a transcending element of our social world.[17]

Honneth's inability to fully reconcile the principle of equalitarian reciprocity with the particularistic moral compass of solidarity is precisely the same limitation that Habermas encountered when he attempted to mobilize solidarity in the interest of retaining "a remnant of good at the core of the right" (see chapter 1). For Honneth, too, solidarity cannot mean that "we esteem each other to the same degree."[18]

Honneth faults Benhabib, for one, for being drawn to exactly this sort of desideratum when she recommends extending the boundaries of moral discourse to the point where "visions of the good life underlying conceptions of justice and assumptions about needs and interests sustaining rights claims become visible."[19] Honneth is quite prepared to acknowledge solidarity "as an interactive relationship in which subjects mutually sympathize with their various ways of life because, among themselves, they esteem each other symmetrically."[20] However, he maintains that Benhabib's proposal risks contravening the limits of the Kantian conception of justice insofar as it entreats the unilateral relation of care to envelop the entire field of moral discourse— an outcome that Benhabib, who remains in the end a moral universalist, is herself unwilling to countenance (see chapter 1). If they are to successfully negotiate their views and beliefs publicly, Honneth stresses, dialogic subjects must at some point dissociate themselves from affective attachments and pursue the goal of equal treatment through an appeal to symmetrical norms of moral discourse. We can arrive at a just settlement of conflicting interests, "only if all persons involved show one another the same amount of respect *without allowing feelings or sympathy and affection to come into play.* Thus attitudes of asymmetrical responsibility, on which, for instance, care and benevolence are based, must remain excluded from the procedure of a practical discourse."[21]

Corollary to the model of recognition just outlined, Honneth demarcates three forms of "misrecognition," or "disrespect," each of which is said to be uniquely injurious to its corresponding domain of recognition. With respect to affective attachments, misrecognition involves some form of damage to the integrity of the bodily self (e.g., through physical abuse); with legal relations, it entails the denial of rights and various measures of exclusion; and with regard to social esteem, acts of denigration and insult are the salient harms.[22] Although manifest in different ways, a common self-other orientation undergirds all three forms of misrecognition—namely, the "tendency to perceive other persons as mere insensate objects."[23] In fact, Honneth finds that in each instance, our reflexive actions have lost "consciousness of their origin in an act of antecedent recognition" and crossed "the threshold to pathology, skepticism, or—as Adorno would have called it—identity thought."[24] In portraying the "amnesia," or the "forgetting," of the antecedent recognitional stance as a *pathological* tendency, Honneth endeavors to reconstruct the idea that Lukács, appealing to Marx and Weber, attempted to work out under the rubric of "reification" more than eighty years ago.

RECONSTRUCTING HABERMAS AND DERRIDA ON RECOGNITION-THEORETIC TERMS?

The foregoing overview has brought into relief a number of interesting points of resonance and disparity between Honneth's recognition theory and the discourse-ethical perspective of Habermas.[25] As Honneth suggests, their conceptual compatibility appears to reside in their joint allegiance to the tradition of a certain "left Hegelianism." Consonant with the latter, both authors attempt to locate within contemporary societies a partially articulated normative framework of "emancipatory interests" against which the task of establishing domination-free social relations is understood to take its moral bearings. Indeed like Habermas, Honneth maintains that a principal aim of critical social theory is to identify those elements of practice or experience that amount to "socially embodied reason insofar as [they] possess a surplus of rational norms or organizational principles that press for their own realization."[26] The effort to immanently expose existing normative principles as carriers of a moral claim for just social relations that is "broader and more demanding than what has already been realized in society" is, for both writers, precisely what gives critical theory its *critical* impulse.[27]

There is a significant break with Habermas, however, in that Honneth sees this transcending potential as residing not so much in the normative presuppositions of language-based validity claims as in a core of sociohistorically variable expectations of recognition, whose underlying principles frame the terms in which individuals receive and accord approval to one another. All such epochal "recognition orders" are marked, moreover, by a struggle over the appropriate application and interpretation of the surplus validity specific to the three general principles of recognition (love, law, and achievement) identified in Honneth's model. Honneth takes as a case in point the individualist achievement principle, which on his account has become associated with the recognitional orientation of social esteem in modern societies. On the one hand, the achievement norm has been appropriated by elites within bourgeois-capitalist society to justify a highly unequal distribution of goods and life chances. On the other hand, although it has been mobilized to propagate social inequality and legitimate the privileged appropriation of particular resources, this principle contains at its normative foundation "a claim to consider the individual achievements of all members of society fairly and appropriately in the form of mutual esteem"—a standard to which countless contemporary social movements have appealed in their efforts to secure legal and political rights.[28] In order to position itself as a framework of immanent social critique, Honneth contends that a theory of justice must wield the achievement norm, as well as the general recognitional principles of love and law, "against the facticity of their social interpretation."[29]

Habermas, argues Honneth, fails to theorize recognition in such terms and instead subsumes the concept within his account of the transcendental-emancipatory properties of communicative reason *as such*. This emphasis on the normative presuppositions of human language leads Habermas to demote the perspective of recognition in favor of a model in which the sphere of social integration is differentiated from that of system integration. As we have noted (see chapter 3), on this move Habermas distinguishes between the instrumental-rational organizing imperatives of the state and the economy (undergirded by the delinguistified steering media of political power and money, respectively) and the noninstrumental type of communicative rationality that characterizes the sociation of the lifeworld. The price paid for this categorical bifurcation is inattention to what Honneth views as the expressly *normative* dimensions of the so-called subsystems, whose organizational framework Habermas would like to stylize as anonymous and value free. From the latter vantage point, we are hard pressed to "discover the principles of normative integration in the institutionalized spheres of society that open up the prospects of desirable improvements."[30] For Honneth, that is to say, social struggles over the scope and direction of the putatively value-neutral steering imperatives of the state and the economy entail an appeal to the normative assumptions that underlie these very directives. Habermas's system/lifeworld paradigm is accused of losing sight of this possibility entirely. In fact, according to Honneth, the theory of reification that Habermas constructs on the basis of this model[31] harbors a decidedly functionalist bias, insofar as it enjoins moral actors to determine when the "functionally necessary" steering directives of the subsystems overstep their remit of benign action coordination and begin to colonize the communicative norms of the lifeworld: "The question concerning the point at which objectifying attitudes unfold their reifying effects cannot be answered by speaking of functional requirements in an apparently nonnormative way."[32] Against Habermas, then, Honneth pleas for a recognition-theoretic "moral monism" that collapses the distinction between social integration and system integration, thereby allowing us to fully acknowledge the normative expectations that undergird action in, to use Habermas's terminology, both the lifeworld and system spheres of society.

These differences over the terms in which the contemporary social field and the social struggles within it are to be conceptualized are indeed significant. Honneth and Habermas are nevertheless united in what I have just characterized as a left-Hegelian endeavor to retain within critical theory a normative yardstick against which the domination of human subjects can be at once diagnosed and called into question as a pathology to be overcome through processes of social transformation. Although theorized from different conceptual vantage points, each author views *measurable equality* as a normative orientation already at play in modern capitalist societies, one to whose unrealized or "surplus" validity moral agents are enjoined to appeal in their efforts to establish a more just society. In both, the principle of equal treatment is thus valorized as a starting point for a political ethic and an attendant critique of contemporary social conditions. To Honneth, the privileging of this standpoint is consonant with, and is in fact justified by, the "moral grammar" of the overwhelming majority of contemporary social conflicts (including so-called identity-political struggles), which entail the public mobilization and justification of "moral arguments somehow tied to the equality principle."[33] *Pace* communitarian thinkers such as Michael Sandel, for example, he argues that a culture, community, or social group that demands that its particular value convictions, ways of life, and constitutive practices should be esteemed *for their own sake* is culpable of exceeding the equal treatment ideal's normative horizon. In fact, because claims for this sort of unqualified social esteem are not amenable to adjudication in accord with norms of equality and fairness, they, like gestures of affective sympathy, issue from "a process of judgment that escapes our control" and are therewith denied legitimacy at the level of moral argumentation.[34] No less than Habermas, then, Honneth seeks to subordinate the asymmetrical attitude of care to the universalistic symmetricality of publically adjudicated moral discourses. Indeed, in both writers, relations of symmetrical intersubjectivity are ultimately positioned as a *constraint* on relations of asymmetrical intersubjectivity.

Agreed as they may be on the propriety of a certain left-Hegelian moral universal universalism, Honneth has defended the architectonic preeminence of the equality principle on terms that appear to redress some of the care-theoretic weaknesses of Habermas's approach. Indeed, in conceptualizing asymmetrical relations of care as conceptually and genetically prior to all mature manifestations of love, legal rights, and social esteem, Honneth adds something to our understanding of care that escapes even commentators such as Rehg, who have been at pains to coimbricate the ethics of care with the application of the procedural norms of the Habermasian discourse ethic. Because they are anchored not in the cognitive adjudication of contested validity claims but in an orientation of unconditional felt concern for the "concrete other," Honnethian struggles for recognition expand the compass of morality beyond the goal of mutual understanding and reserve a place for the emotive, empathetic dimension of communicative sociation—the reciprocal recognition of goods, affects, and needs—that accounts for one's willingness to engage in moral deliberation in the first place. Honneth can on these terms rectify the "motivational deficit" of discourse ethics, about which critics such as Sharon Krause have complained, but without inviting—à la Benhabib and others—the prospect of a blurred boundary between affective care and the requirement of impartial, reciprocal respect.

Honneth's approach also seems well equipped to attend to a number of the deficits that we have identified in relation to Derrida's privileging of the standpoint of the incalculably singular. Honneth maintains that while Derrida may be astute to thematize "a degree of reciprocal benevolence greater than that which can be observed in the Kantian requirement of respect,"[35] he errs in presenting the asymmetrical viewpoint of care as a moral guidepost that is oriented, in a "self-correcting manner," toward the practical realization of equal treatment. In fact, in effectively integrating the two different perspectives into a single framework, the deconstructive ethics of radical singularity transgresses the limits of the Kantian ideal of universal justice: it grants unilateral relations of care entrée into the arena of moral discourse to the point where agents are left ill situated to successfully adjudicate their views and beliefs publicly.

Furthermore, Honneth offers a way around the prospect of a re-teleologized encounter with the natural world, which I have attempted to expose, in chapter 3, as a risk of Derrida's antifoundationalist critique of the methodological dualism upheld in the philosophical tradition of Kant. Leaning on Adorno's "libidinally cathected" object attachment theory, Honneth entertains, with Derrida, the possibility of extending the attitude of affective sympathy toward the realm of things. Crucially, however, there is no danger from Honneth's standpoint of "re-enchanting" nature, inasmuch as the sympathy in question is of an expressly "indirect" character, derived from the attitudes that we experience others as displaying toward objects in the noumenal world. As a result, Honneth, allows for the adoption of a certain attitude of "care" for nonspeaking nature, while at the same time demurring from Derrida's depiction of the calculative attitude as always and "forever wounding." [36]

FOREGROUNDING RECOGNITION AT THE COST OF OBSCURING THE OBJECTIVATING ATTITUDE?

While Honneth's framework seems to provide a number of important correctives to the theorizations of care advanced in both Derridean difference ethics and Habermasian discourse ethics, one may nevertheless consider whether something crucial has been given up in the move away from Habermas's dualistic framework of knowledge-constitutive interests. One such drawback has been suggested by Nancy Fraser. Fraser notes that Honneth's theory spreads the compass of recognition so wide as to lose sight of what are in fact the thoroughgoingly objectified organizing principles of the modern political and economic subsystems. With Habermas, she characterizes these domains as marked by the capacity to coordinate action independent of the argumentation procedures to which communicative consociates appeal when they engage in processes of discursive will-formation. Honneth is accused of undergirding the organizing directives of the subsystems with so much normative significance as to implicate him in a broader "cultural turn" in critical theory, in which the utility of concepts such as system integration, political power, and the profit motive is obscured. For his part, Honneth expressly denies that he is participating in any such effort to analyze phenomena such as market processes solely with reference to "cultural recognition." Rather, his aim is to uncover modern capitalist society's "epoch-specific grammar of social justice and injustice," from whose vantage point communication within the political and economic spheres is to a large extent structured. *Contra* both Fraser *and* the so-called cultural turn, Honneth's idea is that

> even structural transformations in the economic sphere are not independent of the normative expectations of those affected, but depend at least on their tacit consent. Like the integration of all other spheres, the development of the capitalist market can only occur in the form of a process of symbolically mediated negotiation directed toward the interpretation of underlying normative principles.[37]

To Honneth, there is thus a greater degree of "normativity" at play within the organizational ambit of the capitalist political economy than received frameworks of Marxism, as well as Habermasian communications theory, have been willing to acknowledge. To underline the extent to which action in the capitalist market is undergirded by normative rules, Honneth interrogates the concept of "deregulation." Within the context of modern welfare state societies, this idea, he argues, quickly presents itself as "a direct indication of the fact that the labor market is organized by legal norms that express the moral interests of those involved."[38] This view stands in sharp distinction to Habermas's portrayal of the subsystems as underlain by autonomous, extranormative steering imperatives. According to the argument initially worked out by Habermas in *Legitimation Crisis* and Claus Offe in *Contradictions of the Welfare State*, the capacities for normative justification and social contestation reside in the lifeworld domain alone. In fact, for both authors, the prospect of a legitimation crisis arises in the contemporary public sphere precisely at the point when the welfare state's effort to administratively coordinate the media-steered activities of competing capitals results in the thematization of counterfactual universal norms—claims that *unintentionally* subvert the prereflexive sociocultural traditions and privatizing/depoliticizing motivational syndromes (consumerism, leisureism, and so forth) that the state is also charged with perpetuating in the interest of system reproduction and maintenance. As Habermas puts it in *Legitimation Crisis*,

> At every level, administrative planning produces unintended unsettling and publicizing effects. These effects weaken the justification potential of traditions

that have been flushed out of their nature-like course of development. Once their unquestionable character has been destroyed, the stabilization of validity claims can succeed only through discourse. The stirring up of cultural affairs that are taken for granted thus furthers the politicization of areas of life previously assigned to the private sphere.[39]

It should be stressed that Habermas has never denied that he is setting forth anything other than Weberian "ideal types" when he distinguishes between the norm-free, purposive-rational logic of system integration and norm-laden logic of social integration.[40] In fact, it seems to me that even on strictly Habermasian premises, one could account for at least some degree of recognitional normativity within the subsystems, although perhaps not enough to satisfy the morally monistic objectives of Honneth's model. Be this as it may, Honneth does in fact go too far, in my estimation, in packing the concept of recognition into what Habermas, Weber, and the Marxist tradition have theorized (if only on an ideal-typic level) as the reified operations of the capitalist market and state apparatus. Even if it is not his express aim to analyze these spheres in terms of cultural recognition alone or to discount the importance of steering directives such as the profit motive, these conclusions are in fact potential by-products of Honneth's endeavor to frontload the concept of recognition while refusing to categorically distinguish the logic of system integration from that of social integration.

This objection points to a more deep-seated conceptual limitation of the moral monism upheld in Honneth's recognition theory. Put briefly, his model risks leaving the status of the "reifying attitude" epistemologically ambiguous. This danger is perhaps unavoidable in view of his break on a metatheoretical level with Habermas's framework of knowledge-constitutive interests. In chapter 3, I considered a number of the advantages that this dualistic perspective offers over its monistic competitors. I noted that the aim of Habermas's theory is to differentiate the scientific-technical, the moral-practical, and the aesthetic-expressive as categorically discrete knowledge domains and to connect each with a corresponding interest intrinsic to our anthropological endowment as language-speaking beings. In the case of the *Naturwissenschaften*, the effort is to constitutively link the empirical-analytic orientation with the human interest in the prediction and control of the nonspeaking world. Habermas can now theorize the encroachment of the objectivating attitude of the modern sciences upon the lifeworld as a pathological development, to the extent that it threatens to distort the latter's noninstrumental norms of communicative sociation. A principal benefit of Habermas's methodological dualism, I argued, is its ability to offer a compelling account of reification in modern societies as well as a critique of positivism that does not leave the status of the natural sciences epistemologically hanging, as is the case with Lukács and much of the ensuing tradition of Western Marxism.

In frontloading the perspective of recognition to the degree that he does, it seems to me that unlike Habermas, Honneth is likewise in jeopardy of allowing the epistemological standing of the reifying perspective to become ambiguous. As we have noted, Honneth is careful to dispute the contention (of Heidegger and Dewey, for example) that adopting a reified stance toward insensate objects is in itself a violation of the normative foundations of our social practices. It is by no means the case, he insists, that "our physical surroundings must always already have been disclosed to us in their qualitative significance before we can relate to them in a theoretical fashion."[41] On this conviction, Honneth appears to reject Lukács's nature-theoretic monism in favor of an epistemological dualism consistent with that set forth in Habermas's theory. However, Honneth's model is in my view hard pressed to defend this position absent an appeal to something like the Habermasian framework of knowledge-constitutive interests. Indeed, establishing a theoretical link between the *knowledge* of reified objects/processes and the human *interest* in their prediction and control is a problem that recedes significantly from the compass of Honneth's recognition-theoretic account of the genetic sequence of care and detached cognition.

The retreat of the knowledge/human interest paradigm is so thoroughgoing, in fact, that objectivating modes of thought and their associated organizational frameworks (science/technics, state/economy) are in danger of being obscured *as such* under the cover of an all-pervasive phenomenology of recognitional experience—Honneth's vehement objections to such charges notwithstanding. It is no doubt the case that at the level of *social integration*, introducing more of the recognitional orientation than can be countenanced on Habermas's premises poses no untoward difficulties.[42] On the contrary, as I have suggested, such a move goes a long way toward redressing the various objections that have been raised against Habermas's attempt to ground moral discourse in the cognitive redemption of language-based validity claims. Moreover, *qua* social integration, Honneth's effort to recast the problem of reification as a pathological "forgetting" of the antecedent recognitional stance is likewise an important addendum to Habermas, who views the matter strictly in terms of the instrumental-technical colonization of communicative norms.

Its advantages vis-à-vis the social integration–theoretic dimensions of communications theory aside, Honneth's framework would be prudent to retain rather than discard Habermas's account of a knowledge-constitutive association between the empirical-analytic attitude and the human interest in the control and mastery of insensate objects and mechanisms. In collapsing the division between system integration and social integration and failing to clarify the status of the objectivating standpoint at the level of epistemology and human interests, the morally monistic vantage point of recognition theory risks opening itself up to an all-encompassing phenomenology of recognitional experience—an accusation that Honneth himself is keen to avoid. Accordingly, my proposal is to allow, with Honneth, more of the "recognitional" attitude into the domain of social integration than Habermas has been willing to countenance. At the same time, I insist, with Habermas and against Honneth, that the epistemological compass of the reifying disposition must remain expressly confined to the extranormative object domains of nature and the media-steered subsystems, and kept, thereby, categorically distinct from both the immeasurable vantage point of care and the noninstrumental type of rationality that undergirds the reciprocative norms of moral argumentation.

Yet before such a move can be undertaken productively, a fundamental conceptual obstacle must be overcome. This difficulty concerns Honneth's insistence upon the genetic-conceptual primacy of the care perspective for *all* detached modes of cognition. This position is in need of refutation if we are to excise the orientation of care from the objectivating attitude's epistemological orbit in the manner just proposed. It is admittedly well beyond the scope of the present discussion to mount such a criticism with reference to the rather expansive body of moral- and developmental-psychology literature bearing on Honneth's argument. One may nevertheless initiate a tentative riposte to Honneth on this score by appealing to the macrosocial perspective of systems theory—a vantage point that, as previously noted, has been invoked by authors like Habermas, Weber, and Marx to account for the organizing imperatives that underlie spheres of life (ideal-typically, the state and the economy) wherein action is directed "behind the backs" of the existential motivations, emotive dispositions, and normative standpoints of the agents involved. From a system-theoretic point of view, the latter orientations are envisaged as "detached" from the organizing logics of the modern economic and political subsystems, which are guided by what Habermas calls the "delinguistified steering media" of money and administrative power, respectively. According to this conception, there is simply no precursive attitude of "care" to be retrieved from the reifying standpoint—either at the level of system integration or with respect to the empirical-analytic investigation of the natural world. In what follows, I shall attempt to explicate this counterargument to Honneth's position, demonstrating why it is advisable to expunge the immeasurable vantage point of care from the conceptual and genetic firmament of the objectivating stance.

THE EPISTEMOLOGY OF CARE

At this point in our argument, something like a schematic for a reconstruction of the Habermasian paradigm is beginning to emerge (see table 5.1). In this outline, key aspects of Honneth's recognition model have been grafted onto to Habermas's framework on terms that leave the latter's overarching conceptual morphology intact. A principal advantage of such a reconstruction, I have argued, is the preservation of the *cordon sanitaire* that Habermas draws between empirical-analytic and historical-hermeneutic problem-solving languages. In chapter 3, I endeavored to explicate the usefulness of Habermas's epistemological dualism with respect to the question of care for the other of nature. I shall now attempt to further elucidate the propriety of Habermas's bifurcated account of human reason with respect to the problem of care for the human other.

It will perhaps be instructive to return in this context to William Rehg's hypothetical account of the plight of John, the professor of philosophy who accepts employment on a year-to-year contract basis at a university in expectation that this work will eventually lead to a tenure-track position (see chapter 1). After several years at the university, officials surprise John by announcing that all tenure-track positions will now be awarded on the basis of a nationwide merit search. According to Rehg, if the agents involved in this scenario were to attempt to decide, from a discourse-ethical standpoint, whether the university's merit norm is justifiably applicable in John's case, they would find themselves immediately and inescapably enmeshed in questions of care ethics. Rehg considers a number of possible circumstances on the basis of which those affected would be justified in amending the university's merit norm so that John and other contract faculty members might be spared from the "weal and woe" of a devastating existential injury (e.g., the loss of longstanding ties to the local community). Let us now complicate the panoply of potential scenarios still further, highlighting a problem that Rehg does not entertain. Suppose that all members of the philosophy department faculty agree that the merit norm should be qualified in x manner in consideration of the needs and concerns of applicants in John's position. They now present their proposed revision to the job search rule to the university's human resources department, but are met with staunch resistance from its administrators. It turns out that the university is in the midst of a severe budgetary crisis; in order to qualify for much-needed federal funding, it must apply the merit norm precisely as initially stipulated (i.e., with no qualifications whatsoever). From the standpoint of the human resources department, there is simply no scope for attending to the "weal and woe" that threatens to befall contract workers like John as a consequence of the rule's application.[43]

Table 5.1. The Epistemology of Care: A Proposed Schematic

ACTION TYPE	INSTRUMENTAL-STRATEGIC	COMMUNICATIVE		AESTHETIC-EXPRESSIVE
ACTION DOMAIN	media-steered subsystems	◄——————— lifeworld ———————►		"nature itself"
TYPE OF ACTION COORDINATION	system integration	◄———— social integration ————►		
RECOGNITION DOMAIN	x	law	solidarity	care
RECOGNITION PATTERN	x	cognitive respect	social esteem	affective sympathy
MORAL STANDPOINT	x	universal norms/justice	ethical values/goods	"goodness"
SELF-OTHER RELATIONS	x	direct	direct	direct
SELF-NONHUMAN OTHER RELATIONS	x	x	x	indirect—"transformed" nature (*Umwelt*); animals
RETRIEVABLE ANTECEDENT ATTITUDE OF CARE?	x	✓	✓	✓
HUMAN INTERESTS	prediction and control ——►	mutual understanding ——►		"world disclosure"
EPISTEMOLOGICAL ORIENTATION	empirical-analytic ——►	historical-hermeneutic ——►		

In such a scenario, the deficits of Honneth's recognitional monism are readily apparent. Having dissolved the distinction between system integration and social integration, his model enjoins us to envisage the actions of the university's human resource bureaucracy as undergirded with as much recognitional significance as action in the philosophy faculty's "lifeworld." Indeed, in Honneth's account, the Habermasian view that action coordination in the bureaucratic sphere is directed by extranormative, delinguistified steering media of administrative power is in danger of being eclipsed by a phenomenology of recognitional experience assumed to pervade all spheres of life. I maintain, against Honneth, that the recognitional orientation is at best of minimal significance with respect to the organizing principles of the system domain, and is therefore rightly jettisoned from the latter's ambit at the level of ideal-typic categorization (see table 5.1). Indeed, Habermas is in my view right to portray action in the modern bureaucratic and economic subsystems as coordinated chiefly by prediscursive organizing imperatives, which do not oblige actors to reach either a universally binding consensus about contested validity claims or evince affective sympathy for the unrepresentable existential sufferings of others. Habermas would thus have little difficulty accounting for the intransigence displayed by our human resource bureaucrats when confronted with a request to amend an officially prescribed rule in the interest of averting the potentially unjust consequences of its application. Circumscribed by the logic of strategic rationality, the department is effectively constrained from abiding by either discourse-ethical principles of moral argumentation or the ethics of care: whatever the personal convictions of its administrators, its juridical remit in this matter is ultimately delimited by the prescribed conditions for the receipt of federal funding.

In his essay on "The Idea of the University," Habermas, recalling the arguments of Max Weber, makes precisely this point: in highly differentiated modern societies, the operations of universities and other bureaucratic institutions depend "on the detachment of organizational goals and functions from the motivations of their members."[44] According to this view, the onus would be on the "lifeworld" agents in our scenario—i.e., those faculty members who remain unconstrained by the organizing imperatives of administrative power—to erect a "democratic dam" against those strategic directives such that they are no longer poised to distort procedures of moral disputation and thereby hinder a just resolution of conflicts. Such intervention might even take the form of an act of nonviolent civil disobedience wherein the resolve of university officials to abide by an unjust norm is challenged. In *Between Facts and Norms*, Habermas refers to intercessions of this sort as acts of "communicative power." Implemented "in the manner of a siege," communicative power, he contends, "influences the premises of judgment and decision making in the political system without intending to conquer the system itself. It thus aims to assert its imperatives in the only language the besieged fortress understands: it takes responsibility for the pool of reasons that administrative power can handle instrumentally but cannot ignore, given its juridical structure."[45]

In contrast, for Honneth the task for our agents would be to recover the "forgotten" antecedent orientation of recognitional care that lies behind and makes possible the detached bureaucratic logic of the university's announced merit norm. Retrieval of this kind is necessary, Honneth would surely argue, inasmuch as this rule promises to subject contract workers like John to the pathology of misrecognition—in this case, through a loss of cognitive respect in the legal sphere. However, precisely insofar as economic and bureaucratic reasoning is constituted by what Habermas rightly understands as "a systemic character [that produces] structures detached from the lifeworld,"[46] I maintain that there is simply no precursive orientation of care to be recovered from the conceptual orbit of an institution like our human resources department. In fact, in insinuating the attitude of care into their conceptual and genetic core, Honneth's approach risks losing sight of the fact that the economic and bureaucratic spheres of modern societies have a purposive-rational "life of their own," which is quite distinct from the hermeneutic-historical discourses characteristic of the lifeworld.

REDRESSING THE "INEFFABILITY" DEFICIT:
TOWARD A CARE-THEORETIC REVIVIFICATION
OF THE KNOWLEDGE/HUMAN INTEREST PARADIGM

In chapter 4, I drew attention to a charge leveled by Martin Morris. In sympathy with Derrida, Morris challenges Seyla Benhabib's understanding of her own approach as a *critical* theory: "One does not get critical theory by coordinating epistemology (social theory) with normative philosophy; one gets mainstream theories that moralize."[47] I noted that Morris would presumably extend this accusation to Habermas's project, whose overarching philosophical aims Benhabib shares. In view of the arguments that have now been advanced, we are perhaps in a position to turn the tables, as it were, on Morris. If our position is sound, then the critical character of Habermas's communications theory is vouchsafed by precisely the robust framework of epistemological dualism that it deploys to account for action in the system and lifeworld spheres of contemporary society. It is this vantage point that makes clear *why* the orientation of care is theorized in such precarious terms by authors like Derrida and—as we have just seen—Honneth. In their writings, the perspective of instrumental measure either fails to be distinguished (Derrida) or is insufficiently distinguished (Honneth) from that of noninstrumental measure at the level of epistemology and human interests. In Derrida's case, not only is there no such segregation of measurability standpoints; the principle of *measure as such* is undermined, such that the gesture of care for the unquantifiably nonidentical is allowed to emerge as a preeminent moral orientation for our dealings with one another and with nature. In Honneth, there is, to be sure, an attempt to valorize the perspective of equal measurement as a normative bulwark against the potential (of deconstruction and other approaches) to permit the care perspective to "go wild"—to infect the impartialist vantage point of justice as well as the reifying stance that modern science and technics adopt toward the external world. Honneth's account is nonetheless lacking in crucial resources: it is devoid of a firm epistemological vantage point from which to differentiate the *immeasurability* of care from the distinct standpoints of *measurability* that circumscribe communicative and instrumental frameworks of interaction. Instead, in Honneth, care is situated as the genetic and conceptual ballast for *all* spheres of measure.

Yet on this move, Honneth, no less than Derrida, has hung far too much on the shoulders of care. He has shunted aside a compelling account of the empirical-analytic and the hermeneutic-historical as clearly demarcated epistemological orientations. Arising equiprimordially from "actual structures of human life," these problem-solving languages are associated, on Habermas's account, with correspondingly distinct knowledge domains (nature/media-steered subsystems and lifeworld) and human interests (prediction/control and mutual understanding). This dualistic epistemological vantage point elucidates precisely why care, in dissociating itself from the principle of measure, cannot be permitted to commingle with either the objectivating attitude of the mathematical sciences or the impartialist perspective of justice, both of which are bound up—albeit on very different terms—in the *logos* of measurability. The theory of knowledge-constitutive interests shows that in a perspective like Derrida's, the gesture of care radically destabilizes the principle of measure—in both its instrumental and noninstrumental incarnations—only to immediately place the approach at risk of sacrificing its own critical aspirations to what Thomas McCarthy has aptly called the "politics of the ineffable."[48] Indeed, while it would like us to imagine care and justice as tensely yet productively affiliated with one another, deconstruction is commanded by its own thoroughgoingly antiuniversalist precepts to contest received notions of rights, justice, tolerance, and reciprocal respect without *express* recourse to the principles of measurable equality that are needed to carry forth this criticism at the level of ethics and politics. From Derrida's standpoint, that is to say, the attitude of immeasurable care for the wholly other cannot help but commandeer and undercut the vantage point of measurable universal justice, precisely because for deconstruction, "democracy to come" must be situated beyond all "calculable relations." As McCarthy observes, "[e]ven if his heart is in the right place, and even if his 'anarchy' is 'responsible,' we know from experience that the devaluation of these modes [of measurability] opens a space, or rather creates a vacuum that can be filled in quite different ways—for example, by a call for submission to some indeterminate authority." In this sense, "Derrida's discourse . . . *lives* from the enormous elasticity, not to say vagueness and ambiguity of his key terms."[49]

Although it seeks to prioritize the principle of equal treatment and thereby stave off the potential for ethicopolitical ineffability to which an approach like Derrida's is prone, Honneth's recognition model is categorically hamstrung in this regard: no less than deconstruction, it provides us with no stable epistemological basis upon which to distinguish instrumental and noninstrumental standpoints of measurability from one another and from the immeasurability of the care perspective. In sharp contrast, Habermas's framework of knowledge-constitutive interests clarifies the epistemological status of the principle of equalitarian measure such that it can be ushered to the fore of social critique and rescued from the nebulous ethicopolitical space to which both Derridean deconstruction and Honnethian recognition theory consign it. That critics like Morris are inclined to accuse the discourse ethic of "moralizing" for coordinating epistemology with normative philosophy is thus the height of irony (and not in the positive "deconstructive" sense). For, as I have been arguing, it is precisely Habermas's well-conceived account of knowledge and human interests that shores up his model's status as a critical theory. Yet while Habermas has himself allowed this crucial philosophical underpinning of his framework to recede from view in recent years, this study has endeavored to situate the latter at the conceptual spine of the discourse-ethical project.

Buoyed by this expressly foregrounded paradigm, our reconstruction can now theorize the orientation of care on what I have characterized as more stable terms. It confines care to the terrain of the immeasurable, distinguishing it, at the level of epistemology, from the sorts of ethicopolitical interventions that can be carried forth only from a standpoint explicitly affiliated with the *logos* of measurability. At the same time, by bringing in the Honnethian idea of "recognition" at the level of social integration, our reconstruction is amenable to the prospect of retrieving a "forgotten" antecedent attitude of care within the recognitional domains of love, law, and solidarity. Our perspective thus affords a rather different view of the "moral grammar" (to use Honneth's term) of contemporary forms of social contestation than that set forth in Habermas's account. Indeed, in theorizing recognitional care as conceptually and genetically antecedent to detached discourse-ethical deliberation, we endow moral actors with the capacity to retrieve the attitude of felt concern for the existential welfare others in cases where this orientation has been overlooked—a capability that is imperative if we are to avoid threatening moral argumentation with the prospect of "banalization." As Habermas himself reminds us, if it is to steel itself against a potential "entropy of meaning," moral discourse must involve more than an appeal to the "transcending power" of dialogical reasonableness alone (see chapter 1).

Thus, within the sphere of social integration (and its subdomains of love, law, and solidarity), our reconstructed model opens a space for the immeasurability of care—or as Alan Bass would have it, its "strangeness"—even as it bars its particularism from taking over and undermining the universalistic standpoint of moral reason. This is indeed precisely the risk of an approach such as Morris's—which, conceived in the shadow of thinkers like Derrida and Adorno—entertains the prospect of aestheticizing ethicopolitical life in order to enhance its capacity to attend to the presumed irreducible nonidenticalness and untranslatablity of the self and its other. With Habermas, our reconstruction insists on derailing the prospect of a wholly aestheticized public sphere, a space that is unreservedly open to what Bonnie Honig calls the "wild, dangerously unscripted futures" of moral actors.[50] It recognizes such incalculable wildness as, in fact, a "danger"—that is, as something that is potentially encumbering of human flourishing rather than facilitative of it. As a result, our model remains cognizant of the epistemological barriers that bar the care orientations and particularistic viewpoints of concrete subjectivities from fusing with the reason and interests of universally measurable justice. In so doing, it upholds what both Honneth and Habermas understand as the critical force of left Hegelian intersubjectivism against the cul-de-sac of ethicopolitical ineffability, a path down which deconstruction and kindred approaches are inclined to lead us.

The analytical implications of our retooled framework should by now be clear. From its standpoint, there is simply no expectation that moral agents will be able to redeem anything like an ethics of care from the steering directives of modern bureaucratic and economic subsystems, which in our hypothetical case are forestalling a just outcome for contract employees like John. If an attitude of "care" for such morally aggrieved individuals is to be recovered at all, this can be accomplished only through an appeal to the recognitional principles of love, rights, and achievement that are at play within the framework of a normatively constituted *lifeworld*. When our faculty contests the legal misrecognition of John and his fellow contract workers, it does so within the context of a public sphere endowed with a distinct *life of its own*, one whose underlying normativity is epistemologically disjoined from the strategic *ratio* of capital accumulation and administrative power. The emancipatory *interests* of the actors in our lifeworld are envisaged, from this vantage point, as inimical to the reifying organizing principles of the modern bureaucracy and marketplace, which have crossed the threshold from benign extranormative action coordination and are now threatening to treat employees like John as little more than insensate objects. The acknowledgement of this crucial epistemological difference between the two domains of life is precisely what positions our actors to resist the unjust consequences of a "misapplied" objectivating attitude.

However, as noted, in our model the moral grammar of this resistance has taken on a rather different cast than that of the struggles undertaken by Habermasian agents. From our perspective, we can imagine, with Rehg, a philosophy faculty that is moved to object to the human resources department's announced merit rule out of affective sympathy for contract employees like John, who would face potentially devastating existential losses were this norm to be applied without any qualifications. In fact, our view is consistent with Rehg's account of the care-justice relationship, but with a crucial advantage: it reminds us that the faculty's attitude of felt concern for John is genetically and conceptually prior to the abrogated norm of equal treatment. As such, care is theorized as not only recuperable from the sphere of detached moral cognition, but as an orientation that *makes possible* the impartialist standpoint of justice in the first place. One can of course point to innumerable struggles within contemporary lifeworld contexts that are aimed at recapturing precisely this nullified prior attitude of recognitional care. This objective is evident, for example, in demands by women's groups for the implementation of just maternity leave policies; in the efforts of animal rights campaigners to secure more humane living conditions for livestock reared in large agribusiness abattoirs; in collective actions undertaken by factory workers seeking to defend themselves and their families from the loss of livelihood that accompanies precipitous plant closures; and even in arguments (such as those championed by President Obama) for the inclusion of an "empathy standard" on the judicial bench.

Consistent with the proposals of Habermas and Derrida alike, our reconstruction is also amenable to the idea of leaving the detached procedures of moral argumentation open to "the shock of what is absolutely strange, cryptic, or uncanny," to forms of world-disclosive transcendence that "refuse to be assimilated to pregiven categories."[51] This is precisely the potential that resides, as Habermas notes, within the "negativity" of modern art, which—as manifest in many contemporary films, musical compositions, community murals, and so forth—has the capacity to emotively depict the moral injury of reification and inspire feelings of "care" for the existential plight of the individuals affected (Picasso's *Guernica* is an iconic example).

Yet owing to its insistence upon a distinction between two disparate vantage points of knowledge and human interests—and its attendant clarity about where the boundaries of the system and lifeworld spheres of society "begin and end"—our perspective is well positioned to adjudge when the attitude of care has, for its part, crossed the epistemological threshold such that its immeasurable, particularistic moral compass is now depriving agents of the capacity to appeal to the *logos* of noninstrumental measurability to reach universally binding agreements about contested validity claims. Ultimately, this study has argued, it is exactly the discourse-ethical standpoint of measurable, egalitarian reciprocation that enables moral actors to adjudicate the normative principles in the name of which they speak and act. The principle of equal measurement is in this sense *contributory* to human flourishing. It is neither something to be undermined entirely (Marcuse); acknowledged but then subsumed within an axiologically preeminent moral orientation of incalculably unconditional care (Derrida); or defended from the latter two frameworks of social critique on epistemologically unstable grounds (Honneth). Indeed, it is precisely from the vantage point of reciprocal respect and impartial, equal treatment that we are poised to take the measure of care.

NOTES

1. Axel Honneth, "Love and Morality," in *Disrespect: The Normative Foundations of Critical Theory* (Cambridge, UK: Polity Press, 2007), 172.

2. Honneth, "Love and Morality," 173.

3. Axel Honneth, *The Struggle for Recognition: The Moral Grammar of Social Conflicts* (Cambridge, UK: Polity Press, 1992), 107.

4. Honneth, "Love and Morality," 173.

5. Honneth, *The Struggle for Recognition*, 107.

6. Axel Honneth, *Reification: A New Look at an Old Idea* (Oxford: Oxford University Press, 2008), 50.

7. Honneth, *The Struggle for Recognition*, 95.

8. Honneth, *The Struggle for Recognition*, 118.

9. Honneth, *The Struggle for Recognition*, 118–19.

10. Honneth, *The Struggle for Recognition*, 120.

11. Honneth, *The Struggle for Recognition*, 122.

12. Honneth, *The Struggle for Recognition*, 123, 126.

13. Honneth, *The Struggle for Recognition*, 128.

14. Honneth, *The Struggle for Recognition*, 127; my emphasis.

15. Honneth, *The Struggle for Recognition*, 129; my emphasis.

16. Axel Honneth, "Integrity and Disrespect: Principles of the Conception of Morality Based on the Theory of Recognition," *Political Theory* 20, no. 2 (1992): 195.

17. Honneth, "The Other of Justice: Habermas and the Ethical Challenge of Postmodernism," in *Disrespect*, 123–24.

18. Honneth, *The Struggle for Recognition*, 129.

19. Seyla Benhabib, *Situating the Self: Gender, Community and Postmodernism in Contemporary Ethics* (New York: Routledge, 1992), 170.

20. Honneth, *The Struggle for Recognition*, 128.

21. Honneth, "The Other of Justice," 122; my emphasis.

22. Honneth, *The Struggle for Recognition*, 129.

23. Honneth, *Reification*, 57.

24. Honneth, *Reification*, 57.

25. The discussion that follows draws on arguments set forth in *Redistribution and Recognition*, where Honneth criticizes Nancy Fraser's defense of "redistribution" as a vantage point from which to theorize contemporary forms of social contestation. In addition to engaging with Fraser's work, Honneth takes advantage of this forum to confront Habermas, upon whom Fraser relies for many of her own positions.

26. Axel Honneth, "The Point of Recognition: A Rejoinder to the Rejoinder," in Nancy Fraser and Axel Honneth, *Redistribution or Recognition? A Political-Philosophical Exchange* (London: Verso, 2003), 240.

27. Honneth, "The Point of Recognition," 258.

28. Honneth, "Redistribution as Recognition: A Response to Nancy Fraser," in *Redistribution or Recognition?*, 149.

29. Honneth, "Redistribution as Recognition," 186.

30. Honneth, *The Struggle for Recognition*, 254.

31. See the discussion of Habermas's version of the "misapplication thesis" in chapter 3.

32. Honneth, *Reification*, 55.

33. Honneth, "Redistribution as Recognition," 169.

34. Honneth, "Redistribution as Recognition," 168.

35. Honneth, "Love and Morality," 178.

36. Jacques Derrida, *Politics of Friendship*, trans. George Collins (London: Verso, 1997), 22.

37. Honneth, "The Point of Recognition," 250–51.

38. Honneth, "The Point of Recognition," 254.

39. Jürgen Habermas, *Legitimation Crisis*, trans. Thomas McCarthy (Boston: Beacon Press, 1973), 72.

40. Jürgen Habermas, *The Theory of Communicative Action, Volume 1: Reason and the Rationalization of Society*, trans. Thomas McCarthy (Boston: Beacon Press), 102.

41. Honneth, *Reification*, 61.

42. On this count, I favor Honneth's analysis over Nancy Fraser's. Unlike Honneth, Fraser sees contemporary social conflicts as oriented toward the attainment of "participatory parity," an overarching norm that in her view encompasses claims for "recognition" as well as demands for the just redistribution of wealth, resources, and life chances. See Nancy Fraser, "Social Justice in the Age of Identity Politics: Redistribution, Recognition, and Participation," in Fraser and Honneth, *Redistribution or Recognition?*, 7–109.

43. This modification of Rehg's hypothetical was conceived prior to the April 2010 decision of Middlesex University, London, to close its philosophy department in light of funding cuts and financial pressures. Although purely coincidental, the parallels between the Middlesex case and our imagined situation are obvious.

44. Jürgen Habermas, "The Idea of the University: Learning Processes," in *The New Conservatism: Cultural Criticism and the Historians' Debate*, trans. and ed. Shierry Weber Nicholsen (Cambridge, UK: Polity Press, 1989), 101–2.

45. Jürgen Habermas, *Between Facts and Norms: Contributions to a Discourse Theory of Law and Democracy*, trans. William Rehg (Cambridge, Mass.: The MIT Press, 1996), 486–87.

46. Habermas, "The Idea of the University," 116.

47. Martin Morris, *Rethinking the Communicative Turn: Adorno, Habermas, and the Problem of Communicative Freedom* (New York: The State University of New York Press, 2001), 204n.

48. Thomas McCarthy, "The Politics of the Ineffable: Derrida's Deconstructionism," in *Hermeneutics and Critical Theory in Ethics and Politics*, ed. Michael Kelly (Cambridge, Mass.: The MIT Press, 1991), 146–68.

49. McCarthy, "The Politics of the Ineffable," 162; my emphasis.

50. Bonnie Honig, "Dead Rights, Live Futures: On Habermas's Attempt to Reconcile Constitutionalism and Democracy," in *The Derrida-Habermas Reader*, ed. Lasse Thomassen (Chicago: The University of Chicago Press, 2006), 169.

51. Habermas, *Between Facts and Norms*, 490.

Bibliography

Apel, Karl-Otto. "The Conflicts of Our Time and the Problem of Political Ethics." Pp. 81–102 in *From Contract to Community: Political Theory at the Crossroads*, edited by Fred R. Dallmayr. New York: Marcel Dekker, 1978.

Aronowitz, Stanley. "The Production of Scientific Knowledge: Science, Ideology, and Marxism." Pp. 519–41 in *Marxism and the Interpretation of Culture*, edited by Cary Nelson and Lawrence Grossberg. Chicago: University of Illinois Press, 1988.

Bass, Alan. *Interpretation and Difference: The Strangeness of Care*. Stanford: Stanford University Press, 2006.

Benhabib, Seyla. *Critique, Norm, and Utopia: A Study of the Foundations of Critical Theory*. New York: Columbia University Press, 1987.

———. *Situating the Self: Gender, Community and Postmodernism in Contemporary Ethics*. New York: Routledge, 1992.

———. "Subjectivity, Historiography, and Politics: Reflections on the 'Feminism/Postmodernism Exchange.'" Pp. 107–25 in Seyla Benhabib et al., *Feminist Contentions: A Philosophical Exchange*. New York: Routledge, 1995.

———. "Democracy and Difference: Reflections on the Metapolitics of Lyotard and Derrida." Pp. 128–58 in *The Derrida-Habermas Reader*, edited by Lasse Thomassen. Chicago: The University of Chicago Press, 2006.

Benjamin, Walter. *Illuminations*, edited by Hannah Arendt. New York: Schocken, 1969.

———. "The Critique of Violence." Pp. 277–300 in *Reflections: Essays, Aphorisms, Autobiographical Writings*, edited by Peter Dements and translated by Edmund Jephcott. New York: Schocken, 1986.

Bernstein, Richard J. "An Allegory of Modernity/Postmodernity: Habermas and Derrida." Pp. 71–97 in *The Derrida-Habermas Reader*, edited by Lasse Thomassen. Chicago: The University of Chicago Press, 2006.

Bhabha, Homi K. *The Location of Culture*. New York: Routledge, 1994.

Bloch, Ernst. *Subjekt-Objekt: Erlauterung zu Hegel*. Berlin: Suhrkamp, 1952.

———. *Heritage of Our Times*, translated by Neville Plaice and Stephen Plaice. Cambridge, UK: Polity Press, 1991.

Bookchin, Murray. *Post-Scarcity Anarchism*. Berkeley: Ramparts Press, 1971.

———. *The Ecology of Freedom*. Palo Alto: Cheshire Books, 1982.

Borradori, Giovanna, ed. *Philosophy in a Time of Terror: Dialogues with Jürgen Habermas and Jacques Derrida*. Chicago: The University of Chicago Press, 2003.

Bronner, Stephen Eric. "Utopian Projections: In Memory of Ernst Bloch," Pp. 165–74 in *Not Yet: Reconsidering Ernst Bloch*, edited by Jamie Owen Daniel and Tom Moylan. New York: Verso, 1997.

Calarco, Matthew. 2004. "Deconstruction Is Not Vegetarianism: Humanism, Subjectivity, and Animal Ethics." *Continental Philosophy Review* 37, no. 2: 175–201.

Cohen, Jean L. "Critical Social Theory and Feminist Critiques: The Debate with Jürgen Habermas." Pp. 57–90 in *Feminists Read Habermas: Gendering the Subject of Discourse*, edited by Johanna Meehan. New York: Routledge, 1995.

Conley, Verena Andermatt. *Ecopolitics: The Environment in Poststructuralist Thought*. London: Routledge, 1997.

Cornell, Drucilla. *The Philosophy of the Limit*. London: Routledge, 1992.

Critchley, Simon. "Habermas and Derrida Get Married." Pp. 267–80 in *The Ethics of Deconstruction: Derrida and Levinas*. Edinburgh: Edinburgh University Press, 1999.

———. "Frankfurt Impromptu—Remarks on Derrida and Habermas." Pp. 98–110 in *The Derrida-Habermas Reader*, edited by Lasse Thomassen. Chicago: The University of Chicago Press, 2006.

Derrida, Jacques. *Writing and Difference*, translated by Alan Bass. Chicago: The University of Chicago Press, 1978.

———. *Positions*, translated by Alan Bass. Chicago: The University of Chicago Press, 1981.

———. *Given Time: Counterfeit Money*, translated by Peggy Kamuf. Chicago: The University of Chicago Press, 1992.

———. *The Other Heading: Reflections on Today's Europe*, translated by Pascale-Ann Brault and Michael B. Naas. Bloomington: Indiana University Press, 1992.

———. *Specters of Marx: The State of the Debt, the Work of Mourning, and the New International*, translated by Peggy Kamuf. New York: Routledge, 1994.

———. *On the Name*, edited by Thomas Dutoit and translated by David Wood et al. Stanford: Stanford University Press, 1995.

———. *Points . . . Interviews, 1974–1994*, translated by Peggy Kamuf et al. Stanford: Stanford University Press, 1995.

———. "Remarks on Deconstruction and Pragmatism." Pp. 77–88 in *Deconstruction and Pragmatism*, edited by Chantal Mouffe. New York: Routledge, 1996.

———. *Of Grammatology*, translated by Gayatri Chakravorty Spivak. Baltimore: Johns Hopkins University Press, 1997.

———. *Politics of Friendship*, translated by George Collins. London: Verso, 1997.

———. "Hospitality, Justice and Responsibility: A Dialogue with Jacques Derrida." Pp. 65–83 in *Questioning Ethics: Contemporary Debates in Philosophy*, edited by Richard Kearny and Mark Dooley. New York: Routledge, 1999.

————. *Cosmopolitanism and Forgiveness*, edited by Michael Collin Hughes. New York: Routledge, 2001.

————. *Acts of Religion*, edited by Gil Anidjar. New York: Routledge, 2002.

————. "Deconstructing Terrorism," Pp. 137–72 in *Philosophy in a Time of Terror: Dialogues with Jürgen Habermas and Jacques Derrida*, edited by Giovanna Borradori. Chicago: The University of Chicago Press, 2003.

————. "The Animal That I Therefore Am." Pp. 116–33 in *Animal Philosophy*, edited by Matthew Calarco and Peter Atterton. New York: Continuum, 2004.

————. *Paper Machine*, translated by Rachel Bowlby. Stanford: Stanford University Press, 2005.

————. *Rogues: Two Essays on Reason*, translated by Pascale-Anne Brault and Michael Nass. Stanford: Stanford University Press, 2005.

Derrida, Jacques, and Richard Kearney. "Dialogue with Jacques Derrida." Pp. 105–26 in Richard Kearney, *Dialogues with Contemporary Continental Thinkers: The Phenomenological Heritage*. Manchester: Manchester University Press, 1984.

Derrida, Jacques, and Giovanna Borradori. "Autoimmunity: Real and Symbolic Suicides—A Dialogue with Jacques Derrida." Pp. 85–136 in *Philosophy in a Time of Terror: Dialogues with Jürgen Habermas and Jacques Derrida*, edited by Giovanna Borradori. Chicago: The University of Chicago Press, 2003.

Dewey, John. *Experience and Nature*. Whitefish, Mt.: Kessinger Publishing, 2003.

Dews, Peter. *Logics of Disintegration: Post-structuralist Thought and the Claims of Critical Theory*. New York: Verso, 1987.

Durst, David C. "Ernst Bloch's Theory of Nonsimultaneity." *The Germanic Review* 77, no. 3 (2002): 171–94.

Elden, Stuart. *Speaking Against Number: Heidegger, Language and the Politics of Calculation*. Edinburgh: Edinburgh University Press, 2006.

Feenberg, Andrew. "Marcuse or Habermas: Two Critiques of Technology." *Inquiry* 39 (1996): 45–70. www-rohan.sdsu.edu/faculty/feenberg/marhab.html (14 July 2010).

Ferrechio, Susan. "Sotomayor: 'Wise Latina' Line Was a Rhetorical Flourish That Didn't Reflect Her Real Views." *The Washington Examiner*. 14 July 2009. www.washingtonexaminer.com/opinion/blogs/beltway-confidential/Sotomayor-wise-Latina-line-was-rhetorical-flourish-that-didnt-reflect-her-real-views-50732192.html (12 July 2010).

Finlayson, James Gordon. "Women and the Standpoint of Concrete Others: From the Criticism of Discourse Ethics to Feminist Social Criticism." Unpublished manuscript, cited with permission from the author.

Flax, Jane. *Thinking Fragments: Psychoanalysis, Feminism, and Postmodernism in the Contemporary West*. Berkeley: The University of California Press, 1990.

Forst, Rainer. "Situations of the Self: Reflections on Seyla Benhabib's Version of Critical Theory." *Philosophy and Social Criticism* 23, no. 5 (1997): 79–96.

Foucault, Michel. *Power: The Essential Works of Foucault, 1954–1984, Volume 3*, edited by James D. Faubion. New York: The New Press, 1994.

Fox, Warwick, "Deep Ecology: A New Philosophy of Our Time?" Pp. 153–65 in *Philosophical Dialogues: Arne Naess and the Progress of Ecophilosophy*, edited by Nina Witoszek and Andrew Brennan. Lanham, MD: Rowman & Littlefield, 1999.

Frank, Manfred. *Was ist Neostrukturalismus?* Frankfurt: Suhrkamp-Verlag, 1984.

Fraser, Nancy. "False Antitheses: A Response to Seyla Benhabib and Judith Butler." Pp. 59–74 in Seyla Benhabib et al., *Feminist Contentions: A Philosophical Exchange*. New York: Routledge, 1995.

———. "Social Justice in the Age of Identity Politics: Redistribution, Recognition, and Participation." Pp. 7–109 in Nancy Fraser and Axel Honneth, *Redistribution or Recognition? A Political-Philosophical Exchange*. London: Verso, 2003.

Fraser, Nancy, and Axel Honneth. *Redistribution or Recognition? A Political-Philosophical Exchange*. London: Verso, 2003.

Fritsch, Matthias. *The Promise of Memory: History and Politics in Marx, Benjamin, and Derrida*. New York: The State University of New York Press, 2005.

Ganis, Richard. "Derrida and Habermas: Asymmetry and Accord." Review of *The Derrida-Habermas Reader*, ed. Lasse Thomassen. *Radical Philosophy Review* 10, no. 2 (2007): 197–203.

———. "Interpretative Care and the Postmetaphysical Tradition: The Legacy of Two Freuds." Review of Alan Bass, *Interpretation and Difference: The Strangeness of Care*." *H-Ideas, H-Net Reviews*, February 2009. www.h-net.org/reviews/showpdf .php?id=22980 (15 July 2010).

———. "Caring for Nature in Habermas, Vogel, and Derrida: Reconciling the Speaking and Nonspeaking Worlds at the Cost of 'Re-enchantment'?" *Radical Philosophy Review* 13, no. 2 (2010), in press.

Gaon, Stella. "Pluralizing Universal Man: The Legacy of Transcendentalism and Teleology in Habermas's Discourse Ethics." *The Review of Politics* 60, no. 4 (2005): 685–718.

Gare, Arran E. *Postmodernism and the Environmental Crisis*. London: Routledge, 1995.

Gilligan, Carol. *In a Different Voice: Psychological Theory and Women's Development*. Cambridge, Mass.: Harvard University Press, 1993.

Gutmann, Amy, ed. *Multiculturalism: Examining the Politics of Recognition*. Princeton: Princeton University Press, 1994.

Habermas, Jürgen. *Toward a Rational Society: Student Protest, Science, and Politics*, translated by Jeremy J. Shapiro. Boston: Beacon Press, 1970.

———. *Legitimation Crisis*, translated by Thomas McCarthy. Boston: Beacon Press, 1973.

———. "A Postscript to *Knowledge and Human Interests*." *Philosophy of the Social Sciences* 3 (1973): 157–89.

———. *Communication and the Evolution of Society*, translated by Thomas McCarthy. Boston: Beacon Press, 1979.

———. "A Reply to My Critics." Pp. 219–83 in *Habermas: Critical Debates*, edited by John B. Thompson and David Held. Cambridge, Mass.: The MIT Press, 1982.

———. "The Entwinement of Myth and Enlightenment: Re-Reading *Dialectic of Enlightenment*," in *New German Critique* 26 (Spring-Summer 1982): 13–30.

———. *Philosophical-Political Profiles*, translated by Frederick G. Lawrence. Cambridge, Mass.: The MIT Press, 1983.

———. *The Theory of Communicative Action, Volume 1: Reason and the Rationalization of Society*, translated by Thomas McCarthy. Boston: Beacon Press, 1984.

————. *Knowledge and Human Interests*, translated by Jeremy J. Shapiro. Cambridge, UK: Polity Press, 1987.

————. *The New Conservatism: Cultural Criticism and the Historians' Debate*, edited and translated by Shierry Weber Nicholsen. Cambridge, UK: Polity Press, 1989.

————. *Moral Consciousness and Communicative Action*, translated by Christian Lenhardt and Shierry Weber Nicholsen. Cambridge, Mass.: The MIT Press, 1990.

————. *The Philosophical Discourse of Modernity: Twelve Lectures*, translated by Frederick G. Lawrence. Cambridge, Mass.: The MIT Press, 1990.

————. "Justice and Solidarity: On the Discussion Concerning 'Stage 6.'" Pp. 32–52 in *Hermeneutics and Critical Theory in Ethics and Politics*, edited by Michael Kelly. Cambridge, Mass.: The MIT Press, 1991.

————. "Further Reflections on the Public Sphere." Pp. 421–61 in *Habermas and the Public Sphere*, edited by Craig Calhoun. Cambridge, Mass.: The MIT Press, 1992.

————. *Postmetaphysical Thinking: Philosophical Essays*, translated by William Mark Hohengarten. Cambridge, Mass.: The MIT Press, 1992.

————. "Struggles for Recognition in the Democratic Constitutional State." Pp. 107–48 in *Multiculturalism*, edited by Amy Gutmann. Princeton: Princeton University Press, 1994.

————. *Between Facts and Norms: Contributions to a Discourse Theory of Law and Democracy*, translated by William Rehg. Cambridge, Mass.: The MIT Press, 1996.

————. *The Inclusion of the Other: Studies in Political Theory*, edited by Ciaran P. Cronin and Pablo De Greiff. Cambridge, UK: Polity Press, 1998.

————. "Reconstructing Terrorism." Pp. 45–84 in *Philosophy in a Time of Terror: Dialogues with Jürgen Habermas and Jacques Derrida*, edited by Giovanna Borradori. Chicago: The University of Chicago Press, 2003.

————. *The Future of Human Nature*. Cambridge, UK: Polity Press, 2003.

————. "On the Relation between the Secular Liberal State and Religion." Pp. 327–38 in *The Frankfurt School on Religion: Key Writings by the Major Thinkers*, edited by Eduardo Mendieta. New York: Routledge, 2005.

————. "Religious Tolerance—The Pacemaker of Cultural Rights." Pp. 195–207 in *The Derrida-Habermas Reader*, edited by Lasse Thomassen. Chicago: The University of Chicago Press, 2006.

Habermas, Jürgen, and Giovanna Borradori. "Fundamentalism and Terror—A Dialogue with Jürgen Habermas. Pp. 25–44 in *Philosophy in a Time of Terror: Dialogues with Jürgen Habermas and Jacques Derrida*, edited by Giovanna Borradori. Chicago: The University of Chicago Press, 2003.

Habermas, Jürgen, and Jacques Derrida. "February 15, or What Binds Europeans Together: A Plea for a Common Foreign Policy, Beginning in the Core of Europe." Pp. 270–77 in *The Derrida-Habermas Reader*, edited by Lasse Thomassen. Chicago: The University of Chicago Press, 2006.

Habermas, Jürgen, and Eduardo Mendieta. "America and the World: A Conversation with Jürgen Habermas." *Logos* 3, no. 3 (Summer 2004): 101–22. www.logosjournal.com/issue_3.3.pdf (14 July 2010).

Hardt, Michael, and Antonio Negri. *Multitude: War and Democracy in the Age of Empire*. New York: The Penguin Press, 2004.

Heidegger, Martin. *Being and Time*, translated by John Macquarrie and Edward Robinson. New York: Harper & Row Publishers, 1962.

———. *Pathmarks*, edited by William McNeil. Cambridge, UK: Cambridge University Press, 1998.

———. *Contributions to Philosophy: From Enowning*, translated by Parvis Emad and Kenneth Maly. Bloomington: Indiana University Press, 1999.

Hendley, Steven. *From Communicative Action to the Face of the Other: Levinas and Habermas on Language, Obligation, and Community*. Lanham, Md.: Lexington Books, 2000.

Honig, Bonnie. "Dead Rights, Live Futures: On Habermas's Attempt to Reconcile Constitutionalism and Democracy." Pp. 161–75 in *The Derrida-Habermas Reader*, edited by Lasse Thomassen. Chicago: The University of Chicago Press, 2006.

Honneth, Axel. "Integrity and Disrespect: Principles of the Conception of Morality Based on the Theory of Recognition." *Political Theory* 20, no. 2 (1992): 187–201.

———. *The Struggle for Recognition: The Moral Grammar of Social Conflicts*. Cambridge, UK: Polity Press, 1992.

———. "The Point of Recognition: A Rejoinder to the Rejoinder." Pp. 237–68 in Nancy Fraser and Axel Honneth, *Redistribution or Recognition? A Political-Philosophical Exchange*. London: Verso, 2003.

———. "Redistribution as Recognition: A Response to Nancy Fraser." Pp. 110–97 in Nancy Fraser and Axel Honneth, *Redistribution or Recognition? A Political-Philosophical Exchange*. London: Verso, 2003.

———. *Disrespect: The Normative Foundations of Critical Theory*. Cambridge, UK: Polity Press, 2007.

———. *Reification: A New Look at an Old Idea*. Oxford: Oxford University Press, 2008.

Horkheimer, Max, and Theodor W. Adorno. *Dialectic of Enlightenment: Philosophical Fragments*, translated by Edmund Jephcott. Stanford: Stanford University Press, 2002.

Ingram, David. *Habermas and the Dialectic of Reason*. New Haven: Yale University Press, 1987.

Kant, Immanuel. *Perpetual Peace*, translated by Mary Campbell Smith. New York: Cosimo, 2005.

Kearney, Richard. *Dialogues with Contemporary Continental Thinkers: The Phenomenological Heritage*. Manchester: Manchester University Press, 1984.

Kovel, Joel. "The Dialectic of Radical Ecologies." *Capitalism, Nature, Socialism* 14, no. 1 (2003): 75–87.

Krause, Sharon. "Desiring Justice: Motivation and Justification in Rawls and Habermas." *Contemporary Political Theory* 4, no. 4 (2005): 363–85.

Lacan, Jacques. *The Seminar of Jacques Lacan: Book II: The Ego in Freud's Theory and in the Technique of Psychoanalysis, 1954–55*, edited by Jacques-Alain Miller and translated by Sylvana Tomaselli. Cambridge, UK: Cambridge University Press, 1988.

Levinas, Emmanuel. *Totality and Infinity: An Essay on Exteriority*, translated by Alphonso Lingis. Pittsburgh: Duquesne University Press, 1969.

Lukács, Georg. *History and Class Consciousness*, translated by Rodney Livingstone. Cambridge, Mass.: The MIT Press, 1971.

Mahmood, Saba. *Politics of Piety: The Islamic Revival and the Feminist Subject*. Princeton: Princeton University Press, 2005.

Maihofer, Andrea. "Care." Pp. 383–92 in *A Companion to Feminist Philosophy*, edited by Alison M. Jaggar and Iris Marion Young. Oxford: Blackwell, 1998.

Marcus, George E., and Michael J. Fischer. *Anthropology as Critique: An Experimental Moment in the Human Sciences*. Chicago: The University of Chicago Press, 1986.

Marcuse, Herbert. *Eros and Civilization: A Philosophical Inquiry into Freud*. New York: Vintage Books, 1962.

———. *One-Dimensional Man: Studies in the Ideology of Advanced Industrial Society*. Boston: Beacon Press, 1964.

Martin, Bill. *Matrix and Line: Derrida and the Possibilities of Postmodern Social Theory*. New York: The State University of New York Press, 1992.

Marx, Karl. *Economic and Philosophic Manuscripts*, in *Marx and Engels: Collected Works, Vol. 3*. New York: International Publishers, 1975.

Matuštík, Martin. "Between Hope and Terror: Habermas and Derrida Plead for the Im/Possible." Pp. 278–96 in *The Derrida-Habermas Reader*, edited by Lasse Thomassen. Chicago: The University of Chicago Press, 2006.

McCarthy, Thomas. 1990. "The Politics of the Ineffable: Derrida's Deconstructionism." Pp. 146–68 in *Hermeneutics and Critical Theory in Ethics and Politics*, edited by Michael Kelly. Cambridge, Mass.: The MIT Press, 1991.

Meehan, Johanna, ed. *Feminists Read Habermas: Gendering the Subject of Discourse*. New York: Routledge, 1995.

Mendieta, Eduardo. "Globalizing Critical Theory of Science." Pp. 187–208 in *Globalizing Critical Theory*, edited by Max Pensky. Oxford: Rowman & Littlefield, 2005.

Morris, Martin. *Rethinking the Communicative Turn: Adorno, Habermas, and the Problem of Communicative Freedom*. New York: The State University of New York Press, 2001.

———. "Between Deliberation and Deconstruction: The Condition of Post-National Democracy." Pp. 231–56 in *The Derrida-Habermas Reader*, edited by Lasse Thomassen. Chicago: The University of Chicago Press, 2006.

Mouffe, Chantal. "Democracy, Power, and the Political." Pp. 245–56 in *Democracy and Difference: Contesting the Boundaries of the Political*, edited by Seyla Benhabib. Princeton: Princeton University Press, 1996.

Obama, Barack. "The President's Remarks on Justice Souter." *The White House Blog*, 1 May 2009. www.whitehouse.gov/blog/09/05/01/The-Presidents-Remarks -on-Justice-Souter/ (12 July 2010).

Oelschlaeger, Max, ed. *Postmodern Environmental Ethics*. Albany: The State University of New York Press, 1995.

Offe, Claus. *Contradictions of the Welfare State*, edited by John Keane. Cambridge, Mass.: The MIT Press, 1984.

Ortner, Sherry B. "Theory in Anthropology since the Sixties." Pp. 372–411 in *Culture/ Power/History: A Reader in Contemporary Social Theory*, edited by Nicholas B. Dirks, Jeff Eley, and Sherry B. Ortner. Princeton: Princeton University Press, 1994.

Ottman, Henning. "Cognitive Interests and Self-Reflection: The Status and Systematic Connection of the Cognitive Interests in Habermas's *Knowledge and Human
Interests*." Pp. 79–97 in *Habermas: Critical Debates*, edited by John B. Thompson
and David Held. Cambridge, Mass.: The MIT Press, 1982.

Quinn, Andrew, and James Vicini. "Sotomayor Cool under Republican Grilling,"
Reuters, 14 July 2009. www.reuters.com/article/idUSTRE56B0TA20090714 (12
July 2010).

Rehg, William. *Insight and Solidarity: The Discourse Ethics of Jürgen Habermas.*
Berkeley: University of California Press, 1994.

Rorty, Richard. "Habermas and Lyotard on Postmodernity." Pp. 161–75 in *Habermas and Modernity*, edited by Richard J. Bernstein. Cambridge, Mass.: The MIT
Press, 1985.

———. "Habermas, Derrida and the Functions of Philosophy." Pp. 46–65 in *The
Derrida-Habermas Reader*, edited by Lasse Thomassen. Chicago: The University
of Chicago Press, 2006.

Rosenfeld, Michel. "Derrida's Ethical Turn and America: Looking Back from the
Crossroads of Global Terrorism and the Enlightenment." *Cardozo Law Review* 27,
no. 2 (2005): 815–45.

Schmidt, Alfred. *The Concept of Nature in Marx.* London: New Left Books, 1971.

Sessions, Jeff. "Confirmation Hearing: 'Our Chance to Get It Right.'" *Richmond
Times-Dispatch*, 12 July 2009. www2.timesdispatch.com/news/2009/jul/12/
ed-sessions12_20090710-195407-ar-37551 (12 July 2010).

Spivak, Gayatri Chakravorty. *In Other Worlds: Essays in Cultural Politics.* New
York: Routledge, 1988.

Thomassen, Lasse, ed. *The Derrida-Habermas Reader.* Chicago: The University of
Chicago Press, 2006.

———. "'A Bizarre, Even Opaque Practice': Habermas on Constitutionalism and
Democracy." Pp. 176–94 in *The Derrida-Habermas Reader*, edited by Lasse Thomassen. Chicago: The University of Chicago Press, 2006.

Thompson, John B., and David Held, eds. *Habermas: Critical Debates.* Cambridge,
Mass.: The MIT Press, 1982.

Trey, George. "Communicative Ethics in the Face of Alterity: Habermas, Levinas and
the Problem of Post-Conventional Universalism." *Praxis International* 11, no. 4
(1992): 412–27.

Tronto, Joan C. *Moral Boundaries: A Political Argument for an Ethic of Care.* New
York: Routledge, 1993.

Vogel, Lawrence. *The Fragile "We": Ethical Implications of Martin Heidegger's
Being and Time.* Chicago: Northwestern University Press, 1994.

Vogel, Steven. *Against Nature: The Concept of Nature in Critical Theory.* New York:
State University of New York Press, 1996.

———. "Nature as Origin and Difference: On Environmental Philosophy and Continental Thought." *Philosophy Today, SPEP Supplement* (1998): 169–81.

Warren, Mark E. "The Self in Discursive Democracy." Pp. 167–200 in *The Cambridge Companion to Habermas*, edited by Stephen K. White. Cambridge, UK:
Cambridge University Press, 1999.

Wellmer, Albrecht. *Critical Theory of Society*, translated by John Cumming. New York: Continuum, 1971.

West, Robin. *Caring for Justice*. New York: New York University Press, 1997.

White, Stephen K., ed. *The Cambridge Companion to Habermas*. Cambridge, UK: Cambridge University Press, 1999.

Whitebook, Joel. "The Problem of Nature in Habermas." *Telos* 40 (Summer 1979): 41–69.

Wildman, Sarah. "Closed Sessions: The Senator Who's Worse than Lott." *The New Republic*, 30 Dec. 2002. www.tnr.com/politics/story.html?id=8dd230f6-355f -4362-89cc-2c756b9d8102 12 (12 July 2010).

Wyschogrod, Edith. *An Ethics of Remembering: History, Heterology, and the Nameless Others*. Chicago: The University of Chicago Press, 1998.

Young, Iris Marion. "Communication and the Other: Beyond Deliberative Democracy." Pp. 120–36 in *Democracy and Difference: Contesting the Boundaries of the Political*, edited by Seyla Benhabib. Princeton: Princeton University Press, 1996.

———. "Asymmetrical Reciprocity: On Moral Respect, Wonder, and Enlarged Thought." *Constellations* 3, no. 3 (1997): 340–63.

Index

Adorno, Theodor W., 10, 48, 49, 78, 79, 81, 92n62, 101, 102, 106, 107, 121, 127, 131, 142; libidinal cathexis, concept of, 86; on nature, 66–67; on reification, 48

animals, 3; Derrida, Jacques on, 81–83, 116n22; Habermas, Jürgen on, 79–80, 92n59; Honneth, Axel on, 86, 87

Apel, Karl-Otto, 70, 84

Arendt, Hannah, 30

Aristotelian ethics, 27, 79

Aronowitz, Stanley, 75, 77

Aufhebung. *See* Hegel, Georg Wilhelm Friedrich

Bass, Alan, 97–98

Benhabib, Seyla, 15, 16–17, 25, 36, 43, 55–56, 95, 117n38, 130, 139; on care and gender, 39n12; criticisms of, 30–33, 40n31, 126–27; on enlarged mentality, Hannah Arendt's concept of, 30; on friendship, 30, 32–33; Habermas, Jürgen, feminist critique of, 28–30, 39n23; on interactive universalism, 29–30; moral universalism of, 29, 32

Benjamin, Jessica, 123

Benjamin, Walter, 19, 33, 34, 96, 109, 119n62; on *Jetztzeit*, 10, 106–7; on law, 107–9; messianism of, 106–7, 108; on violence, 107–8

Bernstein, Richard J., 15, 57–58, 78, 110

Bloch, Ernst: 19, 67, 96, 107, 109; broader physics, concept of, 106; nonsimultaneity theory of, 10, 104–6

Bookchin, Murray, 71

Borradori, Giovanna, 8, 104

Bronner, Stephen Eric, 105

care: feminism and, 3, 16, 28, 39n12, 39n23; immeasurability and, 10, 16, 19, 45–49, 53, 57, 63, 84, 99, 112, 121, 135, 140–44; justice and, 3, 11, 16–17, 25–38, 41n45, 46–57, 60n31 63, 79–80, 104, 108–9, 114–15, 121, 126–28, 131, 140–44; nature and, 3, 18, 19, 49, 63–93, 104, 106–7, 131, 134–35, 140; terrorism and, 17, 44, 54–57, 112. *See also* Benhabib, Seyla; Derrida, Jacques; ecological ethics; Habermas, Jürgen; Honneth, Axel; reciprocity; Rehg, William

Cavell, Stanley, 123

cognitive centrism. *See* Habermas, Jürgen

Cohen, Jean L., 39n23

comprehensive pluralism. *See* Rosenfeld, Michel

constitutional patriotism. *See* Habermas, Jürgen
constructivism. *See* Vogel, Steven
co-originality thesis. *See* Habermas, Jürgen
Cornell, Drucilla, 101
Critchley, Simon, 5, 18, 60n31, 95, 120n85; on third party, Emmanuel Levinas's concept of, 59n25, 114–15

Dasein. *See* Heidegger, Martin
deconstruction. *See* Derrida, Jacques
deep ecology, 71
democracy/justice-to-come. *See* Derrida, Jacques
Derrida, Jacques: on animals, 81–83, 116n22; on democracy/justice-to-come, 9–10, 47, 50, 104, 105, 109; *différance*, concept of, 21n16, 45, 60n34, 63, 82, 92n62, 100–101, 117n26, 118n45; ecological ethics in, 81, 84; on *Ereignis*, Martin Heidegger's concept of, 99; on forgiveness, 8–9; on friendship, 9, 45–46, 50, 63, 81, 85, 87; on gift giving, 44–45, 50, 63, 81, 85, 87; Habermas, Jürgen, critique of, 15–18, 43–49, 80–83, 87, 97–98, 101–4, 109; on hospitality, 7–10, 46–47, 50, 81, 85, 87; on *khôra*, 22n25, 45, 102, 104–6, 107; on law, 9, 10, 47, 48, 50–52; messianism of, 9–10, 98, 106; monism of, 60n34, 64, 92n62, 101, 118n45; on nature, 18, 64, 81–85; on ontotheology, 6–7, 8, 9, 45, 83, 99, 113, 116n22; on terrorism, 54–56; on violence, 11–12, 13, 30, 46, 48, 49, 51–52, 55, 83, 107–9, 121. *See also* care (and justice); Habermas, Jürgen; Honneth, Axel; Levinas, Emmanuel; reciprocity; toleration; Vogel, Steven
Dewey, John, 86, 93n84, 134
Dews, Peter, 60n34, 92n62, 100–101, 117n26, 118n45

différance. *See* Derrida, Jacques
discourse ethics. *See* Habermas, Jürgen
dualism: Bookchin, Murray, critique of, 71; Derrida, Jacques, critique of, 18, 64, 131; Fox, Warwick, critique of, 71; in Habermas, Jürgen, 18, 22n30, 68–69, 76–78, 133–34, 136, 139–40; in Honneth, Axel, 86, 87, 134; in Kantianism, 50, 110; in Lukács, Georg, 66, 71; Vogel, Steven, critique of, 18, 64, 71–74, 84

ecological ethics: in Apel, Karl-Otto, 70, 84; in Derrida, Jacques, 81, 84; in Habermas, Jürgen, 18, 64, 79, 85, 88; in Marcuse, Herbert, 74, 84, 90n17; Vogel, Steven on, 71, 74, 77, 84. *See also* Bookchin, Murray; Fox, Warwick; Kovel, Joel; Ottman, Henning; Whitebook, Joel
Elden, Stuart, 99
Engels, Friedrich, 65, 66, 71
Enlightenment, 7, 12, 16, 18, 21n16, 43, 58, 63, 66, 73, 88, 91n50, 97, 110
environmental ethics. *See* ecological ethics
Ereignis. *See* Heidegger, Martin

Feenberg, Andrew, 76, 90n17
feminism. *See* care (feminism and)
Feyerabend, Paul, 72, 75
Finlayson, James Gordon, 17, 25, 32
forgiveness. *See* Derrida, Jacques
Forst, Rainer, 40n31
Foucault, Michel, 22n25
Fox, Warwick, 71
Frank, Manfred, 117n26
Fraser, Nancy, 39n23; Honneth, Axel, critique of, 131–32; on redistribution, 145n42. *See also* Honneth, Axel
friendship: Benhabib, Seyla on, 30, 32–33; Derrida, Jacques on, 9, 45–46, 50, 63, 81, 85, 87; Honneth, Axel on, 122, 123

Fritsch, Matthias, 22n24
Fürsorge (neo-Aristotelian concept of), 79

Gaon, Stella, 17, 25, 31–32, 41n45, 43, 122, 126
Geisteswissenschaften. See human sciences
gift giving. *See* Derrida, Jacques
Gilligan, Carol, 16, 28–29, 39n12
Göring, Hermann, 81

Habermas, Jürgen: on animals, 79–80, 92n59; cognitive centrism in, 16, 19, 38, 95, 122; on constitutional patriotism, 34, 113; co-originality thesis of, 103; Derrida, Jacques, critique of, 14–16, 96–97, 100–101; dualism in, 18, 22n30, 68–69, 76–78, 133–34, 136, 139–40; ecological ethics in, 18, 64, 79, 85, 88; on law, 11, 12, 103, 113; Levinas, Emmanuel and, 59n25, 114; Marcuse, Herbert, critique of, 12–13, 14, 69, 121; on Marxism, 13–14, 93n90, 133–34; misapplication thesis of, 68, 78; moral universalism of, 4, 95, 102, 121; motivational deficit in, 33, 37, 130; on nature, 68–69, 106; psychosocial deficit in, 70–71, 85–87; on reification, 12–13, 64, 68, 78, 129; on science and technology, 12–13, 18, 64, 68–69, 76, 78, 88; on solidarity, 13, 26–27, 126; on terrorism, 56–57; on toleration, 11–12, 15, 113. *See also* Benhabib, Seyla; care (and justice); Derrida, Jacques; Heidegger, Martin; Honneth, Axel; hospitality; Levinas, Emmanuel; reciprocity; Vogel, Steven
Hardt, Michael, 112
Hegel, Georg Wilhelm Friedrich: 14, 27, 30, 60n34, 65, 66, 105, 117n26; *Aufhebung*, concept of, 13, 110;

intersubjectivism of, 128, 129, 140; *Realphilosophie* of, 123
Heidegger, Martin, 6, 19, 21n16, 37, 85, 86, 95, 110, 134; *Dasein*, concept of, 60n26, 97–100, 116n22; *Ereignis*, concept of, 99; Habermas, Jürgen on, 96–97
Hendley, Steven, 17, 25, 35, 36, 51, 59n25, 60n31, 120n85
Hobbes, Thomas, 118n40
Honig, Bonnie, 103, 142
Honneth, Axel, 4–5, 56, 60n31, 142, 144; on animals, 86, 87; on care, derivative orientation of, 18, 64, 87, 88; on care, genetic and conceptual primacy of, 16, 19, 122–27, 135, 140–41; Derrida, Jacques, critique of, 50, 52–53, 131; dualism in, 86, 87, 134; Fraser, Nancy, critique of, 145n25; on friendship, 122, 123; Habermas, Jürgen, critique of, 36–38, 115, 128–30, 132, 139; on law, 124–25, 127, 128, 130, 132, 141; on libidinal cathexis, Theodor Adorno's concept of, 86, 131; on Marxism, 132; misapplication thesis of, 85; on misrecognition, 54, 85, 87, 127, 139; moral monism of, 19, 133, 138; on nature, 85–87; on objectivating attitude, 86, 131–35; recognition theory of, 122–27; on reification, 85–86, 87, 129, 134 ; on solidarity, 124, 125–26. *See also* Fraser, Nancy
Horkheimer, Max, 10, 78, 81; on nature, 66–67; on reification, 48
hospitality. *See* Derrida, Jacques; toleration
human sciences, 49, 68–69, 84. *See also* natural sciences

Ideologiekritik, 106–7
immeasurability. *See* care (and immeasurability)
Ingram, David, 100

interactive universalism. *See* Benhabib, Seyla

Jetztzeit. *See* Benjamin, Walter
justice. *See* care (and justice); Derrida, Jacques (on democracy/justice-to-come); law

Kant, Immanuel: moral universalism of, 4; on perpetual peace, 7; on toleration, 7–9, 15, 46–47, 120n76
Kantianism, 15, 47, 50, 55, 71, 73, 81. *See also* dualism
khôra. *See* Derrida, Jacques
Kohlberg, Lawrence, 25–27, 28, 29
Kovel, Joel, 70–71, 85
Krause, Sharon, 17, 25, 33–34, 37–38, 41n45, 130
Kuhn, Thomas, 72, 75

Lacan, Jacques, 20n6
law, 2–3, 9, 10, 11, 12, 48, 50, 103, 113, 107–9, 118n40, 124–25, 127, 128, 130, 132, 139, 142. *See also* care (and justice)
Levinas, Emmanuel: Derrida, Jacques and, 8, 17, 43–44, 50–53, 55, 60n31, 114, 116n22; Habermas, Jürgen and, 59n25, 114; on law, 50–52. *See also* Critchley, Simon
libidinal cathexis, 86, 131
Locke, John, 118n40
Lukács, Georg, 37, 67, 68, 69, 73, 74, 77, 78, 85, 86, 105, 107, 134; dualism in, 65–66, 71; misapplication thesis of, 65–66; on reification, 65, 127
Lysenkoism, 72, 73, 76

Mahmood, Saba, 120n76
Marcuse, Herbert: ecological ethics in, 74, 84, 90n17; on instrumental rationality, 13, 14, 48, 63, 121, 144; on nature, 18, 63, 67, 69, 73–74, 82, 84, 90n17; on reification, 13; on

science and technology, 18, 67, 69, 73–74
Martin, Bill, 13, 23n37, 49, 100
Marx, Karl, 13–14, 22n24, 44, 69, 105, 127, 135; on nature, 67, 89n8
Marxism, 7, 9, 65, 132, 134. *See also* Derrida, Jacques (on ontotheology)
Matuštík, Martin, 5, 18, 110–11
McCarthy, Thomas, 6, 56, 140–41
Mead, George Herbert, 123
measurability. *See* natural sciences; reciprocity (symmetrical)
Mendieta, Eduardo, 76
messianism: in Benjamin, Walter, 106–7, 108; in Derrida, Jacques, 9–10, 98, 106
misapplication thesis: in Habermas, Jürgen, 68, 78; in Honneth, Axel, 85; in Lukács, Georg, 65–66
moral universalism, 3, 7; in Benhabib, Seyla, 29, 32; in Habermas, Jürgen, 4, 95, 102, 121
Morris, Martin, 19, 101–3, 104, 117n38, 139, 141, 142
Mouffe, Chantal, 45

natural sciences: Habermas, Jürgen on, 68–69; Honneth, Axel on, 86, 131–35; objectivating attitude of, 20, 28, 49, 66, 71, 77, 83, 85, 86, 134, 135, 140, 143; postempiricist critique of, 71–73, 75–77, 91n50; re-teleologization of, 4, 16, 18, 64, 78, 85, 121; value neutrality and, 65, 71–73, 77, 85. *See also* human sciences; nature
nature: Benjamin, Walter on, 107; Derrida, Jacques on, 18, 64, 81–85; disenchantment of, 66; Habermas, Jürgen on, 68–69, 106; Honneth, Axel on, 85–87; Horkheimer, Max and Theodor Adorno on, 66–67; Lukács, Georg on, 65–66, 67, 68, 69, 71, 73, 74, 77, 78, 86, 107, 134; Marcuse, Herbert on, 18, 63, 67, 69,

73–74, 82, 84, 90n17;
re-teleologization of, 4, 16, 18, 64,
78, 85, 107, 121, 131; Vogel, Steven
on, 18, 71–74, 76, 77, 80, 84, 91n50.
See also ecological ethics; natural
sciences
nature dialectics. *See* Engels, Friedrich
Naturphilosophie, 116
Naturwissenschaften. *See* natural
sciences
Negri, Antonio, 112
nonsimultaneity theory. *See* Bloch, Ernst

Obama, Barack, 1–2, 143
objectivating attitude. *See* natural
sciences
Offe, Claus, 132
ontotheology. *See* Derrida, Jacques
organized crime syndicates, 3, 29, 55
Ottman, Henning, 70

Pascal, Blaise, 104
Plato, 45
postempiricism. *See* natural sciences

Rawls, John, 29, 37, 41n45
Realphilosophie. *See* Hegel, Georg
Wilhelm Friedrich
reciprocity: asymmetrical, 16, 44,
50–51, 81, 127; symmetrical, 4, 7–8,
13, 17, 19, 23n35, 26, 27, 30, 31,
44–47, 50–54, 56–57, 59n25, 63, 78,
111, 114, 120n85, 122, 125–27, 130–
31, 135, 140, 144. *See also*
toleration; Young, Iris Marion
recognition theory. *See* Honneth, Axel
Rehg, William, 17, 25, 28; on care and
justice, 35–36, 37, 130, 136, 143
reification, 143; Habermas, Jürgen on,
12–13, 64, 68, 78, 129; Honneth,
Axel on, 85–86, 87, 129, 134;
Horkheimer, Max, and Theodor
Adorno on, 48; Lukács, Georg, 65,
127; Marcuse, Herbert on, 13
Rorty, Richard, 109–10

Rosenfeld, Michel, 12n76, 17, 44; on
comprehensive pluralism, 111–12,
113; on terrorism, 54–55, 56, 112
Rousseau, Jean-Jacques, 118n40

Sandel, Michael, 130
Schelling, Friedrich Wilhelm Joseph,
67, 105, 106, 107, 118n45
Schleiermacher, Friedrich, 72
Schmidt, Alfred, 107
Sessions, Jeff, 1–2
social ecology, 71
social integration, 16, 19, 38, 129, 133,
134, 135, 138, 141, 142. *See also*
system integration
solidarity: Habermas, Jürgen on, 13,
26–27, 126; Honneth, Axel on, 124,
125–26
Swabian Pietism, 67
system integration, 19, 129, 132, 133,
135, 138. *See also* social integration

terrorism, 3, 17, 44, 54–55, 56–57
Thomassen, Lasse, 19, 103–4
Thomistic ethics, 27
toleration: in Habermas, Jürgen, 11–12,
15, 113; in Kant, Immanuel, 7–9, 15,
46–47, 120n76. *See also* Derrida,
Jacques (on hospitality)
Trey, George, 59n25
Tronto, Joan C., 39n12
Tugendhat, Ernst, 122

value neutrality. *See* natural sciences
violence: Benjamin, Walter on, 107–8;
Derrida, Jacques on, 11–12, 13, 30,
46, 48, 49, 51–52, 55, 83, 107–9, 121
Vogel, Lawrence, 98
Vogel, Steven: on Derrida, Jacques, 80,
84; on ecological ethics, 71, 74, 77,
84; Habermas, Jürgen, constructivist
critique of, 18, 64, 71–74, 91n50;
Marcuse, Herbert, constructivist
critique of, 74, 84; on science and
technology, 72–76, 77

Weber, Max, 12, 48, 49, 64, 127, 133, 135, 138

Wellmer, Albrecht, 23n41

West, Robin, 39n12

Whitebook, Joel, 70

Winnicott, Donald, 123

Wyschogrod, Edith, 6

Young, Iris Marion, 45; on asymmetrical reciprocity, 17, 44, 50, 52. *See also* Derrida, Jacques (on hospitality); reciprocity

About the Author

Richard Ganis is a visiting professor of political philosophy at the Lahore University of Management Sciences, Pakistan. He holds a PhD in politics from the University of Salford; an MA in social and cultural anthropology from the California Institute of Integral Studies; and a BA in political science from Rutgers University. His research interests encompass a wide range of movements and idioms within contemporary European philosophy and social theory, with emphasis on the intersection between the Frankfurt School tradition and philosophies of postmodernity. He is the editor of *Displacement and Belonging in the Contemporary World* and has written articles for *Radical Philosophy Review*, among other publications. He is currently at work on a number of projects, including a contribution to an anthology aimed at assessing the thought of Jürgen Habermas from "non-Western" perspectives (forthcoming).

Breinigsville, PA USA
17 December 2010
251611BV00003B/5/P